# The Archaeology of Jerusalem

# The Archaeology of
# Jerusalem

*From the Origins to the Ottomans*

Katharina Galor and Hanswulf Bloedhorn

Yale UNIVERSITY PRESS   NEW HAVEN AND LONDON

Published with assistance from the Louis Stern Memorial Fund.

Yale University Press books may be purchased in quantity for educational, business, or promotional use. For information, please e-mail sales.press@yale.edu (U.S. office) or sales@yaleup.co.uk (U.K. office).

Designed by Nancy Ovedovitz and set in Janson type by Keystone Typesetting, Inc.
Printed in the United States of America.
Frontispiece photo: Detail of plate 2. Photo H. Bloedhorn.

Library of Congress Cataloging-in-Publication Data
Galor, Katharina.
The archaeology of Jerusalem : from the origins to the Ottomans / Katharina Galor and Hanswulf Bloedhorn.
pages cm
Includes bibliographical references and index.
ISBN 978-0-300-11195-8 (cloth : alk. paper) 1. Excavations (Archaeology) — Jerusalem — History. 2. Jerusalem — Antiquities. I. Bloedhorn, Hanswulf. II. Title.
DS109.15.G35 2013      956.94'42 — dc23      2013011381

A catalogue record for this book is available from the British Library.

This paper meets the requirements of ANSI/NISO Z39.48-1992 (Permanence of Paper).

10  9  8  7  6  5  4  3  2  1

*To our respective sons,*
*Alon, Yuval, Omri*
*and*
*Constantin*

# Contents

# Preface

The complexity of Jerusalem's history and of the relationship between the city's material culture and written documents can be paralleled with other major capitals in the ancient world, such as Athens, Rome, Constantinople, Cairo, and Damascus. Yet, something beyond the material and written remains has contributed to the long-lasting effects of Jerusalem's cultural and religious developments. Whether guided by the desire to prove or disprove a certain spiritual presence and its physical manifestations, and regardless of whether one is a religiously inspired or scientifically trained scholar, the goal is always to reconstruct "the truth" as closely as possible. It is not our intention here to rehash the many contributions that have been made to the archaeology of Jerusalem, nor shall we claim that we have now come closer than others before us to understanding the past. We have strived to create a tangible retrospective of the archaeology of the city from the beginnings through the Ottoman period. One of our most difficult tasks was to include only the information we deemed necessary for obtaining a general understanding of the city's history without overwhelming the reader with facts that are indeed interesting but nonetheless tangential.

The wealth of the textual evidence and the ever-growing material data exposed by archaeologists over nearly 175 years has caused the field to become increasingly dichotomized and fragmented, making the general reader's grasp and familiarity with Jerusalem's myriad archaeological finds difficult and unwieldy. It is not surprising, then, that the generation of scholars excelling in both the textual and material cultures of the city is waning and that scholars working in the biblical periods no longer venture into the classical and later periods, and vice versa. More importantly for the framework of this book, specialists of the biblical periods are usually trained differently and work independently of scholars of the classical periods, and the scope and knowledge of specialists working in the early periods rarely overlap with the cultural, religious, and chronological frameworks of those studying the medieval period. The large number of monographs dealing with minor topics and specific periods is the result of an almost insuperable amount of material remains uncovered in Jerusalem to date. As in many other parts of the ancient world, scholarly activity — preliminary and final reports, as well as the more theoretical and analytical studies — seems to be lagging behind the seemingly bottomless pit of the city's ancient treasures. The need to assimilate this wealth of ancient material culture and organize it in an accessible fashion has been articulated by many, yet the few publications that indeed cover most of the city's more than three thousand years of existence are either clearly outdated or too concerned with religious, political, or touristic aspects of the city.

Our primary goal in this book is, therefore, to create a newly updated survey of Jerusalem's archaeology that will serve a large readership: those who are familiar with only a sub-category of archaeological findings or a particular chronological time span as well as those who are new to this field.

In order to organize the material in an accessible way, we decided to proceed chronologically, devoting each chapter to a major period. We open with a brief historical outline based primarily on the written texts and then proceed to describe in detail the material culture, mainly architecture and a selection of representative and/or unique small finds.

Given the importance of Jerusalem to three major monotheistic religions, we felt it essential to cover a wide time span, beginning with the Chalcolithic period in the fourth millennium B.C.E. and ending with the Ottoman period in 1917 C.E. The range of periods demanded that all the chapters offer a distinct treatment of the material evidence. The nature of the remains from each period and the resulting agendas of the various archaeological reports and analyses largely determined the focus of individual chapters. Whereas a more detailed treatment of water and fortification systems was deemed necessary for the early periods (Bronze and Iron Ages), a stronger emphasis on city planning and monumental architecture was required for the later periods (most importantly the Graeco-Roman period); unlike the focus on civic architecture in the Graeco-Roman period, a more attentive treatment of sacral architecture was necessary for the Byzantine period; finally, the archaeology of standing monuments characterizing the latest periods covered here, the Early Islamic through the Ottoman period, warranted a slightly different approach.

Other than in the introduction, where some of the leading archaeologists who have conducted fieldwork in the city are mentioned, names of individual scholars appear almost exclusively in the notes. With more than 1700 excavations carried out in Jerusalem over the last decade and a half, and nearly as many archaeologists heading those efforts, exhaustive lists and descriptions would have compromised the clarity of the text.

The nomenclature appearing in this volume was chosen according to the most widely accepted and internationally used terms in the field. The chronological division into the First and Second Temple periods used by the majority of Israeli scholars and a progressively smaller group of American scholars, and almost completely eschewed by European scholars, was avoided as much as possible. While appropriate for the study of historical documents, the use of this terminology is particularly problematic when the archaeological material is viewed within its larger geographical and cultural contexts. The chapter headings instead follow the universal chronological terminology used and understood by scholars and nonprofessionals alike. The historical outlines are based on written sources only (which are not always complemented by the material evidence) and therefore use the names and titles (kings, emperors, sultans, dynasties, etc.) appearing therein.

The heated debates among specialists dealing with the biblical periods (Bronze and Iron Ages) in Jerusalem have swamped the scholarly literature. Minimalist and maximalist views suggest very different reconstructions of the city's early developments and challenge long-established chronologies. One of the main reasons for these intense controversies is that the biblical texts were compiled and edited hundreds of years after the events they describe; distortions and exaggerations can be expected. In contrast, for the later classical and postclassical periods, contemporary sources are the norm. Even if a certain bias or subjectivity transcends the writing, the reliability of the later historical documents has been questioned less. This accounts clearly for more moderate controversies among scholars regarding the postbiblical periods. The relatively more recent interest in the city's medieval archaeology, architecture, and art explains the more restricted use of scholarly references. Although we have taken into account the discrepant evaluations and interpretations of Jerusalem's archaeology, it is our objective here to present the data to the reader as coherently as possible rather than to overload and confuse him or her with a disarray of opinions. The footnotes and bibliographical references should serve as a helpful guide for those interested in exploring the scholarly controversies more thoroughly.

Having lived, worked, and taught in Jerusalem for many years, we found it essential to capture our immediate physical and visual contact with the sites and objects we describe and to transmit them to the reader in a tangible way, not only in words but also in images. The numerous photographs, plans, sections, drawings, and reconstructions throughout the volume are therefore an important component of our work.

This book is the result of our joint efforts, a collaboration that would not have been possible without the generous help, assistance, and guidance of many. For the illustrative part of this book, we are most indebted to the hard and meticulous work of a young and very talented artist, Jennifer Dillon. Jennifer spent five months with us in Jerusalem, drawing, copying, interpreting and translating numerous previously published figures that were adopted for the present volume. Margit Speidel has contributed several additional drawings to our volume. Jean-Michel de Tarragon guided us in the selection of images from the collection of the École biblique et archéologique française for the Ottoman and British Mandate periods. His impressive knowledge of historic photography and Jerusalem around the turn of the century has benefitted us greatly. During our repeated visits to the photo archives of the Rockefeller Museum, and with the helpful guidance of Arieh Rochman-Halperin, we were able to locate additional images from the British Mandate period that appear here. Yael Barschak of the Israel Antiquities Authority assisted us with the selection of more recent photographs that postdate the establishment of the State of Israel. Erin Christensen, Vera Mayerczik, and Yael Richardson helped us with many practical aspects of this book. We are most thankful to our colleague Robert Schick for his review and helpful comments of the chapters on the Mamluk and Ottoman periods. We also thank Hani Davis and Michael Steinberg for their editorial comments, as well as Deborah Bruce-Hostler for her insightful copyediting. Many thanks also to Christina Tucker, Ann-Marie Imbornoni, and Christopher Rogers of Yale University Press for all their advice and patience during the editorial process. Last, but not least, we are grateful to our families for enduring the many months, days, and nights of our hard work and for showing understanding, patience, and respect for a passion we both share: the exploration of ancient Jerusalem as expressed in its physical remains.

The Archaeology of Jerusalem

# 1 ✦ Introduction

## History of the Research

Jerusalem . . . by far the most famous city of the East and not of Judaea only.

PLINY THE ELDER, *Natural History*, V, 70

Turning to the past to enhance one's perspective of the present is not a modern invention. From early on, Jerusalem has beckoned numerous historians, explorers, and adventurers. Whether to illuminate one's ancestral heritage or to revisit sites that shaped world religions, the quest to uncover Jerusalem's mysterious legacy has been a source of inspiration for many (fig. 1.1).[1]

Flavius Josephus (ca. 37–95 C.E.) may be considered a pioneer in the exploration of Jerusalem's history, described in the course of his work to record the history of his people for the contemporary Roman reader.[2] Byzantine and medieval pilgrims attempted to locate those sites associated with Jesus and recorded their observations (plate 1).

Fig. 1.1. Aerial view of Jerusalem (on August 31st, 1934). Courtesy of the Israel Antiquities Authority.

Theoderich, in his *Libellus de locis sanctis* (1172 C.E.), sought to reconstruct first-century C.E. Jerusalem using Josephus's description of the city. Mujir al-Din in the fifteenth century C.E. should be considered as the most important author recording the history of the city from an Islamic perspective. The earliest physical explorations of the East began with Napoleon's campaign in Egypt (1798–99).[3] After attention to Egypt and Mesopotamia, interest to explore Palestine archaeologically was sparked only in the mid nineteenth century.[4]

In 1838, Edward Robinson, professor of biblical literature at Union Theological Seminary in New York, made his first trip to Palestine, followed by a second journey in 1852.[5] With his numerous identifications of places mentioned in the Bible he was able to establish the foundations for a historical topography of Palestine. Although Robinson was one of the first modern investigators to study Jerusalem, his most valuable contributions were for Palestine as a whole.[6]

More relevant for the investigation of Jerusalem proper are the studies conducted by the Swiss physician Titus Tobler.[7] In the course of his visits to Palestine,[8] first in 1835–36 and then in 1845–46, he compiled a detailed description of the city.[9] His visual observations, combined with a systematic study of late antique and medieval pilgrim accounts, resulted in a standard reference work. Two additional journeys, in 1857–58 and 1865, led to the organized collation and publication of all known and relevant pilgrim reports,[10] as well as the production of a comprehensive chronologically sequenced bibliography of Palestine.[11]

The earliest field investigations of the city were conducted by Conrad Schick. Although trained as a locksmith and clockmaker, he was sent to Jerusalem in 1846 in the service of the Mission Society of St. Chrischona (near Basel)[12] and recorded his valuable architectural observations in numerous articles.[13]

The first excavations proper were undertaken by Félix de Saulcy.[14] In the winter of 1850–51, he began to expose the tomb of the royal family of Adiabene north of the city, which he erroneously identified as the Tomb of the Kings of Judah.[15]

The first institutionalized framework for further field investigations was created in 1864.[16] Under the Ordnance Survey of Jerusalem, Captain Charles W. Wilson[17] was entrusted to supervise the renovation of the city's water supply system.[18] His systematic description of the city, with plans featuring its most important buildings, appeared in the fall of 1865.[19]

Wilson's unexpected success in surveying the city's archaeological remains led to the establishment of the Palestine Exploration Fund on May 12, 1865. The express goal of the Fund was to undertake investigations "for biblical illustration." In the fall of 1865, Wilson, accompanied by Lieutenant Anderson and Corporal Phillips, was again sent to Palestine. His work in 1866 was restricted to Jerusalem, where spectacular results were expected to appear quickly. In 1867, the team was reinforced by the addition of Lieutenant Charles Warren,[20] who soon discovered the shaft behind the Gihon that was later named after him.[21] In the following years, because excavations on the Haram al-Sharif were impossible, numerous risky shaft excavations were conducted outside the Haram's enclosure walls. Warren and Wilson's written report appeared in 1871.[22] The Jerusalem volume of *The Survey of Western Palestine*, with contributions by Wilson as well as by Warren, Conder,[23] and Charles Clermont-Ganneau, was published in 1884, comprising a compendium of the archaeological knowledge of the day.[24]

Clermont-Ganneau served as a secretary at the French consulate in Jerusalem from 1865 to 1872, when he also conducted intensive archaeological investigations in Jerusalem and the vicinity.[25] In 1873–74 he was again in Palestine, sent by the Palestine Exploration Fund. Although he could not obtain an excavation permit, his mission was no less successful through his numerous architectural observations, which he compiled during his journeys in Palestine and published in 1896; his notes about Jerusalem followed three years later.[26]

Following the British model, the Germans founded the Deutscher Verein zur Erforschung Palästinas (German Society for the Exploration of Palestine) in 1877.[27] Hermann Guthe was entrusted with the task of excavating in Jerusalem.[28]

In the 1870s the debate heightened as to whether the Canaanite city captured by David was to be sought on the Southwest Hill, the traditional Mount Zion, or whether the settlement had begun on the Southeast Hill, which include the Gihon and the water installations. This question remained in the background of the ensuing excavations conducted by the Palestine Exploration Fund. Frederick J. Bliss, former assistant to William M. F. Petrie, came to Jerusalem after the end of his work at Tall al-Hasi in May 1894 and, together with Archibald C. Dickie, began his excavations on the Southwest Hill. Bliss and Dickie did not use Petrie's pioneering stratigraphic method in his excavations but rather Warren's older technique of shaft and tunnel excavations. Despite these apparent methodological drawbacks, however, Bliss and Dickie's excavations mark a considerable stride in research because of their precise documentation. The confirmation for their precision was recently reestablished by the renewed excavation of the city wall on the southern slope of Mount Zion conducted by Yehiel Zelinger.[29]

A unique excavation project was undertaken by Montague B. Parker beginning in 1909. Less interested in illuminating the settlement history, he was determined to uncover the treasure of King Solomon's temple.[30] Louis-Hugues Vincent of the École biblique et archéologique française,[31] who accompanied Parker on his adventurous excavations, took the opportunity to make scientific observations and swiftly published the results as a monograph.[32]

Baron Edmond de Rothschild initiated an excavation motivated by his desire to discover the tombs of the kings of Judah. On his behalf, Raymond Weill conducted a first campaign in 1913–14.[33] In addition to various city wall sections, he uncovered the building inscription of what is presumed to have been the Theodotus synagogue.[34] Soon after, he cleared several underground structures, which he claimed were the tombs of the kings of Judah.[35]

Conditions for archaeological excavations in Jerusalem changed decisively in the British Mandatory period. The Department of Antiquities of Palestine was established to allow for several extensive excavations. Methodological innovations were made, which meant, most importantly, that shaft explorations were no longer considered an appropriate means to uncover the ancient city.

The first large-scale exploration, directed by Robert A. S. Macalister and John G. Duncan under the auspices of the Palestine Exploration Fund between 1923 and 1925, was on the top of the Southeast Hill as well as in the area above the Gihon Spring.[36]

Between 1927 and 1929 John W. Crowfoot and Gerald M. Fitzgerald expanded the excavations on the western slope of the Southeast Hill. Unfortunately, their finds were only published in abbreviated form.[37]

Also methodologically deficient and unsatisfactorily documented were the extended excavations undertaken by Eleazar L. Sukenik and Leo A. Mayer on behalf of the Jewish Palestine Exploration Society north of the Old City in 1925–28 and again in 1940.[38] Robert W. Hamilton and Cedric N. Johns advanced the methodological framework of investigations in Jerusalem by introducing the technique of stratigraphic excavations during several soundings and excavations carried out in the 1930s and 1940s.[39]

After a long interruption due to the war, excavations resumed with several projects conducted under the auspices of the British School of Archaeology. Between 1961 and 1967, Kathleen M. Kenyon, in collaboration with Alan D. Tushingham and Roland de Vaux (from the École biblique et archéologique française), directed a number of excavation projects. Her contribution to uncovering Jerusalem was tremendous and her publications will remain a valuable resource for the archaeological history of ancient Jerusalem.[40]

Following the Israeli conquest of East Jerusalem in 1967, Kenyon aborted her work because of the UNESCO charter's stipulation that no further expeditions could be conducted in an occupied territory. Consequently, numerous large-scale and long-term projects were initiated by Israeli archaeologists, conducted first under the auspices of the Israel Department of Antiquities and Museums, and after 1990 the Israel Antiquities Authority.[41] Only the most significant ones are mentioned here.

Soon after the conquest of the Old City, between 1969 and 1982, Nahman Avigad conducted extensive excavations, focusing almost exclusively on the period preceding the 70 C.E. destruction. Unfortunately, most of the post-Herodian building remains had been bulldozed before the beginning of the excavation. With the exception of the Nea Church and sections of the Byzantine *cardo*, the expedition dealt primarily with the earlier periods and thus created a biased picture of the settlement history in this area of the Old City (fig. 1.2).[42]

Around the same time, between 1968 and 1977, an additional large-scale excavation was conducted south of the Haram al-Sharif. Here, Benjamin Mazar, and later, Eilat Mazar, continued the work begun by Kenyon.[43]

Earlier investigations by Johns in the Citadel and by Kenyon and Tushingham in the Armenian Garden, were resumed by a number of Israeli archaeologists: Ruth Amiran and Avraham Eitan,[44] Hillel Geva,[45] Renée Sivan and Giora Solar,[46] Amit Re'em,[47] Magen Broshi,[48] and Dan Bahat and Broshi.[49] All these excavations yielded fascinating results, but so far they have been published only in preliminary reports.

Between 1978 and 1985, Yigal Shiloh resumed excavations on the Southeast Hill. These were first published in several preliminary reports and more recently as final reports.[50]

Since 1995, Ronny Reich and Eli Shukron have conducted extensive excavations around the Gihon Spring; they were the first excavators to dig down to the bedrock in this area. Their work con-

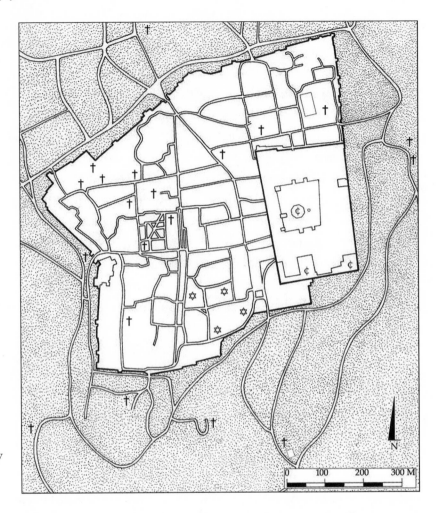

Fig. 1.2. Plan of the
Old City. Drawing by
J. Dillon and
M. Speidel.

tributes primarily to a revised understanding of the early water and
fortification systems.[51] Remains of the Herodian Siloam Pool were
exposed in 2004.[52] Soon after this discovery, Eilat Mazar uncovered
additional Iron Age remains further north on the Southeast Hill.[53]
A number of small and large scale excavations conducted north of
Damascus Gate exposed various sections of an extramural ecclesiastical quarter from the Byzantine period.[54]

   In spite of the ongoing interest in the biblical periods, not all
historical and archaeological studies of Jerusalem are limited to pre-

classical times. Tobler and Schick have already addressed the history of the holy places in late antiquity and the Middle Ages, an effort continued by Melchior de Vogüé,[55] and later by Vincent and Félix-Marie Abel.[56] More recently, Denys Pringle expanded the corpus of the Crusader churches.[57] In contrast to medieval Christian architecture, the interest in Islamic archaeology and architecture is more recent in western scholarship.[58] Since the 1980s a series of studies devoted to the Islamic heritage of the city was sponsored by the British School of Archaeology, since 2001 known as the Kenyon Institute. The survey of Islamic architecture began with Keppel Archibald Cameron Creswell for the Early Islamic period and was continued by Michael Hamilton Burgoyne for the Mamluk period.[59] A complete study on the archaeology and architecture of the Ayyubid period was recently conducted by Mahmud Hawari.[60] Ottoman Jerusalem was studied by a number of archaeologists, historians, art historians, and architects. Their work was compiled and edited by Sylvia Auld and Robert Hillenbrand.[61]

Two important studies devoted to the city's epigraphic heritage are Hannah M. Cotton and Werner Eck's corpus of all pre-Islamic inscriptions and Max van Berchem's survey of Arabic inscriptions.[62]

The work, effort, and studies of all the above-mentioned individuals — in addition to numerous others not mentioned in this context — have set the groundwork for this book. Although many missing pieces of the puzzle have yet to be deciphered, the existing textual and material remains allow us to draw a fairly detailed picture of Jerusalem's fascinating past.

## 2 ✦ Natural and Built City Limits

Jerusalem is emphatically a mountain city. Situated in the heart of
the hill country which extends from the great plain of Esdraelon to
the southern extremity of the Promised Land, surrounded on all
sides by limestone hills whose surface is broken by countless ravines, and only approached by rough mountain roads, its position is
one of great natural strength. This peculiarity in the situation of
the Holy City is frequently alluded to in the Bible, and we may in-
fer from the well-known words of the Psalmist, "As the mountains
are round about Jerusalem, so the Lord is round about his people,"
that importance was attached to the hills as a barrier or protection
against hostile attack.

C. W. WILSON, *Picturesque Palestine*, I, 1–2

Whereas the city's natural topography has remained constant in the period under consideration, the evolving history of the region has repeatedly modified the urban limits and the definition of space within. Factors that have determined the shift in boundaries include the inhabitants' relations with surrounding cultures that were either cordial or hostile at various times; their religious and ethnic affiliations; and the city's socioeconomic, ecological, and demographic conditions.[1]

## Topography and Geology

Palestine lies on a narrow stretch of the Fertile Crescent, at the southern end of the Levantine coast. Located in the center of the country, the Judaean hills mark the dividing line between the drainage basin of the Mediterranean Sea and that of the Jordan Valley. Ancient Jerusalem stands on a promontory enclosed on either side by two valleys that converge near its southernmost protrusion and continue onwards to the Dead Sea. On the crossroads of two regional trade routes, one north–south following the line of the mountain ridge, and the other east–west stretching from the sea toward Transjordan, Jerusalem has often served as the capital of the whole of Palestine. In geographical terms this is surprising, since the city was not easily accessible and there were no easy lines of communication through the hills leading into the city. Furthermore, natural water sources were always limited.

Ancient Jerusalem extended over several hills or spurs surrounded by even higher mountains (figs. 2.1–2).[2] The city's central core of hills is encircled on the west, south, and east by valleys and deep ravines. In ancient times the hills and valleys of Jerusalem were more pronounced than they are today. The numerous acts of destruction and the changes that the city has undergone, as well as the constant accumulation of waste and debris that filled the valleys and

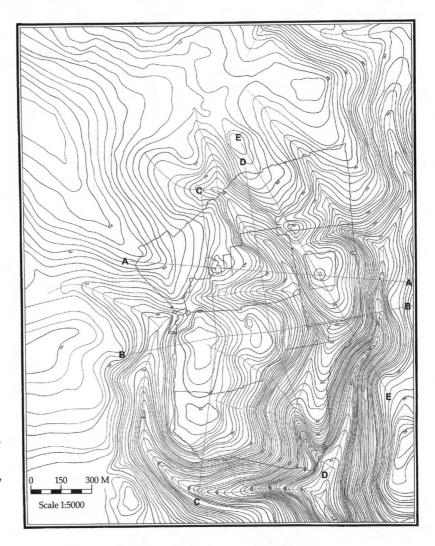

Fig. 2.1. Topographi-
cal map of Jerusalem.
Redrawn by J. Dillon,
after: Vincent and
Steve, *Jérusalem*, I,
plate 1.

consequently lowered the heights, rendered the site the appearance
of a plateau rather than of prominent hills and deep valleys (plate 2).

The eastern border of the ancient city is marked by the Kidron
Valley (Wadi al-Joz in the north and Wadi an-Nar in the east and
south), which separates it from the Mount of Olives ridge (Jabal az-
Zaitun, 830 meters). Its western border is the Valley of Hinnom
(Wadi ar-Rababa), which runs north–south, skirting Mount Zion,

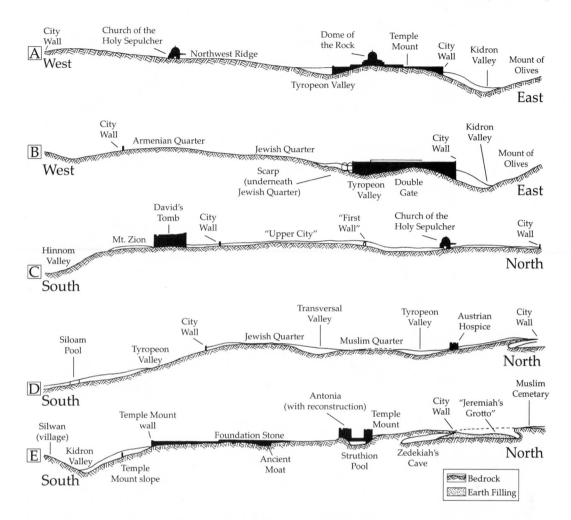

Fig. 2.2. Sections of the Old City. Redrawn by J. Dillon, after: Bahat, *Illustrated Atlas*, 15.

and then turns east along the southern border of the ancient city down until its confluence with the Kidron Valley. The city's northern border has no clear-cut topographical demarcation. The only morphological feature that separated the city from the hills to the north was the (now filled) Transversal Valley. From Late Hellenistic times onward the city's boundaries spread beyond the Transversal Valley. From north to south, the city is divided by the valley (al-Wad), known

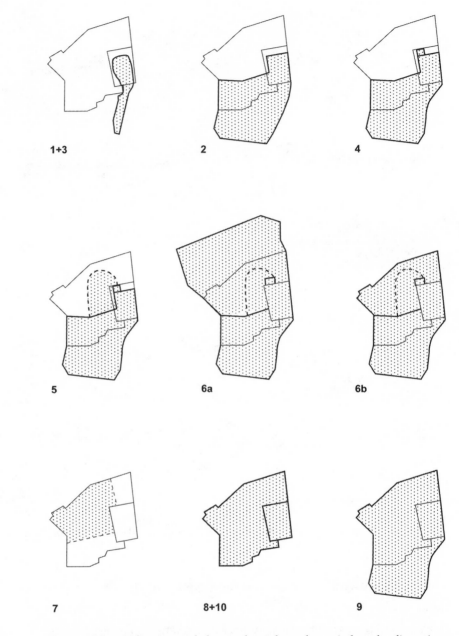

Fig. 2.3. Maps indicating settled areas throughout the periods under discussion.
1. Bronze through Iron Age IIB (3300–725 B.C.E.); 2. Iron Age IIC (725–586
B.C.E.); 3. Babylonian, Persian, and Hellenistic Periods (586–ca. 67 B.C.E.); 4.
Hasmonean Period with First Wall (ca. 67 B.C.E.–ca. 44 B.C.E.); 5. Late
Hellenistic or Hasmonean Period with Second Wall (ca. 44 B.C.E.–ca. 44 C.E.);

later, from the time of Josephus, as the Central or Tyropoeon Valley. It was this depression that separated the so-called Southwest Hill or Upper City (765 meters), now occupied by the Armenian and Jewish Quarters, and Mount Zion further south (770 meters), from the Southeast Hill or Lower City. The latter included the Temple Mount (745 meters) and the City of David to the south (660 meters).[3]

During the early periods of the city's existence, the inhabitants clung tenaciously to its only perennial spring, the Gihon, located on the lower eastern slopes of the Southeast Hill above the Kidron Valley. It was only when greater efficiency was achieved in the utilization of rainwater and in the diversion of faraway spring sources that Jerusalem was able to expand in other directions.

## The City's Physical Growth

Only rough estimates can be made regarding the inhabited area before construction of the city's earliest fortifications around 1850 B.C.E.[4] The city's ancient boundaries can be measured most accurately when the course of the city walls is determined (table 2.1).[5] Additional information on urban development and the ever-changing city limits can be determined by defining the location and extent of Jerusalem's necropolis.[6] The following plans reflect the most commonly accepted opinions with regard to the extent of the city during its various phases of occupation (fig. 2.3). Sources used for the reconstructions of the city and its population are partially historical and partially archaeological.

---

6a. Third Wall north of Ottoman Wall—according to maximalist view (ca. 44–70 C.E.); 6b. Third Wall corresponding to Ottoman Wall — according to minimalist view (ca. 44–70 C.E.); 7. Roman Period with no wall (135–300 C.E.); 8. Late Roman and Byzantine Periods (300–450 C.E.); 9. Late Byzantine and Early Islamic Periods (450–ca. 980 C.E.); 10. Fatimid Period and later (since ca. 980 C.E.). Redrawn by M. Speidel, after: Broshi, "The Expansion of Jerusalem," 12–15.

Table 2.1 Estimates of Jerusalem's size and population, by historical period

| | AREA | | | POPULATION | | | | | |
|---|---|---|---|---|---|---|---|---|---|
| | Broshi | Tarler & Cahill | Lipiński | Broshi | Tarler & Cahill | Lipiński | Asali | Peters | Schölch |
| Bronze Age | 30–45 dunams<br>7.5–11.25 acres<br>3–4.5 hectares | 60 dunams<br>15 acres<br>6 hectares | 45 dunams<br>11.25 acres<br>4.5 hectares | 2,000–2,400 | 1,500–2,400 | 800–1,100 | | | |
| Iron Age IIA/B, including the Temple Mount | 130 dunams<br>32.5 acres<br>13 hectares | 160 dunams<br>40 acres<br>16 hectares | 130 dunams<br>32.5 acres<br>13 hectares | 4,500–5,000 | 4,000–6,400 | 2,600–3,200 | | | |
| Iron Age IIC, including the western expansion | 500 dunams<br>125 acres<br>50 hectares | 620 dunams<br>155 acres<br>62 hectares | 500–650 dunams<br>125–162.5 acres<br>50–65 hectares | 25,000 | 15,500–24,800 | 15,000 | | | |
| Persian period | 120 dunams<br>30 acres<br>12 hectares | 150 dunams<br>37.5 acres<br>15 hectares | 120 dunams<br>30 acres<br>12 hectares | 4,500 | 3,750–6,000 | 4,363 | | | |
| Hasmonean period, including the western expansion | 650 dunams<br>162.5 acres<br>65 hectares | 620 dunams<br>155 acres<br>62 hectares | 650 dunams<br>162.5 acres<br>65 hectares | 30,000–35,000 | 15,500–24,800 | 15,000 | | | |

| Period | | | | | | |
|---|---|---|---|---|---|---|
| Herodian period | 900 dunams 225 acres 90 hectares | 770 dunams 92.5 acres 77 hectares | 750 dunams 187.5 acres 75 hectares | 40,000 | 19,250– 30,800 | >15,000 |
| Eve of destruction (70 C.E.), including the northern expansion (Mayer-Sukenik Wall) | 1800 dunams 450 acres 180 hectares | 1560 dunams 390 acres 156 hectares | 1700 dunams 425 acres 170 hectares | 80,000 | 39,000– 62,400 | 35,000– 40,000 |
| Late Byzantine and Abbasid periods, including the southwestern expansion | 1200 dunams 300 acres 120 hectares | 1050 dunams 262.5 acres 105 hectares | 1000 dunams 250 acres 100 hectares | 55,000– 60,000 | 26,375– 42,200 | 25,000 |
| Mamluk period | c. 1 square km | | | | | |
| Early Ottoman | c. 1 square km | | | | | |
|   –1538 | | | | 7,900 | | |
|   –1553 | | | | 13,400 | | |
|   –1600 | | | | 7,600 | | |
| Late Ottoman | | | | | | |
|   –1806 | | | | 8,800 | | |
|   –1850 | | | | 15,000 | | |
|   –1870 | | | | 22,000 | | |
|   –1890 | | | | 42,000 | | |

# 3 ✦ The Chalcolithic Period and the Bronze Age

To the King, my Lord, say: Thus Abdu-Heba, thy servant. At the
two feet of my lord, the king, seven times and seven times I fall . . .
Behold, the King has set his name in the Land of Jerusalem for
ever; so he cannot abandon the lands of Jerusalem!

AMARNA LETTERS, NO. 287:60–64

## A Canaanite City

Jerusalem first appears in the written sources as a Canaanite city
at the beginning of the second millennium B.C.E. The land of Canaan
consisted of groups of seminomadic tribal confederations and several
cities, each ruled by its own king. The two great empires of Egypt and
Babylonia competed for dominance over Canaan and the entire region.

Egyptian execration texts referring to the city as *ȝwšȝmm* (*ru-
shalimum*) appear on nineteenth-century B.C.E. ceramic bowls and
eighteenth-century B.C.E. clay figurines of bound captives.[1] It was

believed that the power of the enemy whose name was inscribed on the bowls and figurines could be destroyed by smashing them.

Jerusalem is mentioned again in the fourteenth-century B.C.E. Amarna letters, the diplomatic correspondence between the kings of several Canaanite cities and their Egyptian overlords. Some letters contain important information regarding political, military, and economic conditions and the nature of the role of the rulers, including six messages sent by the ruler of Jerusalem confirming the loyalty of the "Land of Jerusalem" (*mât urusalim*) to the Egyptian king.[2] The oldest written document found in Jerusalem dates from the same period. The small fragment (2 × 2.8 centimeters), possibly part of a larger cuneiform tablet, suggests that Jerusalem may have been an important city in the Late Bronze Age.[3]

At the time of the Israelite "conquest" of the hill country of Judah, the Philistines, a "sea people"—most likely of Aegean origin—began to settle along the southern Mediterranean coast. Eventually, they moved inland to the coastal plain in an attempt to conquer the entire region. The books of Judges and 1 and 2 Samuel contain accounts of the relations and battles between the Israelites and the Philistines. The Philistine threat led to the union of the Israelite tribes under a single monarch, King Saul of the tribe of Benjamin (ca. 1012–1004 B.C.E.; 1 Sam 8–10). After the Philistines defeated Saul and his son Jonathan on Mount Gilboa (1 Sam 31), David, a shepherd from Bethlehem of the tribe of Judah, who was anointed by the prophet Samuel during Saul's reign (1 Sam 16:12–13), emerged as king. According to tradition this happened sometime between 965 and 1004 B.C.E. Ongoing rivalries between the tribes, however, delayed the consolidation of his rule.[4]

## Fortifications and Dwellings

The earliest physical remains indicating human presence in Jerusalem go back to the Chalcolithic period and consist of flint tools

Fig. 3.1. Aerial view of the Southeast Hill, looking west. Upper left: area excavated by Weill (A); upper center: Shiloh areas B–E (B); bottom right: the Gihon Spring (C); upper right: entrance to Warren's Shaft (D). Courtesy of the Institute of Archaeology, Hebrew University Jerusalem.

found on the Southeast Hill. The first structural remains on the hill's eastern slope consist of two buildings with beaten earth floors and benches lining the short walls, dating from the Early Bronze Age (figs. 3.1–2).[5]

Sometime later, a more substantial settlement began to develop west of the Gihon Spring. The transition into a town of a certain size and significance is indicated by the presence of a wall constructed around 1850 B.C.E. The appearance of the city's name in contemporary Egyptian texts suggests a demographic and political change that has been viewed by some as concrete evidence that the god Shalim was believed to have founded the city.[6]

A 12-meter-long segment of the Middle Bronze Age city wall was first exposed on the eastern slope of the Southeast Hill, approximately 22 meters above and 40 meters away from the Gihon Spring.[7] An additional 25 meters of the same wall were exposed some 100 meters further south.[8] Measuring between 2.5 and 4 meters in depth, the wall was built over earlier domestic structures. Soon after, the wall was reinforced from within the city. Another 75 meters further south, a 20-meter-long wall segment (4 meters wide) was exposed, most likely representing the continuation of the two aforementioned sections.[9] Only the most recent excavations, however, have established that the Gihon Spring and the adjacent pool complex were protected by their own fortification, which included several monumental towers.[10]

Given the topographical profile of the southern end of the Southeast Hill, the course of the city wall can be reliably reconstructed (fig. 3.3). The gate exposed in the late 1920s is most likely the Valley Gate, which existed in the time of Nehemiah, possibly built above an earlier entrance.[11]

The area encompassed inside the city walls covered a surface of about four hectares. In comparison to other Middle Bronze Age cities in the northern part of the country (such as Hazor and Megiddo) and in the coastal region (such as Gezer and Dor), this area was rather small.[12] Jerusalem was, however, a sizeable regional settlement for the central hill country and was inhabited by approximately two thousand people (see population estimates, table 2.1).

Mount Moriah, which later became the seat of the Temple Mount, may have already been included within the city wall at this point.[13]

Fig. 3.2. Early Bronze Age house in Shiloh area E-1. Courtesy of the Institute of Archaeology, Hebrew University Jerusalem.

Fig. 3.3. Foreground: Bronze
Age city wall in Kenyon area A;
background: Iron Age city wall
and modern retaining walls.
Photo H. Bloedhorn.

## The Water System

The Gihon Spring is the only perennial spring in Jerusalem sup-
plying fresh water to its residents. Originating at the foot of the
Southeast Hill in the Kidron Valley, the source is located in an enlarged cavity (ca. 3.4 × 1.5 meters), with an intermittent flow of about
830 liters per minute (fig. 3.4). It is this source that enabled early
settlement in this semiarid mountainous area.[14]

The spring is mentioned in the context of King Saul's anoint-
ment (1 Kgs 1:33 and 38), which may be indicative of the site's cultic
character. Access to the spring was probably sealed off during the
reign of King Hezekiah or Manasseh, when the water was diverted
through a tunnel to the Central or Tyropoeon Valley (2 Chron
32:30). The Gihon Spring is mentioned for the last time in connection with the construction of the defense system developed under

King Manasseh (2 Chron 33:14).[15] The spring's existence is not mentioned again until ca. 1330 C.E.[16] The pilgrims of the late Middle Ages knew this as the site where Mary washed baby Jesus's undergarments, which gave it the name Spring of Mother Mary (Ain as-Sitt Maryam). It is also called Spring of the Steps (Ain Umm al-Daraj) for its long flight of steps.

The ancient water system could be accessed from inside the city, on the eastern slope of the hill (fig. 3.5). Here, a series of steps built into the natural fissures in the rock runs about 7.5 meters below ground level (fig. 3.6).

The continuation of this tunnel is almost horizontal (fig. 3.7); it is built on top of the harder dolomite stone (*mizzi ahmar*) and is carved out of the ruins in a northeasterly direction and turns southeast for the next 17 meters, winding its way beneath the city wall and bypassing Warren's Shaft. Its route then continues southward (for the next 12.5 meters), at which point it turns eastward (for 5 meters), until reaching the edge of a large pool (ca. 15 × 10 meters) cut some 14 meters into the rock. The pool is protected from the north by a tower (the Pool Tower) constructed of two parallel foundations made of massive stone blocks (fig. 3.8). An additional tower of similar stature

Fig. 3.4. The Gihon Spring. The outlet into Channel VI is from the Iron Age. Photo H. Bloedhorn.

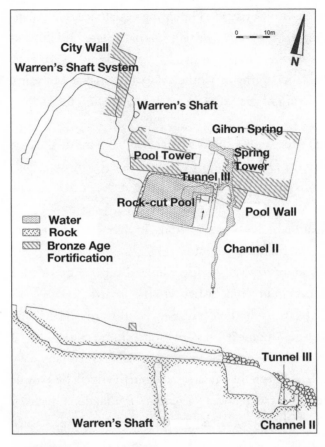

Fig. 3.5. Plan and section of the Warren's Shaft complex in the Bronze Age. Redrawn by J. Dillon, after: Reich and Shukron, "Jerusalem, City of David," 69, fig. 107, and "Jerusalem, Gihon Spring," 137, fig. 179.

Fig. 3.6. Entrance with steps leading down to Warren's Shaft complex. Photo H. Bloedhorn.

Fig. 3.7. The tunnel in Warren's Shaft complex. In the back, the modern staircase built over the original rock-cut steps. Photo H. Bloedhorn.

Fig. 3.8. The pool complex with its surrounding walls. Photo H. Bloedhorn.

might have been positioned south of the pool. Ceramic finds indicate that the tower and pool were built in the Middle Bronze Age. After construction of the Siloam tunnel, the spring pool dried up and was no longer used.

The waters of the Gihon Spring, located just east of the northern tower but some 15 meters deeper, originated from a crack in the rock and from there flowed directly into a cave (fig. 3.9). From here, the water flows through Channel II, opening into the Kidron Valley.[17] Tunnel III supplies the spring pool. A second massive tower (the Spring Tower) embraces and protects the entire area of the spring.

Fig. 3.9. Gihon Channel II, with Dominican priest standing opposite entrance to Tunnel III, Parker Mission 1909–1911. Courtesy of the École biblique.

Despite the spring's location some 35 meters beyond the actual city wall, the bastion ensures optimal protection and can be easily and safely reached by the city's inhabitants.

The new findings, namely that Warren's Shaft was neither used nor accessible in the Bronze Age, renders all scholarly publications — following the shaft's original discovery in 1867 and associating David's conquest of the city to this particular system — outdated. The new discoveries contribute significantly to a better understanding of the ancient water system of Bronze and Iron Age Jerusalem. They do not, however, corroborate the biblical description of David's conquest (2 Sam 5:8 and 1 Chron 11:6).

## Distinctive Finds

Given the absence of historical sources for the Chalcolithic period and the limited chronological value of the biblical narrative for the Bronze Age, our knowledge for these early periods relies almost exclusively on the evaluation of the material culture and the relation between the structural remains and the small finds.

### FLINT TOOLS

Before the appearance of pottery around the middle of the sixth millennium B.C.E., tools were the most important evidence for understanding life and cultural interactions in the early Levant. The majority of tools recovered is made from the hard materials indigenous to the area, the most common being flint (fig. 3.10). The process of making flint tools in Palestine was developed in the Pleistocene period (2,000,000–10,000 B.C.E.). In Jerusalem the earliest stone tools uncovered date to the Chalcolithic period. Although the lithic assemblage of the Southeast Hill excavations may not represent a particularly good chronological indicator, their study can reveal information regarding trade and exchange, and can be used as a basis for the analysis of function and technological change.[18]

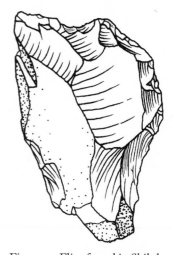

Fig. 3.10. Flint found in Shiloh area E. Redrawn by J. Dillon, after: Rosen, "Flint Implements," 265, fig. 40.8.

### "WHITE PAINTED" POTTERY VESSELS

Pottery production was one of man's great innovations in the later stages of the prehistoric era and one of the most important landmarks in the long transition from a nomadic to a sedentary existence. A group of vessels uncovered in a Jerusalem tomb in the Ophel area and documented by Vincent illustrates the type made during the Early Bronze Age (plate 3).[19] Similar vessels characterized by a cream-colored slip with reddish brown painted wavy or straight lines were found at contemporary Ai and Jericho.[20]

# 4 ✦ The Iron Age

Hezekiah fortified his city, and brought water into its midst; he
tunneled the rock with iron tools, and built cisterns for the water.

BEN SIRACH 48:17

## The Israelite City

According to 2 Samuel 5:7, in the seventh year of his reign (ca.
1000 B.C.E.), David entered Jerusalem, conquering the fortress called
Zion and the surrounding area, which he called the "City of David"
(2 Sam 5:6–9).[1] In a later account (1 Chron 11:4–7), David appointed
Joab son of Zeruiah the chief officer of his army because he was the
first to attack the local population. David united the territory of Israel
and made Jerusalem the political and religious capital of his kingdom
(fig. 4.1).

The Ark of the Covenant, symbol of the unity of the tribes of
Israel and of the covenant between Israel and God, was relocated to

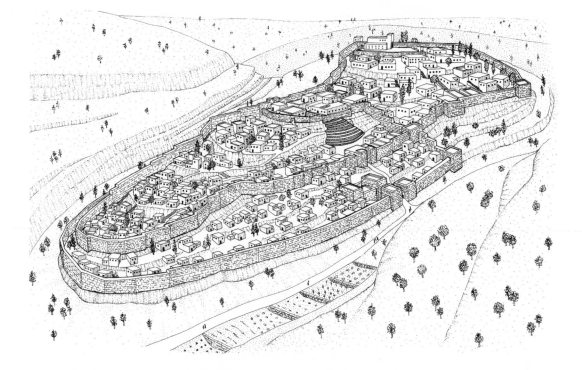

Jerusalem, along with all royal officials, government bureaucrats, important priestly families, and a permanent garrison. Toward the end of his reign, David built an altar on Mount Moriah (the Temple Mount), on the threshing floor that he purchased from Araunah "the Jebusite" (2 Sam 24:18–25; 2 Chron 3:1).[2] This floor may have been considered a sacred place, as its elevation and accessibility were essential features to ancient cultic sites.

On David's death in ca. 970 B.C.E., his son Solomon became king and ruled for forty years (1 Kgs 11:42). His reign was characterized by centralization, territorial expansion, international trade and contacts (particularly with Egypt and Phoenicia), and relative prosperity. Architectural projects in Jerusalem, originally planned during David and Solomon's brief period of joint rule, reached fruition under Solomon and included the Temple, the royal palace, and fortifications. The structure, decorations, and treasures of the Temple and the

Fig. 4.1. Reconstruction of the City of David. Redrawn by J. Dillon, after: L. Ritmeyer, in Shanks, "Everything You Ever Knew," 22–23.

parts of the nearby royal palace are described in great detail in 1 Kings 6–7.

Although most later texts indicate a centralized worship of one God in the Temple under the aegis of David's successor (who was believed to have held divine favor), conducted by the high priest Zadok and the priests and Levites, most scholars would no longer agree that they reflect historical reality. Archaeological evidence suggests that numerous contemporary sanctuaries existed and that monotheism did not develop until after 622 B.C.E.

Toward the end of Solomon's reign, there was a resurgence of tribal factionalism in the north and unrest among the poor. The outbreak of a rebellion of the northern tribes against Solomon's son Rehoboam led to the split of the united monarchy into two separate kingdoms around 930 B.C.E. The Kingdom of Israel was a confederation of the northern tribes, ruled by successive dynasties, with two cultic centers and its capital ultimately in Samaria. The southern Kingdom of Judah consisted of the tribes of Judah and Benjamin and was ruled by the descendants of David, with its Temple and political capital in Jerusalem. The stability of the Davidic dynasty and efforts at centralized worship in the Jerusalem Temple enabled the small Kingdom of Judah to survive tensions with the Kingdom of Israel, foreign invasions, and occasional internal unrest for about 350 years.

Around 926 B.C.E., not long after the schism, the Egyptian king Shishak I (Shoshenk), founder of the Twenty-second Dynasty, attacked Judah and Israel.[3] He plundered the treasures of Solomon in Jerusalem and destroyed other cities, but left the Temple intact.

Problems of succession, palace revolutions, internal conflicts, and other foreign enemies also plagued the Kingdom of Israel. The expanding Assyrian empire conquered and destroyed the Northern Kingdom of Israel in 722 B.C.E. (fig. 4.2). This brought an influx of refugees from the north to Jerusalem and its environs, increasing the population. The Assyrian kingdom continued its campaigns against Judah and neighboring states; this period of conflict contributed to

further construction of fortifications and other development during the reign of King Hezekiah (725–697 B.C.E.) and to the expansion of the borders of Judah to the south. Hezekiah expanded the city to the Southwest Hill, increasing its size tenfold, constructed walls and fortifications, made catchment pools, and dug a tunnel to convey water to the city (2 Chron 32:5; 2 Kgs 18:17, 20:20). These projects served Judah well during the siege of Jerusalem by King Sennacherib of Assyria in 701 B.C.E. The Assyrian army did not conquer Jerusalem, but retreated. The biblical narrative stresses the advice and warnings of the prophet Isaiah — as well as Hezekiah's religious reforms, such as the destruction of altars outside Jerusalem, which enhanced the centrality of the city and the Temple in difficult times. Hezekiah's son Manasseh (697–642 B.C.E.) continued construction of the outer wall (2 Chron 33:14). Assyrian supremacy lasted for nearly a century until the ascendance of Babylonia, the new eastern superpower that conquered the Assyrian capital, Nineveh, in 612 B.C.E. Jerusalem withstood these events and underwent a religious revival under King Josiah (640–609 B.C.E.), who embarked on a policy of repair of the Temple and abolition of foreign cults and sacrifices outside the Temple.

Fig. 4.2. Detail of the "Lachish Relief" in the British Museum, London, representing the conquest of a city. Redrawn by J. Dillon, after: Keel and Küchler, *Orte und Landschaften der Bibel*, 897, fig. 602b.

## Fortifications

According to the written sources, after the Israelites conquered the city, the royal kingdom was established under David with Jerusalem as the capital.[4] Although renewed construction of the city wall should be expected, no archaeological traces of such an endeavor have been found, not even signs of repair of the previously built wall. This lack of evidence may be related to the northern expansion area's serving as a stone quarry in the Roman period. According to some, repeated building modifications and destruction on the Temple Mount — as well as the ultimate reconfiguration of the platform with an enlarged Temple complex under Herod — eradicated all potential building remains of earlier fortifications.[5]

In contrast to the complete lack of evidence from the Early Iron Age, several wall sections can be attributed to the ensuing phase, the period between the death of King Solomon and the beginning of King Hezekiah's rule. One of these sections includes a four-room gate that, given its location, might correspond to the preexilic Water Gate mentioned in Nehemiah 3:26–27.

Although fortification remains on Mount Zion were exposed as early as the nineteenth century C.E., it was not until the Jewish Quarter excavations following the 1967 war that the expanded settlement toward the Southwest Hill was generally accepted among scholars. The 7-meter-wide wall could be traced over a length of 65 meters, stretching from the northeast to the southwest (45 meters) and continuing westward (20 meters) along the contours of the natural terrain (fig. 4.3).[6] The wall was built over houses dating to the beginning of the eighth century B.C.E., erected only several decades earlier, when the Southwest Hill began to be inhabited without a fortified structure surrounding it. Based on the ceramic evidence, the Broad Wall was built toward the end of the eighth or the beginning of the seventh century B.C.E.[7] Shortly after being erected, the wall began to

Fig. 4.3. Northern Broad Wall in Avigad area A during excavation. Courtesy of the Israel Exploration Society.

be dismantled, probably as a result of damage caused during the siege by Sennacherib.[8]

At two different locations some 30 meters further north, archaeologists were able to trace the course of an additional wall. The northern and eastern faces of a tower were partially exposed and, based on the ceramic finds, can be dated to the seventh century B.C.E. Several bronze arrowheads, attributed to the Babylonian siege in 586 B.C.E., were found north of the tower. Here, too, the fortifications were built on top of dwellings from the early eighth century B.C.E.[9]

On the eastern slope of the Southeast Hill, an Iron Age wall situated only slightly higher than the Middle Bronze Age fortification line was uncovered (fig. 3.3).[10] The continuation of this section can

Fig. 4.4. The easternmost Iron Age wall (501) in Reich/Shukron area J. Photo H. Bloedhorn.

be followed further south for some 120 meters. East of this wall segment, several Iron Age domestic structures have hitherto been associated with the refugees surviving the destruction of the Northern Kingdom.[11] New discoveries in the late 1990s, however, completely changed earlier views with respect to the fortification system on the eastern slope of the Southeast Hill. An additional wall dating to the Iron Age period was exposed in the Kidron Valley, east of the Gihon Spring (fig. 4.4). Running in a north–south direction, the fortification line covers a 100-meter-long stretch with sharp indentations at two-meter intervals, creating a distinctive zig-zag pattern similar in appearance to the Broad Wall in the Jewish Quarter. Based on the pottery report, this latter section can be dated to the seventh century B.C.E.[12] The new findings clarify how water from the Gihon Spring was diverted to the settlement's southeastern extremity without making the construction vulnerable to enemy attack. After the city's destruction in 586 B.C.E., no other wall was erected as far down in the valley as the recently discovered Iron Age wall.

Two city gates—Jeremiah's "Potsherd Gate" (Jer 19:1–2) and the "Middle Gate" (Jer 39:3)—can be associated with Hezekiah's westward expansion. The former was probably located in the Tyropoeon Valley and the latter, mentioned in connection with the Babylonian attack, was most likely identified in the center of the northern section of wall exposed in the Jewish Quarter. These represent the only two named gates and cannot be associated with the wall description in Nehemiah 3. Both followed the course of the earlier Iron Age wall. The "Gate between the double walls by way of the King's garden" (2 Kgs 25:4; Jer 39:4; Jer 52:7) mentioned in connection with Zedekiah's escape was probably located between the southern wall of the City of David and the southern extension of Hezekiah's wall, i.e., at the northern end of Birkat al-Hamra's city wall.

## The First Temple

Although we have no physical trace of the original Solomonic Temple, it is one of the most discussed monuments within the context of Jerusalem during the early monarchy (figs. 4.5–6). This overwhelming interest is hardly related to its architectural and decorative value, but more so a result of its unique national and religious role over time. The Temple's gradual development began with a temple form and usage that was well established in the ancient Near East. It is interesting to note that several temples coexisted with Solomon's Temple in Jerusalem and served specialized functions that were not in direct competition with the latter's unique status.[13] These temples, however, were founded long before the belief in a single, divine residence became official doctrine in the last period of the Israelite monarchy.[14]

The two principal sources of information for the plan of the First Temple erected on Mount Moriah during Solomon's reign are the biblical descriptions in 1 Kings 6–8 and 2 Chronicles 2–4. Those accounts, however, differ in several important details. Additional biblical references to the Temple complement these two descriptions (e.g., 1 Kgs 10:12; 2 Kgs 11), while others contradict them. Information regarding the Temple can also be found in Ezekiel's vision of the future Temple (Ezek 40–46), and Josephus recorded a detailed description (*Ant.* VIII, 61–129). The latter text is evidently based on rabbinic tradition, partially influenced by the plan of the Herodian Temple with which some of the rabbis must have been familiar. Far beyond the architectural features of the Temple, its furniture and utensils (i.e., the Ark, the cherubs, the showbread table, the candelabrum, and the curtain) are described in great detail.

Maintaining a sanctuary's location throughout changes of cul-

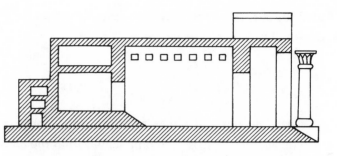

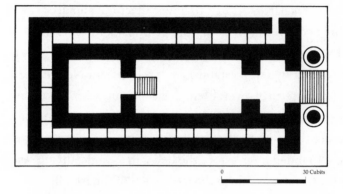

Fig. 4.5. Plan and section of Solomon's Temple. Redrawn by J. Dillon, after: Watzinger, *Denkmäler Palästinas*, fig. 39.

0                                    30 Cubits

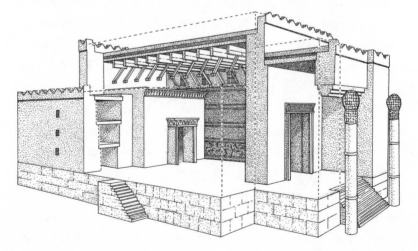

Fig. 4.6. Reconstruction of Solomon's Temple. Redrawn by J. Dillon, after: J. Willbarth, in Zwickel, *Der Salomonische Tempel*, plate 4b.

tural and religious dominion is a well-established custom in antiquity. In Jerusalem we can physically trace this continuity on the Haram al-Sharif, where the Dome of Rock sits on top of the Temple Mount enclosure. Historical evidence suggests that Herod's Temple was built in place of Zerubbabel's Temple, which had been constructed soon after the return from the Babylonian exile and was meant to commemorate the exact spot of the First Temple. The monumental construction of the pre-Hellenistic (i.e., pre-Hasmonean and pre-Herodian) extension of the eastern enclosure wall has been identified as the original Temple Mount platform, which was designed to level off the natural topography and to support the earlier Temple. Whether this construction is part of a preexilic platform supporting the Solomonic Temple is highly debated.[15] All attempts to locate the First Temple, whether by trying to locate the Temple itself (or specific parts of it, such as the Holy of Holies or the sacrificial altar) or, alternatively, by locating the substructure that possibly supported the Temple, remain conjectural.

The Temple compound consisted of the Temple proper, accessed through a porch as well as several courtyards (1 Kgs 7:12). Solomon's Temple is described as being a long-room temple, 60 cubits long, 20 cubits wide, and 30 cubits high (1 Kgs 6:2), with the entrance on the short side and the shrine at the opposite end of the building. Its three main architectural elements were the portico or porch (*ulam*) in the east, the main hall (*hekhal*) in the center, and the inner sanctuary or Holy of Holies (*debir*) in the west.[16]

Although all the above-mentioned information about Solomon's Temple comes from texts, many of which were compiled centuries after its construction, archaeological finds from other sites provide important parallels to the Jerusalem Temple. The long-room temple was a widespread architectural form in Syria and Canaan that originated in the second millennium B.C.E. Two temples uncovered in northern Syria are the most striking examples: the long-room temple at Tall Tainat consisted of a portico, a main hall, and a small shrine in

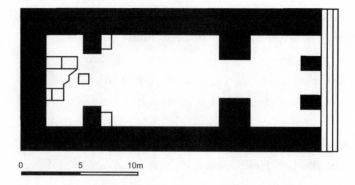

Fig. 4.7. Plan of the temple at Tall Tainat. Redrawn by J. Dillon, after: V. Fritz, "Temple Architecture," 42.

the back of the main hall, opposite the temple's entrance (fig. 4.7).[17] The recently excavated temple at 'Ain Dara contained a portico, two columns, and a main hall.[18] Similar features can be seen in a number of Canaanite temples uncovered at Arad, Bet Shean, Hazor, Lachish, Megiddo, and Shechem.[19]

Despite biblical references mentioning that Phoenician builders helped construct Solomon's Temple (1 Kgs 5:18), this area as yet has not yielded any substantiating archaeological evidence.

## Dwellings

Most intramural sections excavated in the area of the Southeast Hill have produced evidence of occupation at the end of the Iron Age. Several prominent building remains, however, are particularly important for exemplifying both the city's material culture and the intensity of the 586 B.C.E. Babylonian destruction (fig. 4.8). These are the House of Ahiel, the Burnt Room, and the Bullae House uncovered above the Gihon Spring.[20] Additional remains of contemporary dwellings were uncovered on the Southwest Hill.

The House of Ahiel followed the so-called four-room or four-pillared house plan typical of Israelite architecture (fig. 4.9).[21] It measured 8 × 8 meters and was situated along the higher of two supportive terraces. Its name derives from a storage jar fragment (ostracon)

Fig. 4.8. Shiloh area G, looking west. Left and right: two corners of the Hasmonean city wall, in-between the "stepped stone structure" of the Early Iron Age, later built over by the House of Ahiel with two standing pillars (left) and the Burnt Room (right); under the wooden footpath the nonvisible Bullae House. Courtesy of the Israel Exploration Society.

with a Hebrew inscription bearing the name Ahiel. The walls of this building are made of roughly dressed fieldstones and ashlars. Two stone monoliths and two built piers supported the ceiling above the first level and separated the central courtyard from two side chambers. Adjacent to the northern wall of the House of Ahiel was a three-room annex, including a storeroom with over fifty restorable ceramic vessels, mostly storage jars. The floor of a small chamber adjoining the storeroom was paved with a thick layer of lime plaster. A limestone toilet with a plaster-lined cesspit beneath it was embedded in one side of this floor (fig. 4.10).

The Burnt Room is separated from the House of Ahiel by a narrow alleyway and is named after the accumulation of charred debris covering its floor. A staircase built of finely cut ashlars abutted the southern wall of the house and led to its second story. The rec-

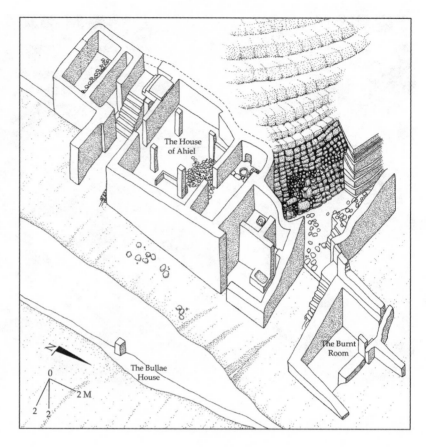

Fig. 4.9. House of
Ahiel in Shiloh area
G, reconstruction.
Redrawn by J. Dillon,
after: Cahill and Tar-
ler, "Excavations," 38.

tangular Burnt Room is located north of the wall delimiting the
external staircase and forms the southern, ground-floor room of a
partially excavated building. Evidence for the second story was provided by the position of the landing above the external staircase as
well as of the corresponding ledge in the western wall, located some
2.5 meters above the floor. The carbonized remains of wooden ceiling beams were found on the ground surface. Among the charred
debris extracted from this room were pieces of burnt wood that included fragments that had been carved with motifs similar to those
known from carved ivories. The majority of the wood came from
indigenous trees; some of the more finely carved pieces were identi-

fied as boxwood (*buxus*), a species found in Cyprus, northern Syria, and southern Turkey.

The Bullae House lies east of the House of Ahiel, on the next, lower, terrace. It was named after a hoard of over fifty bullae, or clay seals, found hidden in the northwestern corner of the house. These artifacts represent the first assemblage of legible Hebrew seal impressions to be found in a clear stratigraphic and datable context. Since all that was excavated consisted only of a narrow strip (ca. 8 × 1 meters) located at the structure's western edge, little can be said about its original plan. Nevertheless, it is clear that its western wall served both as the external wall of the structure and the revetment for a street or alleyway leading to the upper terrace buildings. As in the Burnt Room, a thick layer of charred debris covered the house's hard plaster floor.

The massive destruction of Jerusalem by the Babylonians is evi-

Fig. 4.10. Toilet in the House of Ahiel. Courtesy of the Israel Exploration Society.

dent not only in the thick layers of burnt remains uncovered in buildings such as the Burnt Room and the Bullae House, but also in the
deep stone rubble from collapsed houses scattered over the eastern
slope. The biblical narrative of Jerusalem's destruction (2 Kgs 25:8–
10; Jer 39:8; 2 Chron 36:18–19) parallels the archaeological finds,
confirming the 586 B.C.E. date for the city's collapse as documented in
additional historical sources. The ceramic evidence uncovered in the
destruction layer found over most areas of the eastern slope of the
Southeast Hill is identical to that characteristic of the last phase of the
Iron Age at other Judaean sites.[22]

## The Water System

The entrance shaft and the spring pool of the Bronze Age water
system continued to be used throughout the Iron Age period. The
material remains of the period associated with David's conquest and
his son Solomon's building activities do not reveal any changes with
respect to the city's water installations. In fact, it was not before the
end of the eighth or the beginning of the seventh century B.C.E. that
the initiative was taken to modify the access to the system. Until then,
the upper surface of the harder rock formation served as the walking
ground (fig. 3.5). Now, the tunnel beginning at the bottom of the
staircase was dug right into the rock (fig. 4.11). The intention was
probably to create a more direct access to the spring. After beginning
the construction of this tunnel (for a length of 25 meters and descending some 3.2 meters), the top entrance to a natural vertical
shaft — later to be known as Warren's Shaft — was uncovered by chance
(fig. 4.12).

In order to reach the spring directly, a tunnel (following a crack
winding its way southward and then eastward toward the spring) was
hewn from the bottom of the shaft. At the same time, a fissure in the
rock was followed from the Spring Pool with the goal to connect the
tunnel simultaneously from both directions. The meeting point is

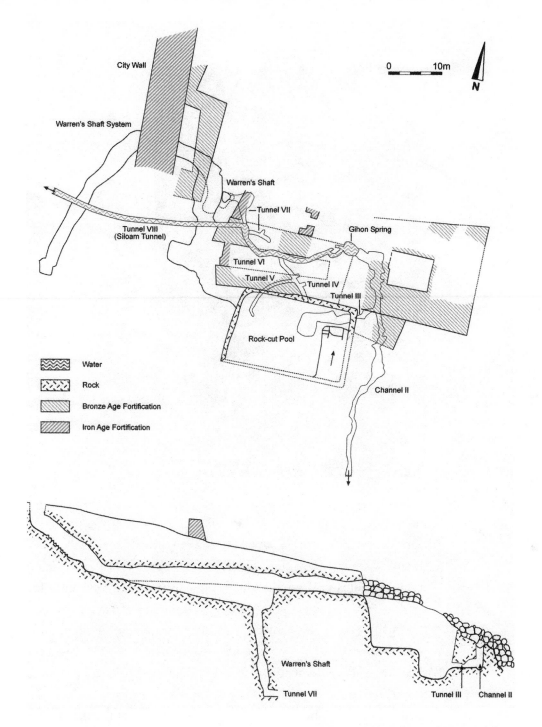

City Wall

Warren's Shaft System

0    10m

N

Warren's Shaft

Tunnel VII

Tunnel VIII
(Siloam Tunnel)

Gihon Spring

Tunnel VI

Tunnel V

Tunnel IV

Tunnel III

Rock-cut Pool

Channel II

Water

Rock

Bronze Age Fortification

Iron Age Fortification

Warren's Shaft

Tunnel VII

Tunnel III

Channel II

Fig. 4.11. Plan and section of the Iron Age water system. Redrawn by J. Dillon and M. Speidel, after: Reich and Shukron, "Jerusalem, City of David," 69, fig. 107, and idem, "Jerusalem, Gihon Spring," 137, fig. 179.

Fig. 4.12. Top of Warren's Shaft, with upper edge of hard dolomite stone visible on top, serving as ground surface of the Bronze Age tunnel. Photo H. Bloedhorn.

located ca. 2.5 meters from the pool. On the wall of the pool, just right of the mouth of Tunnel IV, is a smoothed surface, possibly intended for an inscription (fig. 4.13). A Hebrew inscription found inside the Siloam Tunnel is usually cited as supportive evidence for attributing the tunnel's construction to the reign of King Hezekiah (fig. 4.14).[23] The text, however, commemorates the dramatic moment when the two crews of tunnel diggers met. It does not mention the name of the ruler who initiated the ambitious project. The letters are written in the ancient Hebrew script (Paleo-Hebrew), which was used before the Babylonian exile.[24] The beginning of the inscription is missing and the entire upper portion of the panel was left blank (fig. 4.15).[25] The inscription reads:

[The day of] the breach. This is the record of how the tunnel was breached. While the excavators were wielding (2) their pick-axes, each man toward his co-worker, and while there were yet three cubits for the breach, a voice was heard, each man (3) calling his co-worker, because there was a cavity[26] in the rock (extending) from the south to the north. So on the day (4) of the breach, the excavators struck, each man to meet his co-worker, pick-axe against pick-axe. Then the water (5) flowed from the spring to the pool, a distance of one thousand and two hundred cubits. (6) One hundred cubits was the height of the rock above the heads of the excavators.[27]

Until recently, scholars have associated the construction of the Siloam Tunnel with the Assyrian siege by King Sennacherib. The

Fig. 4.13. Entrance to Tunnel IV at the bottom of the rock-cut pool. Upper right: the smoothed rock face, which may have been intended for an inscription. Photo H. Bloedhorn.

Fig. 4.14. Siloam Tunnel, several meters away from the southern exit. The inscription was positioned between the two fissures on the left rock scarp. Courtesy of the Israel Antiquities Authority.

Fig. 4.15. Siloam Tunnel inscription in the Archaeological Museum, Istanbul. Courtesy of the École biblique.

biblical text describes how King Hezekiah prepared the city for the imminent threat by blocking the flow of Jerusalem's water source (2 Chron 32:2–4). He apparently sealed the existing water outlets and constructed a new tunnel (the continuation of Channel II) that cut through the southeastern slope (2 Kgs 20:20; 2 Chron 32:30; Sir 48:17).

In the opinion of the present authors, however, the actual Siloam Tunnel was the result of an extensive, long-term building project that must have been planned years in advance. A parallel to the Jerusalem system can be found on the island of Samos, where a 1036-meter-long underground passageway connects the spring to the settlement. Here, too, evidence of two teams working in opposite directions is clearly visible. Eupalinus created this masterpiece of ancient engineering toward the end of the sixth century B.C.E.[28] It took him about six years to complete the project. The Jerusalem tunnel is only about half the length, yet its serpentine route and difficult access underground clearly made the planning and execution process far more complicated and time consuming. One should also bear in mind that it was dug some two centuries before its Greek counterpart. The available archaeological evidence therefore seems to suggest that the Siloam Tunnel was not the result of hasty construction in response to the approaching enemy. It is far more likely that Hezekiah's successor, King Manasseh, would have been the initiator of the construction. His long and peaceful reign make him a much more probable candidate for this major long-term building project.[29]

### Necropolis

The necropolis of Iron Age Jerusalem forms a ring around the city. The largest concentration of tombs can be found beyond the settlement limits of the Southeast Hill on the eastern slope of the Kidron Valley (fig. 4.16). Today, this area of the Silwan village is almost completely built over with houses.[30] Only a few tombs can be

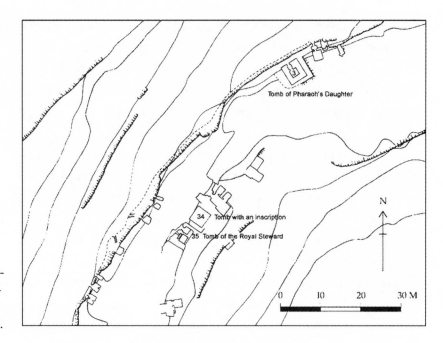

Fig. 4.16. Plan of the northern part of the Silwan necropolis. Redrawn by J. Dillon, after: Ussishkin, *Village of Silwan*, 24, fig. 6.

located in the southern and western Hinnom Valley; most of them are poorly preserved.[31] An additional cemetery is located outside the Old City, north of today's Damascus Gate.[32]

The majority of Iron Age burials are represented by rock-cut tombs. Other practices, such as cremation or interment in anthropomorphic clay coffins or sarcophagi, attested at many other contemporary sites in Palestine, are completely absent here. Problematic for our understanding of this era's burial customs is that among all published tombs in Jerusalem, only six were not disturbed by robbery (figs. 4.17–18). It should also be noted that all excavated tombs can be dated no earlier than the Late Iron Age or the transition between the Late Iron Age and the Persian period.

The most common Iron Age burial form, still in use in the Persian and Early Hellenistic periods, consisted of a single underground chamber with steps descending from ground level on one of the short sides. Initially of irregular shape but later developed into a well-designed rectangular plan, this chamber was equipped with rock-cut

Fig. 4.17. The undisturbed Iron Age burial cave 25 in the Hinnom Valley necropolis, looking west. From the central chamber an opening leads into cave 25 with benches on three sides, on the right with six omega-shaped head supports. Below this bench is a repository that contained bones of over 95 individuals, pottery, seals, coins, and two inscribed silver plaques with the priestly benediction of Num 6:24–26. Photo H. Bloedhorn.

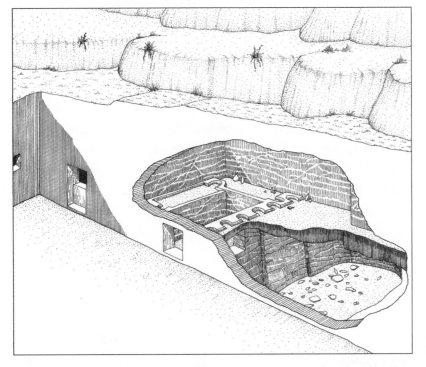

Fig. 4.18. Reconstruction of burial cave 25 in the Hinnom Valley necropolis. Redrawn by J. Dillon, after: Barkay, *Ketef Hinnom*, 24.

burial benches lining three sides, which were used for primary burials. Toward the end of the Iron Age, a niche or repository for secondary burial of the bones, usually placed underneath one of the benches, began to appear.

An additional type, again pertinent only to the latter part of the Iron Age, has flat burial troughs with omega-shaped supports for the head of the deceased. Previously interpreted as Hathor wigs[33] or stylized representations of a mother's womb, they might have simply functioned as headrests, a kind of embracing pillow.[34] Especially well-furnished tomb complexes of this group sometimes have ceilings decorated with cornices (*cyma recta*) as well as profiled doorframes.

Both burial types, those with benches along the walls and those equipped with flat burial troughs and headrests, can also be found together in larger tomb complexes. The latter are usually entered through a vestibule with no burial installations that gave access to various chambers with installations. The most elaborate burial site of this kind is the École biblique tomb complex, considered by some to represent the royal tombs of Manasseh (d. 642 B.C.E.) and Amon (d. 640 B.C.E.).[35]

Unlike tombs with shaft access known from other contemporary sites in the coastal areas and unlike those with troughs and headrests or benches that are paralleled by numerous tomb complexes in the Judaean hills, another group of tombs in Jerusalem is otherwise unknown in the region. These are located near the village of Silwan on the eastern slope of the Kidron Valley and are characterized by the occasional appearance of pyramids and monumental entrances with framed doorways and windows.

### Distinctive Finds

In addition to those objects that can be associated with activities of daily sustenance, such as agricultural and other tools or vessels for eating, drinking, and cooking, many of the finds included in the regular archaeological repertoire from Jerusalem and the surrounding region inform us about the political, administrative, and religious frameworks.[36]

### THE *LMLK* SEAL IMPRESSIONS

The royal seal impressions on storage jar handles, commonly known as *lmlk* (*lamelekh*) seal impressions, have been found at most Late Iron Age sites excavated within the Kingdom of Judah (fig. 4.19). About 1800 such stamped handles are known from excavations, surveys, and collections, of which approximately 300 come from excavations in Jerusalem, the majority coming from the City of David and the Jewish Quarter excavations.[37] The impressions contain an emblem representing either a four-winged beetle or a two-winged solar disc, as well as an inscription above the emblem with the word *lmlk*, meaning "belonging to the king." Beneath the emblem is one of four place-names; *hbrn* (Hebron), *zp* or *zyp* (Ziph), *swkh* (Socoh), or *mmsht* (unidentified).

Although the exact purpose of the stamped jars and the role of the four cities named on the seal impressions remain unclear, there is general agreement among scholars that the word *lmlk* indicates royal ownership or authority. It is unclear, however, whether the jars were intended for taxation, emergency food provisions, or from royal estates producing wine, oil, or other products. The stamped jars first appear around the end of the eighth century B.C.E. (reign of Hezekiah, king of Judah) and continue into the seventh century B.C.E. They constitute an important example of the extensive use of seals in a statewide royal administrative system of the Kingdom of Judah.

Fig. 4.19. Four-winged *lmlk* seal impression of the *hbrn* (Hebron) type. Redrawn by J. Dillon, after: Shoham, *Seal Impressions*, 78, M1.

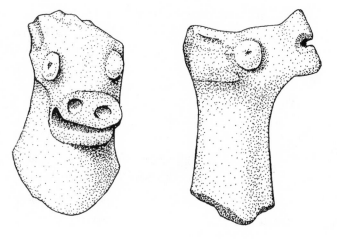

Fig. 4.20. Horse figurine from Avigad area A. Redrawn by J. Dillon, after: Geva, *Jewish Quarter Excavations*, II, 81, F 79.

### CLAY FIGURINES

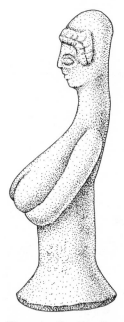

Figurines, either zoomorphic or anthropomorphic, are among the most common pottery finds from the Late Iron Age.[38] The animal figurines are rather schematic, depicting horses (sometimes with riders) and other unidentified quadrupeds (fig. 4.20). The statuettes of women depict their two hands clutching their breasts, and the head is either handmade (i.e., pinched) or molded separately and then attached to the cylindrical body (fig. 4.21). In Jerusalem, the animal figurines comprise approximately 75 percent of all excavated figurines, while anthropomorphic pillar figurines constitute the balance. It should be stressed that the very large number (some two thousand figurines) uncovered thus far in Judah, and Jerusalem in particular, is disproportionate to other areas in Palestine. These figurines can be understood as an expression of popular beliefs whose traditions were rooted in the political and cultural development of Judah, a reality that stands in contrast to the biblical injunction against the making of graven images (Exod 20:4).[39] Recently published excavation reports have shown that the figurines have appeared in similar concentrations in residential buildings and locations considered to have been ritual sites.

Fig. 4.21. Fertility figurine from Avigad area A. Redrawn by J. Dillon, after: Geva, *Jewish Quarter Excavations*, II, 78, F 57.

## INSCRIBED SILVER PLAQUES

In an Iron Age necropolis excavated in the Hinnom Valley and dated to approximately the seventh century B.C.E.,[40] archaeologists uncovered an undisturbed repository in a hollowed area hewn beneath one of the burial benches (figs. 4.17–18). In addition to the bones of the deceased, the repository contained burial gifts consisting of some one thousand items, such as pottery vessels; jewelry (plate 4); arrowheads; bone and ivory artifacts; alabaster vessels; beads of various sizes, colors and materials; a piece of pre-blown glass; and one rare, sixth-century B.C.E. coin (fig. 4.22). Among the rich finds of the repository were two small rolled-up silver plaques (97 × 27 millimeters and 39 × 11 millimeters) featuring inscriptions that were delicately incised with a sharp instrument.[41] Two similar versions of the well-known priestly benediction (Deut 7:9; Num 6:24–26), biblical verses that are still recited to this day (as part of the eighteen benedictions of the daily prayer), could be deciphered. A paleographic study of the script indicates that the strips of silver are contemporaneous

Fig. 4.22. Pottery from the Hinnom Valley necropolis. Courtesy of the Israel Museum.

with the use of the chambers, which were probably hewn sometime in the mid seventh century B.C.E.

The character of the inscription and the shape of the plaques — when rolled up, a string could be threaded through the center space — indicates that they were used as amulets or charms. Similar rolled-up metal plaques (though usually of bronze or lead) containing inscriptions of amuletic character have been found in other excavations in Israel but date to the Roman period and later. These silver plaques constitute the earliest-known copies of the biblical text and represent some of the oldest objects bearing the name of the God of Israel, YHWH.

# 5 ✦ The Babylonian and Persian Periods

Thus said King Cyrus of Persia: The Lord God of Heaven has
given me all the kingdoms of the earth and has charged me with
building Him a house in Jerusalem, which is in Judah. Anyone of
you of all His people — may his God be with him, and let him go up
to Jerusalem that is in Judah and build the House of the Lord God
of Israel, the God that is in Jerusalem.

Ezra 1:2–3

## The Reduced City

The small Kingdom of Judah vacillated between policies of sub-
mission to and revolt against Babylonian domination. In 597 B.C.E.,
King Jehoiachin, his family, and entourage — the elite of Judah — as
well as many of the Temple vessels and royal treasures, were taken
to Babylon (2 Kgs 24:12–16). Jehoiachin's uncle, Mattaniah, re-

named Zedekiah, was appointed king of Judah by the Babylonians and reigned in Jerusalem for eleven years in the service of the king of Babylonia (2 Kgs 24:17–18).[1] In 588 B.C.E., however, he rebelled against Nebuchadnezzar with a coalition of several states, including Egypt, against the advice of the prophet Jeremiah. In the winter of 587 B.C.E. (on the tenth of Tevet), the Babylonian forces placed Jerusalem under siege. The city held out until the summer of 586 B.C.E. (the ninth of Tammuz), when its walls were breached from the north, and hunger and thirst weakened the resistance of its inhabitants.[2] One month later (on the ninth of Av), Nebuchadnezzar ordered the burning of the city, the walls, the Temple, and the royal palace. The accounts in 2 Kings 25:1–21, 2 Chronicles 36:11–21, and Jeremiah 52:1–27 describe the siege and devastation of Jerusalem; many were killed or exiled to Babylonia, and Temple furnishings and parts of the structure were also removed to that country. The Babylonians humiliated Zedekiah and appointed Gedaliah governor of Judah. Gedaliah was assassinated when he advocated compliance with Babylonian rule (2 Kgs 25:22–26).

In Babylonia, the deported Jews founded communities and religious institutions, established themselves in commerce and agriculture, and kept the memory of Jerusalem alive through worship and prophetic discourse (such as that of Ezekiel). Thus, in 538 B.C.E., when Cyrus, King of Persia, conquered the Babylonian empire and issued a decree allowing the Jews to rebuild the Temple (Ezra 1:2–4), a group of exiles returned to Jerusalem. Their return and the reconstruction of the Temple occurred in stages over several generations under the Persian kings Cyrus (ca. 559–530 B.C.E.), Darius I (522–486 B.C.E.), and Artaxerxes I (465–424 B.C.E.). Under Cyrus, an altar was erected, sacrifices were resumed (conducted by the high priest Joshua, a descendant of Zadok), and Passover was celebrated. In 515 B.C.E., during the reign of Darius I, and with the encouragement of the prophet Haggai, the Jews rebuilt the Temple. The Persians appointed Zerubbabel, who was of Davidic descent, as governor of

Yehud (the Aramaic name of the province of Judah in the Persian period). The royal house of David, however, was not restored, and the governor and high priest served as leaders of the Jews in the Persian province.

The most important wave of returnees arrived from Babylonia under the leadership of Ezra the Scribe in 458–57 B.C.E. (Ezra 7). In addition, Artaxerxes appointed his Jewish cup-bearer Nehemiah as governor. His arrival in Jerusalem in 445 B.C.E. saw far-reaching changes. He supervised the quick rebuilding of the city walls and gates despite the protests of local peoples (Neh 3–4). The city, however, remained small and underpopulated. Nehemiah's ability to accomplish the task quickly and efficiently is related to the reduced size of the city and most sections' not requiring more than repair.

Between 445 B.C.E. and 398 B.C.E., Nehemiah and Ezra implemented an ambitious program of religious reforms that affected Jerusalem.[3] These included the public reading of the Torah, the abolition of mixed marriages, the reestablishment of festivals and Temple-related rituals, the enforcement of Sabbath observance, and provisions for the maintenance of the Temple and its sacrifices, as well as for the priests, Levites, and Temple staff. Such a grandiose plan required the imposition of an annual tax on Jewish households throughout the world (Neh 10:29–40). Nehemiah also provided for the repopulation of Jerusalem with returnees and their descendants, stipulating that one-tenth of the Jews in the country must settle in the city (Neh 11:2). Thus, the Temple and Jerusalem achieved greater importance as the center of world Jewry.

After Nehemiah, the Persians and the high priest appointed a governor to take command in Jerusalem and Yehud. A new class of scribes, whose task was to interpret the Torah, followed in the footsteps of Ezra. At the end of the fifth century B.C.E., the Jewish temple in Elephantine, Egypt (Yeb) was destroyed, and in 408 B.C.E. Jewish soldiers in the Persian garrison corresponded with the Jewish governor Bagohi and the high priest Yohanan in Jerusalem.[4] Their letters, written in Aramaic, attest to the importance of Jerusalem as the religious center of the Jewish people.[5] Little is known about Yehud during the rest of the Persian period.

## Fortifications

To rebuild the destroyed city wall that had been lying in ruins since the conquest by Nebuchadnezzar in 586 B.C.E., Nehemiah, son of Hacaliah, was sent from Babylonia to Jerusalem in the twentieth year of Artaxerxes I (445 B.C.E.; Neh 2:1–8). Upon his arrival, he immediately proceeded to reconstruct the city wall, an undertaking that was completed in only fifty-two days (Neh 2:11–4:17; 6:15–16; 7:1–3) and subsequently dedicated with a celebratory procession (Neh 12:27–43).

The narrative of the nightly search for the damaged wall (Neh 2:11–20), its reconstruction (Neh 3:1–7:3), and ensuing dedication (Neh 12:27–43) is based on Nehemiah's firsthand report and thus constitutes the most valuable biblical description of the city, including detailed information about its topography.

The systematic description of each building section allows for a relatively reliable reconstruction. Nehemiah's city wall did not follow the same course as the earlier walls of the Bronze or Iron Ages, which ran through the middle of the eastern slope and in the valley.[6] Maintaining, for the most part, its original location on the western side, following the course of the Central Valley, the eastern boundary was now moved up to the eastern ridge of the Southeast Hill.

In contrast to the detailed literary description of the city's reconstruction, archaeological remains are very sparse. Various wall segments, which are hesitantly attributed to the reconstruction under Nehemiah, were uncovered on the eastern slope of the Southeast Hill.[7] More decisively Persian are the remains of a gate — possibly the rebuilt Valley Gate — uncovered on the western slope of the Southeast Hill (fig. 5.1).[8]

Fig. 5.1. The Valley Gate on the western slope of the Southeast Hill, 1923–1925. Crowfoot and Fitzgerald, *Excavations in the Tyropoeon Valley*, plate 1.

The so-called Solomonic stone quarries beneath a section of today's northern Old City wall have been associated with postexilic fortification efforts, as indicated by sphinx graffiti from the Persian period.[9]

## The Second Temple

Despite the fundamental role of the postexilic Second Temple, built by Zerubbabel, in the history of ancient Jerusalem, archaeological remains of this edifice are lacking. Given that in Jewish tradition the rebuilt Herodian Temple is also considered the Second Temple, merely the location and size of the original structure from the end of the sixth century B.C.E. were adopted; the actual structure and construction materials from the Persian period did not survive the Herodian replacement. It has been suggested that the stretch of wall north of the so-called straight joint, visible 32 meters from the present southeastern corner of the platform, is Persian (fig. 5.2). Unlike the Herodian and Hasmonean ashlars left and right of the seam, the stones of the earlier wall, ca. 73 meters north of the southeastern

Fig. 5.2. Eastern wall of today's Haram al-Sharif, considered the oldest part of the retaining wall: the enormous stones of the two bottom courses immediately south of the Golden Gate. Photo R. Schick.

corner, have a flat margin with an irregularly protruding, sometimes very heavy, boss.[10] Although this kind of masonry is known at other Persian period sites in Lebanon, most scholars are still hesitant to associate this wall segment with the rebuilt Temple whose construction was completed around 516 B.C.E.

## Distinctive Finds

Most of the few objects associated with the Babylonian and Persian periods in Jerusalem clearly evince the occurrence of an administrative change. The intentional repetitive character of words and symbols on seals and coins is obvious.

### SEALS AND SEAL IMPRESSIONS

Most of the seals and seal impressions from the Persian period in Palestine fall into two categories: private seals and official seals con-

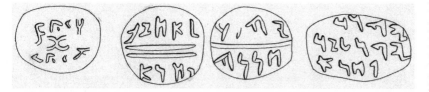

Fig. 5.3. Four seal impressions from Ramat Rachel containing a legend telling the province name, Yehud, as well as a personal name and the word *phw'*—which translates as "the governor." Redrawn by J. Dillon, after: Stern, *Material Culture*, 202.

nected with the administration apparatus of the provinces of Judah and Samaria.[11] The first category includes seals imported from Babylonia, Persia, Egypt, and Greece, as well as local seals with a mixed style. The second consists of a large number of impressions (and one seal) that are interpreted as having been used for tax collection by the Persian administration in Judah. A survey of the contexts in which they were found reveals that they first appeared in Palestine at the end of the seventh century B.C.E., were widespread in the sixth, and continued to be used in the fifth. Most official seal impressions found in Jerusalem (in the excavations of the Ophel, the Tyropoeon Valley, the Southern Wall, the Armenian Garden, the Jewish Quarter, and the City of David) are engraved with the Aramaic name of the province, Yehud, written in full or in various abbreviated formulas in Aramaic or Hebrew script. Several are stamped with monograms, imprints of officials, and figures of animals (fig. 5.3). The few isolated finds of Persian seal impressions on the Western Hill confirm the long-established suggestion that the city boundaries at this time did not extend beyond the Eastern Hill.

### YEHUD COINS

The earliest coins found in Palestine are attributed to the end of the sixth century B.C.E. They became more common in the second half of the fifth century B.C.E., attesting to a great variety of coin types. It is difficult to ascertain whether coins were in wide circulation among the populace in the first century of Persian rule in Palestine or if they were restricted to use by a minority such as merchants, officials, and soldiers. Although coins were already in every-

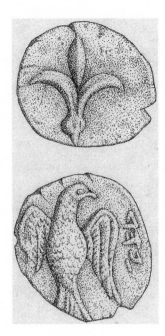

Fig. 5.4. Yehud coin. Obverse: a falcon standing with outspread wings; to its right is a *yhd*
inscription; reverse: a lily. Redrawn by J. Dillon, after: Stern, *Material Culture*, 225, fig. 375.

day use by the fifth and fourth centuries B.C.E., metal ingots were still
being used by weight as currency in business transactions. The coins
in circulation in Palestine in the Persian period included Greek coins,
coins of Phoenician cities, and coins minted in Palestine.[12] Coins
belonging to a separate group among the locally minted ones bear the
legend "Yehud," apparently struck by the governor of Jerusalem with
the authorization of the Persian royal treasury (fig. 5.4). This body
also granted the governors of the other provinces of Palestine the
right to issue an independent coinage. Most are, on the whole, crude
imitations of the Attic drachm, although the head of a bearded male
in Oriental style or even that of the king of Persia generally appears
instead of the head of Athena and the falcon instead of the owl.

## 6 ✦ The Hellenistic Period

Whoever has not seen the [Temple] building erected by Herod has
not seen a beautiful building in his lifetime.

BABYLONIAN TALMUD, BAVA BATRA 4A

### Hasmonean and Herodian Jerusalem

In 332 B.C.E., Alexander the Great conquered Judaea (the Greek
name for Yehud, or Judah) from the Persians and made it part of his
empire, which extended from Greece to India. His conquest led to
the colonization of the Near East by Greeks and the spread of Greek
language, architecture, culture, and lifestyle throughout the region.[1]
Local and Greek customs merged, creating a fusion called Hellenism,
albeit with a predominance of Greek elements.[2] With Alexander's
death in 323 B.C.E., his vast empire split into several kingdoms.[3] Although at first contested, Judaea eventually came under the rule of the
Ptolemaic dynasty of Egypt from 301 to 198 B.C.E. and subsequently
under the Seleucid dynasty of Syria from 198 to 63 B.C.E.[4]

The Seleucids and the Ptolemies allowed the Jews to live by their own laws, granting the Jewish communities autonomy. The status of the temple and recognition of the leadership of the high priest and Temple staff were confirmed in an edict issued by the Seleucid ruler Antiochus III after his conquest of Jerusalem in 198 B.C.E. (Josephus, *Antiquities* XII, 138–46).[5]

Under the Ptolemies, Hellenism penetrated slowly into the upper classes of Jewish society in Judaea.[6] When Judaea came under Seleucid rule, particularly after the accession of Antiochus IV Epiphanes in 175 B.C.E., adoption of Hellenistic culture and lifestyles by the wealthy aristocracy and Temple priests proceeded more rapidly, as related in Maccabees 1 and 2.[7] In 169–68 B.C.E., on his return from a raid on Egypt, Antiochus IV plundered the Temple in Jerusalem, destroyed parts of the city, massacred its people, and placed a garrison of pagan soldiers in a fortress called the Akra to rule the city (1 Macc 1:20–40).[8] Antiochus's policy of actively encouraging the dissemination of Greek culture and religion, combined with the pro-Hellenistic sympathies of the priests — as well as the presence of foreign troops — set the stage for unprecedented royal decrees against Judaism and the ultimate dedication of the Temple to the pagan god Zeus Olympius.[9]

Antiochus IV's decrees incited an armed revolt by Jews who wished to remain faithful to their ancestral laws. The revolt was led by a priestly family, the Hasmoneans of Modi'in, a town located northwest of Jerusalem.[10] In December, 164 B.C.E., exactly three years after Antiochus's edict, the Hasmonean Judah the Maccabee and his troops entered the city, purified and reconsecrated the Temple, offered sacrifices, and prayed (1 Macc 4:37–60).[11] For over two decades, Hasmonean control of Jerusalem fluctuated because of several Seleucid victories, some Jewish hesitation and opposition, and the presence of foreign troops in the Akra. In 142 B.C.E., Simon rose to power, and in 141 B.C.E., shortly after expelling the foreigners from the Akra and destroying it (1 Macc 14:49–50), he was recognized as high priest and ethnarch by both the Seleucids and an assembly of

Jews in Jerusalem (1 Macc 14:25–15:9). He established Judaea as a sovereign state and founded the Hasmonean Dynasty, which would rule over a prosperous society and an increasingly expanding country (annexing Idumea, Samaria, the Galilee, and parts of Transjordan).[12]

In 104 B.C.E., Simon's grandson Judah Aristobulus I adopted the title of "king." Subsequently, the Hasmoneans served as both kings and high priests. According to Josephus, their roles as high priests and their policy of territorial expansion, compounded by military and financial burdens, caused contention and civil strife, particularly under Alexander Jannaeus (103–76 B.C.E.).[13] Social and ideological rifts created ongoing tension between the Sadducees, the wealthy, pro-Hasmonean priestly aristocracy, and the Pharisees, the latter being interpreters of the Torah who cultivated religious observance and were closer to the masses.[14] Other groups, such as the Essenes and the Dead Sea sect, removed themselves from Jerusalem society, seeking a purer life without political involvement.

Under Hasmonean rule, Jerusalem expanded greatly in size and population, as it was both the capital of an independent kingdom and a holy city for all Jews. The Hasmoneans extended the city walls, built a palace, fortifications, and public buildings, and dug aqueducts and reservoirs. The importance of Temple ritual increased with the pilgrimage festivals of Passover, Shavuot (the Pentecost), and the Feast of Tabernacles, drawing large crowds to the Temple from Judaea, the Galilee, and the Diaspora. The Hasmoneans levied a half-shekel annual tax on all Jewish households for Temple maintenance and may have convened sessions of the high courts and their representative body in the Temple Mount area.

The independent Hasmonean kingdom of Judaea was a casualty of Roman expansion in the Near East and of the bitter power struggle between the sons of Alexander Jannaeus, Hyrcanus II, and Aristobulus II.[15] In *War* I, 123–54 and *Antiquities* XIV, 34–79, Josephus vividly describes the intervention of the Roman general Pompey (at the request of Hyrcanus), his siege of Jerusalem, and entry into the city and the Temple in 63 B.C.E. Pompey appointed Hyrcanus II as high priest and ethnarch, to rule only over Judaea and the Galilee, where Jews were the majority population.[16] The rest of the country remained mostly under Roman rule. However, Hyrcanus's adviser, Antipater the Idumean, a descendant of forced converts to Judaism, held the real power and ruled the country with the support of the Romans.

With the assassination of Antipater in 43 B.C.E., Herod became the leading contender for power over the entire country. He fought his Jewish opponents with merciless brutality and skillfully made his way through the various changes of power in Rome, from Cassius to Mark Antony, and finally, to Gaius Octavian (later Augustus). In 40 B.C.E., Mark Antony appointed Herod king of Judaea, giving him massive Roman military, political, and financial support.

The establishment of the Roman Empire in 27 B.C.E. under Augustus led to greater stability and prosperity. Augustus granted Herod additional territory, thereby increasing the size of his kingdom (Josephus, *War* I, 393–400). The king undertook numerous ambitious building projects throughout the country, such as several large fortresses in the Judaean desert; cities in Samaria, the Galilee, and Judaea, including the harbor town of Caesarea; as well as roads, aqueducts, and pagan temples. Jerusalem was transformed by the Herodian works of fortresses, walls, palaces, public buildings, and particularly construction on the Temple Mount and its environs (*War* I, 401–21).

The death of Herod in 4 B.C.E. resulted in massive unrest among the Jews, suppressed harshly by Roman troops who set fire to the porticoes of the Temple (*War* II, 39–54) and by Varus, the Roman governor of Syria (*War* II, 66–75). Augustus subsequently divided the country among Herod's sons. Archelaus was appointed ethnarch in Idumea, Judaea, and Samaria. The rest of the country was divided between Herod's two other sons—Antipas ruled over the Galilee and Peraea, and Philip governed Auranitis, Trachonitis, and Batanea (*War* II, 93–100). From 6–41 C.E., Judaea was placed under direct Roman rule and governed by a prefect. The emperor Claudius (41–54 C.E.) appointed Herod's grandson, Herod Agrippa I, king of the entire country (41–44 C.E.). From 44 C.E. until the outbreak of the First Revolt against Rome in 66 C.E., Judaea was governed by Roman prefects and the Galilee and Transjordan by Herod Agrippa II, son of Herod Agrippa I. The seat of Roman administration was located in Caesarea, but during Jewish pilgrimage festivals the prefects stayed at Herod's palace near the western entrance to the city. Additional troops were lodged in the Antonia fortress, which guarded the northern approach to the Temple Mount (*War* I, 402; *Ant.* XV, 318).

Despite tension between Jewish groups and Roman authorities, Jerusalem continued to grow and develop in the years between Herod's death and the revolt. According to Josephus (*War* V, 136–83), Jerusalem was an impressive city surrounded by walls and towers, its centerpiece the Temple. The Temple Mount construction begun by Herod was completed during the first century C.E. The offices of the Sanhedrin (supreme court) were adjacent to the Temple Mount. Pilgrimage to the Temple and the city increased during the major festivals. Jerusalem had synagogues, academies of Jewish learning, residences, and palaces, and continued to function as a major city in the Near East. The attempt of Herod Agrippa I (41–44 C.E.) to erect a third wall encompassing the newer, northern section of the city was halted by Claudius and later completed by Herod Agrippa II (*War* V, 147–55).

Zealot activism, Jewish discontent, and Roman policies led to a full-scale armed revolt in 66 C.E., mainly in the Galilee and the Jerusalem area. Rebel forces seized control of public buildings, the Antonia fortress, and the Temple Mount and expelled the Roman garrison from Jerusalem (*War* II, 425–56). With the failure of the initial Roman attempt to recapture the city from the west, the Zealots eventually took control. When Roman troops led by Vespasian defeated the Jewish rebels in the Galilee in 67 C.E. (*War* IV, 92–96), Zealot sympathizers and refugees from the Galilee moved into Jerusalem. The city was divided into sections controlled by Zealot leaders who fought against each other, in addition to waging war against the Romans. The suffering and starvation of the inhabitants were further exacerbated as Roman victories continued and Zealot rule grew harsher and more desperate. In the spring of 70 C.E., the Roman general Titus, son of the recently acclaimed emperor Vespasian, brought four legions and large contingents of auxiliaries who set up camps and a siege wall around the city. The siege and conquest lasted for about six months. Titus's forces conquered Jerusalem in several stages: first, by breaching the Third and Second Walls; next, by taking the Antonia fortress and breaching the wall of the Temple Mount; and, finally, by taking the Temple Mount, burning the Sanctuary, the Lower City, and the Upper City (*War* V–VI).

According to rabbinic tradition, the destruction of the Second Temple by the Romans took place on the Ninth of Av, the same day as the destruction of the First Temple by the Babylonians in 586 B.C.E.[17] Titus ordered the destruction of the entire city, with the exception of the three western Herodian towers — Phasael, Hippicus, and Mariamne — that attested to the greatness of the city he conquered (*War* VI, 409–13). The retaining walls of the Temple Mount also remained. Most of the survivors were executed, sold into slavery, or deported (*War* VI, 414–34). Titus held a triumphal procession in Rome, where he displayed the treasures of the Temple (*War* VII, 148–50). As of 75 C.E., these were kept in the newly built Forum Pacis (*War* VII, 158–62), including the famous golden menorah depicted on the Arch of Titus. The latter was erected in 81 C.E. to commemorate Titus's victory over the Jews and his destruction of Jerusalem.[18]

## Fortifications

### THE CITY WALLS

At first, the Hasmonean city was limited to the Southeast Hill, thereby following the course of the city walls rebuilt under the supervision of Nehemiah. According to the literary sources, this was a time of repeated destruction (in the spring of 167 B.C.E.: 1 Macc 1:29–37;

*Ant.* XII, 52; in the fall of 163 B.C.E.: 1 Macc 6:18–62), as well as repair and reconstruction (in 164 B.C.E.: 1 Macc 4:60; under Simon: 1 Macc 13:10; 14:37). Most references, however, remain vague. In the archaeological context, only one wall segment on the western slope of the Southeast Hill can be attributed to this period.[19]

A significant change in the city's landscape occurred in the second half of the second century B.C.E., probably as a result of the limited space available on the Southeast Hill. The city expanded once more, as in the Iron Age, beyond the Tyropoeon Valley to include the Southwest Hill. Based on the archaeological evidence, the construction of the wall — the so-called First Wall — can be dated to the latter part of the second century B.C.E.[20] This leaves us with two potential builders — either John Hyrcanus I (134–104 B.C.E.) or Alexander Jannaeus (103–76 B.C.E.), as they were the only long-term rulers during this period. Josephus attributed this wall to King David and King Solomon:

> Of the three walls, the most ancient, owing to the surrounding ravines and the hill above them on which it was reared, was well-nigh impregnable. But, besides the advantage of its position, it was also strongly built, David and Solomon and their successors on the throne having taken pride in the work. (*War* V, 142–43)

Though not historically founded, Josephus's description of the wall's course (*War* V, 136–45) is corroborated by the topographical features and archaeological remains.

Several segments of the northern wall have been exposed in excavations carried out in the Jewish Quarter.[21] Given the limited excavation areas, it is unclear whether these include the Gennath Gate (fig. 6.1).[22] Toward the northwestern corner of the wall, within today's Citadel, several more wall segments were exposed as early as the 1930s. A continuation was recently uncovered under the old prison.[23]

Fig. 6.1. The First Wall in Avigad area X-2. Courtesy of the Israel Exploration Society.

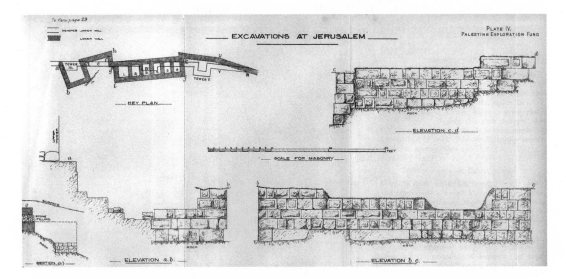

Fig. 6.2. Plan and elevation of the First Wall on Mt. Zion. Drawing by F. J. Bliss and A. C. Dickie, *Excavations at Jerusalem*, plate 4.

Fig. 6.3. Corner 'b' of the same wall, during excavation in 2007. The black hole on the right is one of the F. J. Bliss and A. C. Dickie's re-excavated tunnels. Photo H. Bloedhorn.

Additional segments of the wall came to light further south. Excavations in the area of the so-called Gate of the Essenes on Mount Zion also revealed some sections of the wall. An additional 300 meters of this wall were uncovered 100 meters further east, during the course of underground explorations.[24] Recent excavations exposed this wall (figs. 6.2–3).[25]

The Second Wall mentioned by Josephus (*War* V, 146) was erected under Hyrcanus II (63–40 B.C.E.).[26] The construction was not a result of demographic growth in the Herodian period; rather, the area between the Baris, the Temple Mount area to the south, and the First Wall, passing through the low-lying Tyropoeon Valley, was vulnerable and had to be protected. Only the beginning and end points of this wall are known; its exact course has yet to be identified.[27]

The Third Wall was to overshadow everything known so far (*War* V, 147–60). Begun under Herod Agrippa I in the early 40s to enclose the city's newly developed residential quarters, the endeavor was aborted by Claudius:

This recently built quarter was called in the vernacular Be-
zetha, which might be translated into Greek as New Town.
Seeing then the residents of this district in need of defense,
Agrippa, the father and namesake of the present king, began
the above-mentioned wall; but, fearing that Claudius Caesar
might suspect from the vast scale of the structure that he had
designs of revolution and revolt, he desisted after merely
laying the foundations. Indeed the city would have been im-
pregnable, had the wall been continued as it began. (*War* V,
151–53)

The construction was completed under Herod Agrippa II in 44 C.E.
Remains of a wall associated with the Third Wall were reported as
early as the nineteenth century C.E.[28] Additional sections, from then
on referred to as the Sukenik-Mayer Wall, were exposed in the
1920s,[29] 1960s,[30] 1970s,[31] and most recently in the 1980s (figs. 6.4–
5).[32] The area encompassed by this wall demarcated the populated
area of the city. It is surprising that no Hellenistic archaeological
finds other than the foundations of a large mausoleum (next to the
Arab central bus station on Nablus Road) were discovered in this
extended area.[33]

Josephus's descriptions are inconsistent regarding the walls' ori-

Fig. 6.4. Herodian
ashlar with a flat pro-
truding boss and de-
pressed margins,
reused in the
Sukenik-Mayer Wall.
Courtesy of the Israel
Antiquities Authority.

Fig. 6.5. Sukenik-Mayer Wall (trench 3), restored west of Nablus Road. Photo H. Bloedhorn.

gins and construction (*War* II, 218–19; *War* V, 147–60; *Ant.* XIX, 326–27). As a result, controversy over the dating arose immediately after exposure of the northwestern wall. Other than viewing the sections as the remains of the Third Wall mentioned by Josephus, various other suggestions have been made. Some view them as remainders of the Jewish or Roman barrier wall erected during the First Revolt,[34] or a wall built during the Bar Kokhba Revolt,[35] or a Byzantine fortification line.[36] Opponents to these alternative theories have pointed out the extremely poor building quality, which one would not expect to find in a newly constructed city wall. Moreover, based on the archaeological evidence, the area appears to have remained uninhabited in the late Herodian period. One has to keep in mind, however, that the First Revolt broke out only twenty years after the construction of the wall, and it would have taken some time to populate the area. Based on a recent evaluation of the remains of the Sukenik-Mayer Wall, it was concluded that there is no convincing argument opposing its identification as Jerusalem's Third Wall. None of the alternative theories could be proved convincingly.[37]

Following the destruction of the city in 70 C.E., very little was left of the First, Second, and Third Walls. Around 220 years passed before the idea arose to construct a completely new wall.

### THE AKRA FORTRESS

Two fortresses, the Akra and the Baris, built for monitoring activities on top of the Temple Mount, succeeded each other in one strategic location. The location and history of the Akra is one of the most controversial issues regarding building activity in ancient Jerusalem. The fortress is mentioned in the Letter of Aristeas, in the first, second, and fourth books of the Maccabees, and by Josephus. All these sources mention the Ptolemaic as well as the Seleucid Akra.

The Seleucid Akra constructed under Antiochus IV was located, according to Josephus, in the Lower City (*Ant.* XII, 252) to allow the occupying forces to oversee the local citizens as they ascended from the city to the Temple (*Ant.* XII, 362). The fortress was built on a high place overlooking the Temple courtyards and its gates (*Ant.* XII, 252), obliging one to descend toward the Temple plaza (*Ant.* XII, 406). This suggests that it was located south of the old (pre-Herodian) Temple Mount platform (within the area of today's al-Aqsa Mosque or Solomon's Stables), corresponding to what other sources describe.

The Ptolemaic Akra is mentioned in the Letter of Aristeas (100–104) and by Josephus, who also describes the Jewish expulsion of the Ptolemaic forces from the city (*Ant.* XII, 133–38). The gymnasium, too, was built by Jason at the beginning of Antiochus IV's reign "below the Akra," which would indicate its location south of the Temple.[38]

It is rather surprising that Josephus does not mention the earlier construction in *Antiquities* XII, 252, although he makes an earlier reference to the Ptolemaic fortress (*Ant.* XII 133, 138). It was assumed for a long time that two distinct buildings were described: the earlier one built by Nehemiah (Neh 2:8, 7:2), located north of the Temple platform and referred to by John Hyrcanus I as the Baris fortress, ultimately expanded by Herod to become the Antonia fortress (*Ant.* XV, 403–9); and the later one, located south of the Temple platform. Three points seem to defy this suggestion, however: the fortress of Nehemiah is not referred to as the Akra; there is no mention of its location to the north; and the Hasmonean Baris is referred to as a newly built structure without a precedent (*Ant.* XVIII, 91–92). We should assume, therefore, that a Ptolemaic–Seleucid–Early Hellenistic fortress called the Akra, located south of the Temple Mount platform, was built to serve as a stronghold for the Ptolemaic and Seleucid troops.

No clear reference indicates how long the Akra stood. According to Josephus, it was conquered by Simon in 142 B.C.E. and was demolished, down to its foundations, in only three days and three nights (*Ant.* XIII, 215–17). The book of Maccabees tells us that Simon was the one who cleared the fortress, renovated it, and used it as his royal residence (1 Macc 13:49–52; 14:36–37). Furthermore, according to 1 Maccabees 15:28, Antiochus VII asked Simon to return the fortress, which clearly indicates that the edifice still existed in 138 B.C.E. According to the present authors the Akra was most likely abandoned when the Baris fortress north of the Temple was built, at the very latest, during the Herodian expansion of the Temple platform to the south. By the time of Josephus, no traces of it were left, but its name remained synonymous with the upper part of the Southeast Hill (*War* V, 138–39).

### THE BARIS/ANTONIA FORTRESS

It appears that Simon lived in the old Akra south of the Temple and used it as his palace. However, when the political situation calmed down toward the end of the second century B.C.E., John Hyrcanus I built a new fortress, the Baris. Located on a rock, it allowed for better surveillance of the northwestern corner of the Temple

Mount and of the Temple in particular (*Ant.* XVIII, 91–92).[39] It continued to serve as the royal residence under Alexander Jannaeus (103–76 B.C.E.) and Salome Alexandra (76–67 B.C.E.), and at the beginning of Aristobulus II's rule (67–63 B.C.E.). After the latter (or his brother John Hyrcanus) erected a new palace west of the Tyropoeon Valley, the Baris continued to be used for the supervision of the Temple Mount platform. Considerable reconstruction and renovations were carried out under Herod (*War* V, 238–45), who renamed the structure "Antonia" in honor of Mark Antony (*War* I, 401).[40] Following its destruction by the rebels (*War* V, 83) and after it was razed by Titus in 70 C.E. (*War* VII, 1–2), the entire surrounding area was reconfigured when Hadrian refounded Jerusalem as Aelia Capitolina. Nothing was built on the rock again, nor did it play a role during the Byzantine and Early Islamic periods. It was only in 1170 C.E. that Theoderich identified the location of the Antonia based on Josephus's description.[41] This rock is trapezoidal in shape, measuring 110–120 meters from east to west and 40–45 meters from north to south, rising some 10 meters above the level of the Temple Mount.[42] Inside the buildings south of the rock, the remains of several monumental Herodian ashlars were uncovered (more than 4 meters in width), including the engaged pilaster decoration.[43] Nothing is left, however, of the interior. A pool (52 × 14 meters) adjacent to the northwestern corner was supplied by the conduit in the northwest that overflowed southward. The pool was covered by two vaults in Hadrian's time.[44]

## The Enlarged Temple Mount

Herod was one of the last Hellenistic kings to attempt to immortalize his rule with the construction of glorious monuments. Throughout the eastern Mediterranean, as far flung as the Aegean islands but most importantly in Jerusalem, his "capital," he dedicated temples, theaters, colonnades, and other buildings. Like the Hasmoneans, he built a royal residence in the northwestern corner of the city that surpassed everything that had existed earlier. Yet, as in the case of the Hasmonean royal residences, almost nothing remains.[45] Herod's most ambitious undertaking was undoubtedly the complete reconstruction of the Jewish Temple and increasing the size of the Temple Mount enclosure.[46] This, of course, could not happen without the approval of the Temple priests, who were wise enough to request that all the building material be present on site before beginning construction; there were many incomplete building complexes initiated under Hellenistic rulers whose construction had been terminated because of insufficient funding. Some of these half-finished monuments to Hellenistic glory would be completed only centuries later, usually by Roman emperors.[47]

### ENCLOSURE WALL AND PLATFORM

The Herodian Temple Mount enclosure, supported by its massive retaining walls, was the most prominent and impressive architectural complex in Jerusalem before the city's destruction by the Romans in 70 C.E. Its original appearance is still evident in the outer walls of the Haram, which are preserved to a considerable height and are visible to this day (fig. 6.6). The current height of the esplanade is thought to be approximately the same as it was in the Herodian period. Herod expanded the area of the Temple Mount beyond the natural dimensions of Mount Moriah, bridging the valleys surrounding it.[48]

The Herodian enclosure is rectangular yet has sides of unequal length, measuring 460 meters in the east, 280 meters in the south, 485 meters in the west, and 315 meters in the north (fig. 6.7). The surface area of the esplanade measures 144,000 square meters, which is exceptionally large compared with other well-known sacred enclosures in the classical world. It is evident from the plan that the complex was designed as a symmetric entity incorporating existing

Fig. 6.6. The Temple Mount, looking northwest. Photo H. Bloedhorn.

sections in the east, following the model of an enormous temenos with a temple in its center (fig. 6.8). The enclosure walls, the lower parts of which functioned as retaining walls, were founded on bedrock for their entire length, conforming to the local terrain. A fill, consisting primarily of earth, was used to level the complex's interior. To strengthen the structure, a system of underground vaults (commonly referred to as Solomon's Stables) was built at the southern end to support the platform's surface (fig. 6.9). In some places, the walls' foundations lay deep below the contemporary street level, and the walls themselves stood ca. 30 meters above the street. The towers positioned at the corners, referred to in the sources, measured an additional 5 meters. The walls around the Temple Mount were built of enormous ashlars; their outer faces were dressed with a 10–20-centimeter-wide margin, leaving a smooth boss in the center projecting very slightly from the surface (fig. 6.10). The ashlar blocks were laid beside each other without any bonding material. The size of the most frequently used stones was ca. 1–1.1 meters high and 1.5–2 meters long, each weighing about 2–5 tons. Some of the stones were particularly large, measuring 12 meters in length. Each course in the wall is recessed 2–3 centimeters compared with the one below it, a technique to reinforce the retaining walls of the enclosure and to compensate for possible optical distortion. The outer faces of the walls above the level of the Temple Mount's inner esplanade were decorated with engaged pilasters, some of which can still be seen in a short section of the northern part of the western wall. The

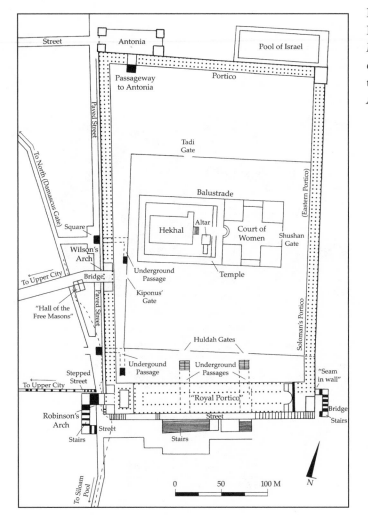

Fig. 6.7. Plan of the Herodian Temple Mount platform. Redrawn by J. Dillon, after: Bahat, *Illustrated Atlas*, 42.

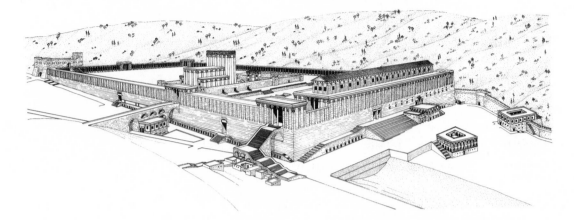

Fig. 6.8. Reconstruction of the Herodian Temple Mount. Redrawn by J. Dillon, after: L. Ritmeyer, in Bahat, *Illustrated Atlas*, 42–43.

Fig. 6.9. Underground vaults (Solomon's Stables) built to support the Herodian Temple Mount platform. Courtesy of the Israel Exploration Society.

Fig. 6.10. Herodian ashlar with flat protruding boss and depressed margins. Photo H. Bloedhorn.

construction of such a solid platform as a means to artificially elevate the surface level is typical of Herodian construction, and was also used for Herod's palace in the Upper City and in other buildings outside Jerusalem and throughout Judaea.

### ENTRANCES

The Temple Mount platform could be accessed via different entrance gates located in the southern, western, and eastern walls of the enclosure. The Antonia fortress was located in the northwestern corner, with an interconnecting passageway to the Temple esplanade.

### THE SOUTHERN ENTRANCES

Two blocked gates are visible today in the southern wall of the Temple Mount: the Double Gate to the west and the Triple Gate 70 meters to the east. Both gates, which were used for entrance and exit, are known as the Huldah Gates, named after Huldah the Prophetess, who lived in Jerusalem in First Temple times and who, according to tradition, was buried nearby.[49] The remaining foundations date to the Herodian period, replacing the original gates from the Hasmonean period located further north. The gates opened into broad tunnels that terminated at a staircase that led to the Temple Mount esplanade some 14 meters above and tunneled below the Royal Stoa. The lintel above the eastern opening of today's western Huldah Gate consists of a large stone topped by a shallow relieving arch. A ceiling consisting of four stone domes supported by arches resting on central columns is preserved inside the gate (fig. 6.11).[50] The Triple Gate leads to a tunnel divided into three sections, narrowing into two about midway through the passageway. The remains of a monumental staircase were exposed at the bottom of the gates (fig. 6.12).[51] The stairs are partly carved into bedrock and partly constructed of smooth, carefully laid stone slabs; the purpose of the alternating use

Fig. 6.11. Inside the western Huldah Gate. De Vogüé, *Temple*, plate 4a.

Fig. 6.12. B. Mazar's Temple Mount excavations, area below the Aqsa Mosque, looking east. Colonnaded street running parallel to the staircase (left) leading up to the Huldah Gates. The preserved row of large ashlars at the top of the stairs is part of the original Herodian enclosure wall. The courses on top of those ashlars date to the Umayyad and later periods. Photo H. Bloedhorn.

of wide and narrow stairs was to regulate the pace of the pilgrims visiting the holy site. This flight of stairs is mentioned in the rabbinic sources: "It happened once that Rabban Gamaliel and the elders were sitting on the stairs on the Temple Mount" (Tosefta, Sanhedrin 2, 6).[52]

## THE WESTERN ENTRANCES

Twelve meters north of the southwestern corner of the Temple Mount enclosure are the remains of the so-called Robinson's Arch (fig. 6.13), named after American scholar Edward Robinson, who first identified it in 1838 as the remains of the eastern end of a bridge he believed spanned the Tyropoeon Valley to connect the Temple platform with the Upper City on the Southwest Hill. That the arch had belonged to a row of arches supporting such a bridge was almost taken for granted, until disproved by more recent excavations (fig. 6.14; for the reconstruction fig. 6.8). The renewed work indicated that the arch was the beginning of a series of vaults designed to support a monumental staircase linking the Royal Stoa on top of the Temple Mount enclosure with the street in the Tyropoeon Valley.[53]

Some 80 meters north of the southwestern corner of the Temple Mount, at the southern end of the present-day Western Wall, the lintel of the so-called Barclay's Gate is still visible (figs. 6.7–8). In the Herodian period, an underground stepped tunnel ran eastward from Barclay's Gate and turned south, toward the Temple Mount esplanade.[54]

Approximately 100 meters north of Barclay's Gate, the so-called Wilson's Arch was uncovered in 1867 (figs. 6.7–8). It is identical in width to Robinson's Arch but is built at a level only slightly lower than the supposed level of the Temple Mount enclosure. Wilson's Arch is considered to have been the beginning of the series of arches supporting a bridge that, at the time of the Herodian Temple, spanned the Tyropoeon Valley and

Fig. 6.13. The western wall with Robinson's Arch and the Herodian street, looking north. The rubble strewn over the street came from the Royal Stoa and the porticoes on top of the Temple Mount. Photo H. Bloedhorn.

Fig. 6.14. Herodian street, looking northwest. The construction on the left was part of the supporting structure of Robinson's Arch and the staircase leading up to the Herodian Temple Mount. Photo H. Bloedhorn.

linked the Upper City in the west with the Temple Mount esplanade in the east. This may be the location of the bridge referred to by Josephus (*War* II, 344; *Ant.* XIV, 58).[55]

The remains of the so-called Warren's Gate (figs. 6.7–8) can be seen in the western wall, about 40 meters north of Wilson's Arch. This was originally an underground staircase providing access from the street level to the esplanade above (as in Barclay's Gate).[56]

### THE EASTERN ENTRANCES

South of the seam separating the Herodian extension from the earlier wall segment are the remains of an arch built in the same style as Robinson's Arch in the western wall; vestiges of a double gate can be seen (fig. 6.15). This may indicate the existence of an eastern flight of stairs that perhaps connected with the structure known as Solomon's Stables.

About 275 meters north of the southeastern corner of the Temple Mount is the so-called Golden Gate (fig. 9.3); the structure standing today dates to the Umayyad period. The remains of an ancient arch discovered by chance were buried below the level of the present-day gate to a point slightly further south. Some scholars attribute this lower-positioned gate to the Herodian era and reconstruct it as the eastern gateway mentioned in Acts 3:2 and 3:10.[57]

### THE ROYAL STOA

In his description of the Temple Mount complex and the stoas (porticoes) that Herod built around the Temple, Josephus describes at length the Royal Stoa that towered above the southern part of the Temple Mount courtyard (*Ant.* XV, 411–16), "and it was a structure more noteworthy than any under the sun" (*Ant.* XV, 412).

The Royal Stoa was built in the form of a basilica consisting of a central nave flanked by two aisles (figs. 6.7–8). This elongated structure was covered with a roof supported by four rows of 162 columns. The southernmost row of columns was integrated into the southern wall of the basilica. The columns had Corinthian capitals, and according to Josephus, it took three people with outstretched arms to encircle a column (*Ant.* XV, 413). The central hall was twice as high as the side halls. Windows in the upper part of the walls of the central hall provided optimal natural lighting. The Royal Stoa itself was not

Fig. 6.15. The beginning of a protruding arch (left) in the eastern wall that originally supported the entrance to the Temple Mount from the Kidron Valley. The seam (center) demarcating the Hasmonean (right) and Herodian (left) walls. Photo R. Schick.

Fig. 6.16. Replica of a cornerstone with the Hebrew inscription: "To the place of the trumpeting . . . ," found at the foot of the southwestern corner of the Temple Mount. Photo H. Bloedhorn.

preserved, but a wealth of decorated architectural elements was found in the collapse that resulted from the destruction of the building, attesting to its former grandeur. The architectural fragments include a rich variety of motifs representing the artistic style characteristic of the Late Hellenistic period in Jerusalem. Among the fragments archaeologists found is an inscribed cornerstone (fig. 6.16). The Royal Stoa served as a center of public activity. It was used mainly for conducting commercial transactions relating to Temple ritual.[58]

### THE TEMPLE

Of the Second Temple itself, which stood in its splendor above the elevated enclosure of the Temple Mount, there is today not a single remnant above the level of the present-day esplanade. Equipped with all the required building materials (*Ant.* XV, 421), the construction of the Second Temple began in 20 B.C.E. and was completed within a year and a half. The additional construction on the Temple Mount compound and its environs, however, took many more years. According to Josephus (*Ant.* XV, 391; XX, 219), the entire building project was completed during the reign of the procurator Albinus (62–64 C.E.).

Reconstructions of the Temple are based on descriptions by Josephus and Talmudic sources. The plan of the Holy of Holies and the main sanctuary remained exactly the same as the First Temple; its height, however, was increased by adding an upper level. The portico was enlarged both in width and height, creating an impressive façade. The Temple's precise location relative to the "foundation stone" (*even ha-shetiyah*; Mishnah, Yoma 5, 2; Jerusalem Talmud, Yoma 5, 42c:34–39) — the rock now enshrined in the Dome of the Rock — is a matter of pure conjecture. The traditional view is that the Temple stood approximately where the Dome of the Rock now stands. An alternative interpretation suggests that the Temple was located slightly north of this site. This theory relies, however, on archaeological evidence erroneously attributed to the Herodian period.[59]

The only material evidence of the Temple complex consists of a Greek inscription and a fragment of another one inserted in the

Fig. 6.17. One of the warning inscriptions from the balustrade (Archaeological Museum, Istanbul) that fenced off the inner court of the sacred enclosure mentioned by Josephus. Courtesy of the Israel Antiquities Authority.

balustrade that fenced off the inner court of the sacred enclosure (fig. 6.17).[60] The stone-carved inscriptions warn Gentiles not to enter the inner court of the Temple Mount. The text reads: "No foreigner shall enter within the balustrade of the Temple, or within the precinct, and whosoever shall be caught shall be responsible for (his) death that will follow in consequence (of his trespassing)."[61]

## Dwellings

### JEWISH QUARTER EXCAVATIONS

Excavations carried out in the Jewish Quarter of the Old City revealed well-preserved remains of domestic structures (fig. 6.18).[62] With the exception of one house that was destroyed in the early first century C.E., most dwellings were built and used throughout the Herodian period. As part of the residential area of the Upper City of Jerusalem, these houses provide evidence of an urban plan for a residential neighborhood, domestic architecture and art, the living conditions of the city's inhabitants, and various aspects of everyday life in the city before its destruction by the Romans in 70 C.E.

Houses were built close together on terraces arranged on the slope of the hill from west to east and are mostly oriented either north-south or east-west. Most houses had two levels, with the living quarters on the ground floor and the service areas in the basement. There are indications that some of the houses had a second story above ground.

One of those structures, the so-called Herodian House, flourished mainly in the days of Herod the Great and may even have been built earlier, toward the end of Hasmonean rule. The building was destroyed at the beginning of the first century C.E., when a road was built through it, and its remains were buried beneath the paving stones. The dwelling, with several rooms arranged around an inner

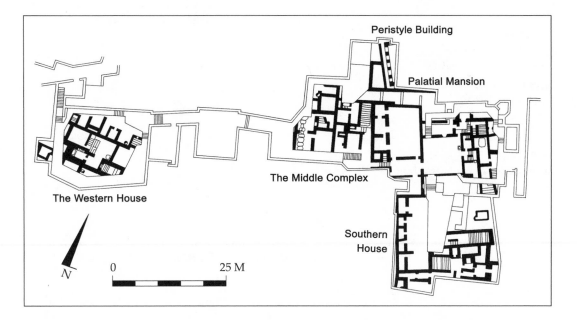

Peristyle Building

Palatial Mansion

The Middle Complex

The Western House

Southern House

0    25 M

N

courtyard, covered an area of some 200 square meters. Four ovens were sunk into the floor of the courtyard. A large ritual pool (*miqveh*), partly vaulted over and accessed by a broad stairway, occupies much of this space, and there is a smaller cistern beside it. In the western wall of the structure, preserved to a height of 1.5 meters, three niches were used as wall cupboards (as indicated by one of them, which contained many broken pottery vessels). The walls were made of fieldstones and partly dressed stones and were plastered over with a plain light plaster. In several rooms such plaster also covered the floors.[63]

The remains of another dwelling, dubbed by the excavator the Peristyle House, differed from all other buildings in the Jewish Quarter in its use of columns (fig. 6.19). A stylobate that retained a few fragments of about six columns coated with fluted stucco in the classical style was uncovered. The corner pillars with two engaged columns indicate that the colonnade turned to the east. A narrow passageway ran between the columns and the parallel wall. Adjoining the wall were two rooms paved with colored stone tiles (*opus sectile*),

Fig. 6.18. Plan of Avigad's Jewish Quarter excavations. Redrawn by J. Dillon and M. Speidel, after: Avigad, *Herodian Quarter in Jerusalem*, 18.

Fig. 6.19. Reconstruction of the Peristyle House in Avigad area F-4, in the Wohl Archaeological Museum, Jerusalem. Redrawn by J. Dillon, after: Avigad, *Herodian Quarter in Jerusalem*, 36–37.

most of which were plundered. The discovery of the Peristyle House is unique since similar structures have been found only in Herodian palaces at Masada, Herodium, Machaerus, and Jericho.[64]

Occupying an area of some 600 square meters, the Palatial Mansion was the largest and best-preserved building discovered in the Jewish Quarter. Remains of two levels were found: the ground floor, which contained the living quarters, and the basement, which contained the water installations, storerooms, and service rooms (figs. 6.20–21). The ground-floor rooms were grouped around a central court paved with stone tiles. The courtyard communicates with various wings in the house, the best preserved of which was the west wing, a well-built ashlar structure. The walls are preserved to an unusual height of up to 3 meters. They were originally adorned with colorful frescoes, which were later plastered over and either left plain or incised with a pattern imitating courses of ashlar masonry. In a large room, apparently a reception hall, the plaster was finished to resemble Herodian-style masonry (fig. 6.22). Many fragments of ornamental stucco were found here as well. Another room yielded fragments of a mosaic floor, and south of it was another room decorated with a frescoed wall preserved to a height of ca. 2.5 meters (plate 5). Remnants of a fire were found in these two rooms, most notably the charred remains of wooden beams. Of the eastern wing of the ground floor, only a small bathroom has remained, including a small pool with steps — probably a sitting-bath. Two stairways led from the courtyard down to a lower level containing several rooms built on a terrace facing east. The distinctive features here are the great number of stepped pools vaulted over with ashlar masonry, as well as deep cisterns hewn into the bedrock. The Palatial Mansion was razed in 70 c.e. with the destruction of Jerusalem. Traces of the fire were found in several rooms in the west, however such evidence was lost in the other parts of the structure because of later building activities. Not many small finds were discovered here, yet the few found are indicative of the status of the inhabitants. Most notable in this connection are the fragments of a splendid glass vessel made by the well-known Phoenician craftsman Ennion (fig. 6.42).[65]

Fig. 6.20. The courtyard of the Palatial Mansion in Avigad area P during the excavation. Courtesy of the Israel Exploration Society.

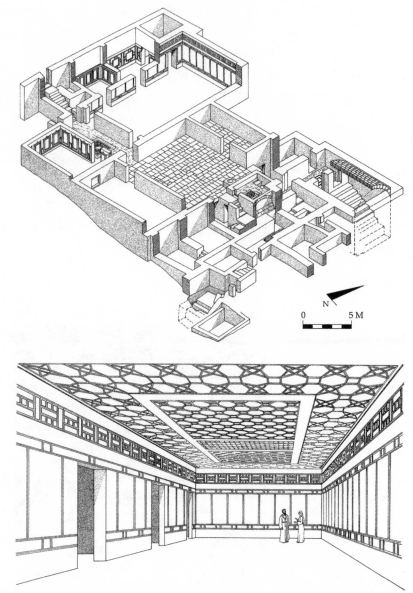

Fig. 6.21. Isometric reconstruction of the Palatial Mansion in Avigad area P, in the Wohl Archaeological Museum, Jerusalem. Redrawn by J. Dillon, after: Avigad, *Herodian Quarter in Jerusalem*, 58–59.

Fig. 6.22. Reconstruction of the reception hall in the Palatial Mansion. Redrawn by J. Dillon, after: Avigad, *Discovering Jerusalem*, 102, fig. 90.

Another building was uncovered north of the Palatial Mansion, adjacent to other houses that were set ablaze by the Romans. This house came to be known as the Burnt House as it includes clear evidence of destruction caused by a huge fire in the year 70 C.E. (fig. 6.23). Only some 55 square meters of this house were exposed; it was

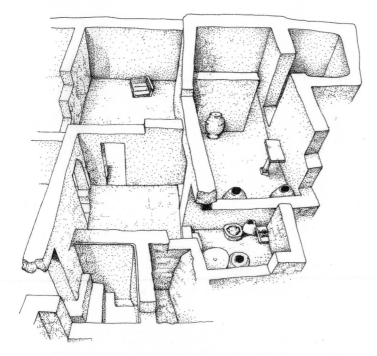

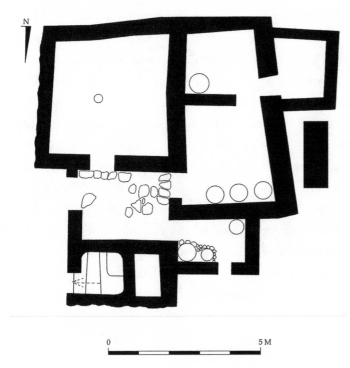

Fig. 6.23. Plan and reconstruction of the Burnt House in Avigad area B. Redrawn by J. Dillon, after: Avigad, *Discovering Jerusalem*, 126, figs. 120 and 121.

0           5 M

N

probably part of a larger structure, but its continuation could not be excavated. The walls were preserved for an average of 1 meter above floor level. The house contains an entrance corridor, four rooms, a small kitchen, and a bathing pool. The rooms excavated were apparently from the basement level; the story above it has not been preserved. According to the excavator, the space had been used as a workshop or laboratory, as indicated by the type and quantity of finds recovered from a thick burnt layer that had not been disturbed by later building and had therefore preserved objects exactly as they had been at the time of the destruction. The finds include numerous stone vessels, stone tables, basalt mortars, stone weights, cooking pots, oil juglets, and perfume bottles. The skeletal remains of the lower arm and hand of a woman were found in the kitchen area. One of the stone weights was engraved with an Aramaic inscription: "(of) Bar Kathros" (fig. 6.24). Tosefta, Menahot 13, 21 mentions the Kathros family as one of the four large priestly families who abused their status by granting positions within the Temple and exploiting the people. It has been suggested that Bar Kathros was a member of the family that worked and possibly lived in this house. Many coins from the First Revolt against Rome were found on the floors of its rooms.[66]

Although the excavator suggested that each of the above-mentioned buildings was owned and used by only one family, the present authors believe that they served as multi-family units. The location on top of the Southwest Hill constituted prime real estate. In numerous dwellings from the Roman and Byzantine periods, some of the internal as well as external spaces were shared by various owners or tenants. This also accounts for the irregular floor plans, the multiple storage areas, bathing installations, and ritual pools (*miqva'ot*).[67]

Fig. 6.24. Stone weight with inscription "(of) Bar Kathros" from the Burnt House. Redrawn by J. Dillon, after: Avigad, *Discovering Jerusalem*, 130, fig. 138.

0   1   2   3 CM

## DECORATION

The strong influence of the Hellenistic building tradition is most obvious in the various decorative media employed.[68] Mosaic floors were in fairly wide use in this affluent residential quarter soon after their introduction into Jerusalem (plate 6). Most were found in bathrooms or other areas connected with the use of water. Some found in rooms or halls had a representational character and were occasionally decorated with opus sectile. Walls were frequently covered with wall paintings employing either the fresco or secco technique; some were decorated with stucco. One feature common to all these techniques is the total absence of animate motifs, which can be attributed to the inhabitants' avoiding contravention of the biblical injunction against graven images. Thus, in spite of the obvious Graeco-Roman stylistic influence, a local trend is apparent.

## Water Installations

Some of the best-preserved structural remains in these dwellings are their water installations, generally subterranean. Since they were usually cut into the rock, rather than built, they would often survive destruction that would otherwise eradicate the rest of the house. It is easy to distinguish between the sewers, cisterns, steam baths, bathtubs, and ritual pools.[69]

Cisterns were used for storing rainwater, which served as the principal source of water in the residential quarters of Jerusalem. The water was drawn through narrow well-holes at the top of the rock-hewn cistern, which was covered with a gray hydraulic plaster containing organic matter such as soot and ash.

Besides the usual bathing rooms, several houses had steam rooms. These chambers were paved with mosaics and had hypocausts beneath their floors, which were supported by upright pottery pipes (instead of the usual small columns generally found in such structures). Several examples of sunken sitting-tubs or built bathtubs, known from other contemporary sites in Palestine, were uncovered in some of the dwellings.

There were many types of miqva'ot in the Upper City. The most common was a stepped rock-cut pool with a vaulted ceiling built of ashlars (fig. 6.25). The lower, stepped part was covered with gray hydraulic plaster, while the vaulted ceiling — which did not come into contact with water — was left bare. Two especially large ritual baths uncovered in the Palatial Mansion had two adjacent entranceways that would enable the bather to enter through one, before purification, and exit through the other, ritually purified after immersion (Mishnah, Shekalim 8, 2). Sometimes the two paths — descending into the pool and ascending from it — were divided down the middle of the steps by a low partition. At least one, and most often two or more, ritual baths were installed in every domestic complex in Jerusalem, attesting to the strict observance of the laws of ritual purity by Jews in this period. According to Jewish religious law (*halakhah*), every Jew was to immerse himself or herself in a ritual bath in order to achieve purification from uncleanness. The ritual bath must hold no less than forty *seah* of spring water or rainwater drawn directly from its source into the bath without being transported. Since the condition regarding the water itself was not always practicable, the water in the bath could be purified by bringing it into contact with ritually pure water. For this purpose, a special storage pool (*otzar*) that held pure rainwater was installed next to the immersion pool. A hole or pipe inserted in the partition wall between the two pools brought the water from one pool into the other, thereby ritually purifying the impure water. Only two such ritual baths with a storage pool were uncovered in the Jewish Quarter excavation; the majority functioned without a secondary pool.[70]

As a result of the expanding city and population, there was a need to increase the water supply. The Gihon and Rogel springs, the ponds from the surrounding areas, and the domestic cisterns were no longer

Fig. 6.25. Ritual pool
in Avigad area T-4.
Courtesy of the Israel
Exploration Society.

sufficient. The waters from the 'Ain Kuwaiziba and 'Ain 'Arrub springs,
located higher in the Judaean hill country to the south of Jerusalem,
had to be brought to the city. A system was designed to carry water
entirely by gravity, even though the drop in height from the springs to
the Temple Mount is only 21 kilometers (11 kilometers aerial distance). By following the contours of the hills, producing a serpentine
system of aqueducts from the springs to the reservoirs known as Solomon's Pools, and from there to the city, the waters could be diverted.[71] The aqueduct is mentioned in the rabbinic sources and is
probably the same one that Josephus tells us Pontius Pilate fixed (*War*
II, 175 and *Ant.* XVIII, 60).[72]

## Necropolis

The tomb complexes in Jerusalem, particularly after the second
century B.C.E., represent the best-surviving structural examples of the
penetration of Hellenistic culture. Since the majority of the surviving
tombs belonged to the upper classes, however, our views about the
Hellenization of the Jews are somewhat skewed. It is very likely that

0                    50 CM

Fig. 6.26. Part of the *opus reticulatum* wall of Herod's mausoleum north of the Damascus Gate and fragments of a cornice and a Doric frieze. Redrawn by J. Dillon, after: Schick, "New Discoveries," plate 3.

acculturation did not affect all Jewish social classes to the same degree. The burial places of the poor may have been no more than simple inhumations and have not been preserved.

Jerusalem was surrounded by a wide ring of tomb complexes, with a particularly high concentration on the slopes surrounding the city from the north, east, and south. Based on a comprehensive survey conducted in Jerusalem, some one thousand ancient burial complexes are known.[73]

Only a few of the Hellenistic complexes are documented in the written sources. The tomb of Alexander Jannaeus was apparently built north of the Temple Mount platform overlooking the Baris, which until the assumption of power by Aristobulus II, served as John Hyrcanus's royal residence (*War* V, 304). The tomb of John the High Priest (referring either to Hyrcanus I or II)—whose residence was in the Hasmonean palace west of the Tyropoeon Valley—was located north of the First Wall, near the Pool of Amygdalon (Birkat Hammam al-Batraq) (*War* V, 258–60). The tomb of Ananus the High Priest, clearly visible from the Temple Mount, was situated on the slope west of the Rogel Spring (*War* V, 506). Finally, north of the city, Herod the Great erected a tomb for his family (*War* V, 108, 507), a circular Roman-type burial structure, similar to Augustus's mausoleum in Rome. Sections of the inner walls were built in *opus reticulatum* (fig. 6.26).[74]

Additional tomb complexes not mentioned in the textual sources but attested by epigraphic evidence can be associated with specific individuals. Such is the case of the priestly family of Benei Hezir (1 Chron 24:15) buried in a tomb with a Doric style façade in the Kid-

ron Valley (fig. 6.27).[75] The tomb was entered through a symmetrically structured portico whose Doric façade shows clear signs of its original decoration, including a still-legible inscription commemorating the Hezir family. The remains of the *nefesh* (a burial marker), found immediately to the left, are too fragmentary to reconstruct its original shape. This kind of façade, with columns supporting decorated friezes, is frequently encountered in the impressive Sanhedriah necropolis north of the Old City.[76] This type can also be seen at the Tomb of Nicanor on Mount Scopus; based on an inscription incised on one of the ossuaries, the tomb was assigned to the Nicanor family from Alexandria, who were sponsors of the eastern gate of the Temple Mount (Mishnah, Middot 1, 4).[77]

In addition to the few tombs that can be associated with specific families, many more upper-class burial complexes have been uncov-

Fig. 6.27. Tomb of the Hezir family (left), Zechariah's Tomb (center), and an unfinished tomb (right) in the Kidron Valley. Photo H. Bloedhorn.

ered whose owners or occupants remain anonymous to us. With the exception of the mausoleum, the majority of the upper-class tomb complexes continue the late preexilic stylistic conventions. Adjacent to the Benei Hezir Tomb is Zechariah's Tomb, a freestanding monolithic structure crowned with an Egyptian-style pyramidal form (fig. 6.27).[78] Some 100 meters further north, Absalom's Tomb employs a similar stylistic feature (fig. 6.28); the freestanding nefesh, composed of a 5 × 5 meter block with a projecting Egyptian cornice, is topped with a squat cylinder which, in turn, is crowned with a concave cone.[79] Some 700 meters north of the city, the tomb of the royal family of Adiabene was also crowned with three pyramids. De Saulcy — who in 1850–51 carried out the first excavation in Jerusalem — associated it wrongly with the Tomb of the Kings.[80] It was later identified as the

Fig. 6.28. Absalom's Tomb in the Kidron Valley. Left: entrance into Yehoshafat's Tomb. Note the decorated pediment with two acroteria above the doorway. Photo H. Bloedhorn.

Fig. 6.29. Courtyard of the tomb of Queen Helena of Adiabene (wrongly identified as the Tomb of the Kings), located some 700 meters north of the Damascus Gate, 1910. Courtesy of the Israel Antiquities Authority.

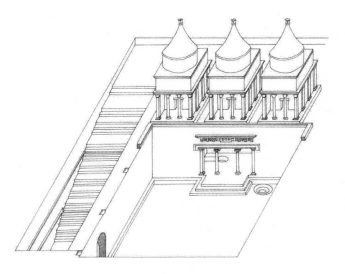

Fig. 6.30. Isometric reconstruction of the tomb of Queen Helena of Adiabene. Redrawn by J. Dillon, after: Vincent and Steve, *Jérusalem*, I, plate 97.

Fig. 6.31. Part of a Doric frieze decorating the portico of the tomb of Queen Helena of Adiabene, 1910. Courtesy of the École biblique.

royal tomb of Queen Helena of Adiabene (figs. 6.29–31) mentioned by Josephus (*War* V, 55, 119, 147 and *Ant.* XX, 17–95).[81] A similar pyramidal superstructure was used to reconstruct Jason's Tomb, located in the western part of the modern city (fig. 6.32).[82]

Many funerary complexes, especially those in the flat areas north and west of the city, were entered through an outer courtyard, where parts of the burial rituals were held. These courtyards were sometimes surrounded by benches lining the walls. In steep areas, especially in the Hinnom Valley, there was simply a portico (instead of a courtyard) that did not include a sitting area. Only some very elaborate tombs were sealed with a rolling stone, such as a large funerary complex with sarcophagi, located on the western slope of the upper Hinnom Valley (figs. 6.33–34).[83] The simpler burial complexes were blocked with rectangular or square stone slabs.

These tombs are usually cut out of the natural rock, which is sometimes friable or easily crumbled and required the walls or ceilings to be reinforced with ashlars. Like the exterior of the burial structure, the interior as well could be more or less elaborate and complex, sometimes containing multiple burial chambers.

Fig. 6.32. Jason's Tomb, located 1400 meters west of the southwest corner of the Ottoman city wall. Courtesy of the Israel Antiquities Authority.

Entrance chambers with surrounding benches, found in a large number of burial complexes (fig. 6.35), are a continuation of an earlier Iron Age tradition. In addition to benches, a number of other installations can be found in Hellenistic tomb complexes. The loculus, or *kokh*-type burial, existed only from the Hellenistic period onward and was first encountered in the second century B.C.E. at Marissa. The niches were used only for primary burials and thus the obligatory closing slabs were not inscribed. Loculi, the most common burial type in use until 70 C.E., consist most frequently of singular niches (fig. 6.36), sometimes of double niches for parallel burials. Since a loculus is cut perpendicular to the wall instead of parallel to it, this practice allowed for a greater number of burials in a limited space than did the bench tradition. A slightly less common type of structure for primary burial is the arcosolium, a bench surmounted by an arch positioned parallel to the chamber wall, attested only from the Hero-

Fig. 6.33. Entrance to Herod's Family Tomb with a rolling stone on the western slope of the Hinnom Valley. Photo H. Bloedhorn.

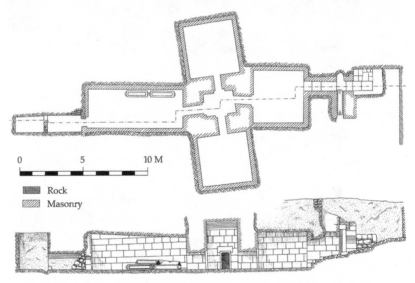

Fig. 6.34. Plan and section of Herod's Family Tomb. Redrawn by J. Dillon, after: Vincent and Steve, *Jérusalem*, I, plate 82.

dian period onward. To optimize the use of space, short or long loculi were often placed beneath arcosolia. The bench of the arcosolium was occasionally hollowed out for use as a trough (fig. 6.37). Typical Roman-style sarcophagi, often stone-carved and freestanding (fig.

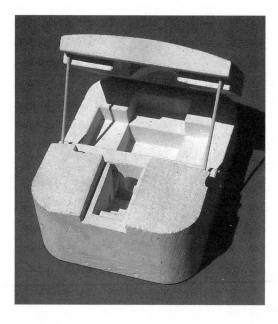

Fig. 6.35. G. Dalman's model of a bench tomb. Note the small entrance giving access to the burial chamber with three benches surmounted by arches (*arcosolia*). Courtesy of the German Protestant Institute of Archaeology, Jerusalem.

Fig. 6.36. G. Dalman's model of a *loculi* tomb with a large courtyard giving access to the burial chamber; note *loculi* behind the benches. Courtesy of the German Protestant Institute of Archaeology, Jerusalem.

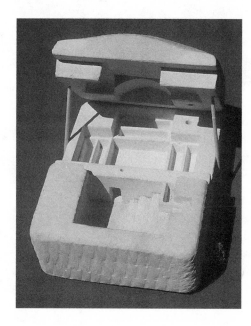

Fig. 6.37. G. Dalman's model of a trough tomb with a staircase giving access to the burial chamber with double-troughs surmounted by arches (*arcosolia*). Courtesy of the German Protestant Institute of Archaeology, Jerusalem.

6.38), and sometimes made of lead, are found in only a few very luxurious burial complexes.

A shorter type of niche existed before the appearance of ossuaries, or stone chests, and was used as an ossilegium; both were meant to receive the bones during the secondary burial stage. As attested in the literary sources, after the decomposition of the flesh, approximately a year after the initial burial, the bones were collected and relocated in a different, permanent setting.

Far more typical for this period than sarcophagi are ossuaries, several thousands of which were found in Jerusalem alone (fig. 6.39).[84] Ossuaries usually take the form of an elongated chest, built either with or without short legs. Originally, they most likely imitated contemporary household chests. Most ossuaries were made of local limestone.

Fig. 6.38. (Above) Sarcophagus found in the Nazirite Family Tomb on Mount Scopus. Courtesy of the Israel Exploration Society.

Fig. 6.39. (Right) Ossuary of a family from Beth Shean, carved with geometric motifs and the names of the deceased in Greek and Hebrew, found in the necropolis of the Syrian Orphanage. Courtesy of the Israel Antiquities Authority.

Only a few examples of clay ossuaries are known, and they appear to be a relatively late development. Ossuaries were between 45 and 70 centimeters long, depending on the length of the human femur. The lids were arched, flat, or gabled, occasionally custom-fitted into grooves carved into the top side of the chest.

Many of the ossuaries were decorated on their long sides with incised, chip-carved, or painted designs, mainly with six-petaled rosettes, floral and geometric motifs, and architectural representations. Occasionally we find names scrawled on their sides, either incised or in charcoal. While the decorations were made by the artisans, the inscriptions, mostly in Aramaic and Greek and only sometimes in Hebrew, were made by the families of the deceased. These were probably added to the prefabricated product. Among the most beautiful and significant ones is the so-called Caiaphas ossuary, twice inscribed "Joseph, son of Caiaphas," and identified by some to have belonged to the high priest Caiaphas (*Ant.* XVII, 33–35).[85]

The great number of ossuaries found in Jerusalem and its vicinity attests to the custom that was clearly prevalent in the Late Hellenistic and Early Roman periods of gathering the bones from a primary burial after the flesh had decomposed and reinterring them in specially prepared receptacles. This custom was practiced by Jews in different parts of the country and in rare cases even beyond its borders, but appears to have waned in the first part of the third century C.E. Any later occurrence of this custom is to be attributed to the transfer of the remains of Jews who had died abroad and were brought to rest in the Holy Land.

Dates of tombs are only approximate since most of them were used for extended periods and reveal several phases. Small finds, such as pottery and glass vessels or jewelry and coins, usually represent only one phase of use and therefore are not reliable dating indicators. The destruction of the city by Titus in 70 C.E. did not halt the use of previously existing burial grounds. The uninterrupted use of the complexes points to a continued presence in the city and a preservation of the same burial rituals. After the suppression of the Bar Kokhba revolt, the majority of the tombs were abandoned, as the Romans avoided using Jewish tomb complexes.

## Distinctive Finds

Although we can see an increased contact with the classical culture imported from Greece, local trends are still present. Apart from some uniquely Judaean objects, we find imports and imitations of foreign products.

### THE STONE INDUSTRY

The well-developed art of working stone in Jerusalem was previously known mainly from sepulchral art. The Jewish Quarter excavations have shown that other branches of the stoneworking craft also flourished in the city and that their products included useful objects such as tables and domestic vessels (fig. 6.40).

The first pieces of furniture from the Hellenistic period found in Jerusalem — the stone tables — come from the Upper City. Most furniture was made of wood and thus has not survived. Therefore, the decorative tables found in almost every house in this residential quarter of Jerusalem provide valuable information.[86] Fragments of two types were found: tables with a rectangular top and a central leg; and small round tables (about 50 centimeters in diameter) that originally stood on tripods. Examples of such tables are well known from Pompeii and other Hellenistic-Roman sites. They usually stood in gardens and reception halls and were used to hold refreshments and food for guests.

Among the material from this period unearthed in the Jerusalem excavations is a prominent group of domestic vessels made of soft white stone. These include large jars, bowls, plates, cups, trays, and lids. Most of the vessels, which are of excellent workmanship, were turned on the lathe while some were handcarved. According to Jew-

Fig. 6.40. Table with an assemblage of stone vessels from the Burnt House in Avigad area B. Courtesy of the Israel Exploration Society.

ish laws of ritual purity, stone was not susceptible to ritual uncleanness (Mishnah, Kelim 10, 1; Parah 3, 2), and for this reason stone vessels were in widespread use throughout the Hellenistic and Roman periods.[87]

### JERUSALEMITE PAINTED POTTERY

The Late Hellenistic material culture in Jerusalem and Judaea, as a whole, consisted mostly of local productions. The limited contact with other Mediterranean cultures is evident in the particularly low number of pottery imports. Though locally produced, the Jerusalemite painted pottery is an excellent example of how artistic traditions from other regions were introduced into the local scene through commercial contacts (fig. 6.41).

Painted pottery vessels dating from the reign of Herod the Great to the destruction of the Second Temple (ca. 20 B.C.E. to 70 C.E.) have been discovered primarily in Jerusalem and its surroundings.[88] This thin, delicate, fine-quality tableware comprises mostly bowls, although some jugs, juglets, and kraters have also been found. The clay is light pinkish brown in color, painted in brown, reddish brown, and black with floral motifs, lines, and dots. In shape, fabric, and decora-

Fig. 6.41. Pseudo-Nabatean pottery from Avigad's Jewish Quarter excavations. Courtesy of the Israel Exploration Society.

tion the Jerusalemite painted bowls are similar to the Nabatean fine ware from the first century B.C.E. onward, found mainly in Petra and other Nabatean towns and caravansaries.[89] Neutron activation analysis conducted on ten pieces of this ware has proven that they were all manufactured in Jerusalem.

### ENNION'S GLASS

The glassware unearthed in the Jewish Quarter excavations is unique. The corpus consists of molded bowls in the Hellenistic tradition, including an almost complete example of a bowl with a ribbed body in imitation of early metal vessels, as well as a few long-necked bottles and small perfume bottles. Several unusual finds indicate that the inhabitants of Jerusalem could obtain the finest glass products of the period, as exemplified by the jug made by the Phoenician glass master Ennion (fig. 6.42). This vessel was found broken and distorted by the fire that destroyed the Palatial Mansion.[90]

## THEODOTUS INSCRIPTION

The Theodotus inscription was discovered out of context in 1913 at the southern end of the Southeast Hill (fig. 6.43). This Greek inscription constitutes the earliest material evidence testifying to the existence of a synagogue in Jerusalem in the first century B.C.E. The text reads:

Theodotus, the son of Vettenus, priest and *archisynagogus*, son of an *archisynagogus*, grandson of an *archisynagogus*, built the synagogue for the reading of the Law (the Torah) and the study of the commandments, and a guesthouse and rooms and water installations for hosting those in need from abroad, it (the synagogue) having been founded by his fathers, the presbyters, and Simonides.[91]

Fig. 6.42. Glass amphora made by Ennion of Sidon, from the Palatial Mansion in Avigad area P. Redrawn by J. Dillon, after: Avigad, *Discovering Jerusalem*, 108, fig. 96.

Fig. 6.43. Theodotus inscription, in the Rockefeller Museum, Jerusalem. Courtesy of the Israel Exploration Society.

Named after the head of the synagogue, the text suggests that the building was multifunctional. It was used for educational and religious purposes, but also accommodated pilgrims visiting the city and Temple.[92]

# 7 ✦ The Roman Period

At Jerusalem he [Hadrian] founded a city in place of the one which had been razed to the ground, naming it Aelia Capitolina.

CASSIUS DIO, *Historia Romana* LXIX, 12:1

## Aelia Capitolina

According to Josephus's description of Jerusalem in the post-destruction era (*War* VII, 1–4), most of the city lay in ruins and was covered by rubble. After the fighting ended, the province was reorganized, land was redistributed and the Tenth Roman Legion Fretensis, responsible for the city's destruction, was now asked to guard it (fig. 7.1). Since neither Josephus nor any other contemporary sources refer to an expulsion, we may assume that the majority of the surviving original population remained in Judah.

During his first voyage to the East between 129 and 131 C.E., the emperor Hadrian spent time in the provinces of Syria, Arabia, and

Fig. 7.1. Coin of Iudaea Capta. Obverse: Head of Titus, laureated, facing right; Greek inscription, for "Caesar Imperator Titus." Reverse: Nike standing to right, resting her left foot on a helmet and writing with her right hand on a shield hanging from a palm tree; Greek inscription, for "Iudaea Capta." Courtesy of the Israel Antiquities Authority.

Judaea.[1] Having founded many new cities (usually only implying the establishment of new neighborhoods), he also decided to reconstruct the destroyed city of Jerusalem under the new name of Aelia Capitolina. In addition to honoring the emperor Aelius Hadrianus himself, this name paid tribute to the three most important gods of the Roman pantheon: Jupiter, Juno, and Minerva (in Greek, Zeus, Hera, and Athena). It is most likely that this caused the outbreak of a renewed revolt against the Romans.[2] This Second Revolt (132–135 C.E.) erupted immediately after the emperor left the East, fifty-eight years after the First Revolt (66–74 C.E.).[3] The rebellion involved many Jewish inhabitants led by one Bar-Kokhba ("son of the star").[4] The quelling of this revolt required three Roman legions reinforced by auxiliary troops that were dispatched all over the southern hill country of Judaea over the course of three years.[5] Given the presence of the Fretensis legion, Jerusalem was not threatened by the rebels.[6] This is archaeologically corroborated by the lack of coins minted by the Jews at this time. A detailed literary source similar to the one Josephus provided for the First Revolt is, unfortunately, lacking.[7]

As soon as things quieted down, the reconstruction of the city could begin. The legion's partial presence in the city eliminated the need for a protective city wall. Thus, builders concentrated their efforts on resurrecting the western part of the city, not paying any attention to the area of the Temple Mount. Although we know of many inscriptions and coins attesting to the presence of numerous temples and other public buildings in Jerusalem, no archaeological traces of such structures have yet been discovered.[8]

Toward the end of the third century C.E., the legion was moved to Aila (today's Aqaba); Jerusalem was then, once again, surrounded by a wall. Based on a few uncovered wall segments and a literary reference (the Bordeaux Pilgrim), the reconstructed course corresponds approximately to the current Old City wall built in the Ottoman period.[9]

## The Camp of the Tenth Legion

According to Josephus (*War* VI, 413; VII, 2–3), the only large structures Titus left standing in the overall destruction of the city were the western city wall and the three towers Hippicus, Phasael, and Mariamne that crowned Herod's palace, as well as sections of the palace itself. These remains survived as testimony to the Roman victory, and served to protect the Tenth Roman Legion Fretensis stationed there.

Based on literary traditions, most scholars have placed the Roman camp within the modern-day Armenian Quarter and part of the Jewish Quarter.[10] The archaeological finds, however, with the exception of isolated wall segments inside the courtyard of the Citadel, are represented by only a few stamped tiles of the Tenth Legion.[11] Recent suggestions locate the camp in the area of the Holy Sepulchre[12] or on the Ophel, south of the Temple platform.[13] Archaeological evidence is insufficient to substantiate the camp's presence in those areas.[14] Stamped tiles and bricks bearing the symbol of the Tenth Legion were found in many public buildings, yet their presence does not automatically imply the existence of military facilities (fig. 7.2). The combined evidence we have from the literature and archaeology indicates that it is rather unlikely that the entire legion was stationed in Jerusalem. One single division or several smaller units would have sufficed. The larger units were stationed in the outskirts of the city at

Fig. 7.2. Roman tile stamped: "Leg(io) X F(retensis)"; above: a ship; below: a boar. Redrawn by J. Dillon, after: Bahat, *Illustrated Atlas*, 58.

Shaikh Badr (Givat Ram), 2 kilometers northwest of the Old City, and at Khirbat Salih (Ramat Rachel), 4 kilometers further south.[15]

## Roman City Planning

With so few archaeological remains attributed to the time of Aelia Capitolina having come to light, and in spite of an abundance of secondary sources, such as the Byzantine Madaba Map and Crusaders' renderings of the city, it is difficult to establish the original plan. The variety of suggested reconstructions is mostly a result of the unresolved location of the camp of the Tenth Legion.

### CARDO AND DECUMANUS

The conventional Roman city plan had two main streets—the *cardo* and the *decumanus*—which crossed each other more or less in the center, usually the focal point of the city. This layout was based on Roman military camps; given the nature of the local terrain, however, Hadrian was not able to implement this classical plan in Jerusalem.[16]

The present-day layout of the Christian and Muslim quarters of the Old City, consisting of streets intersecting each other at right angles, is usually thought to have originated in the Roman period. The decumanus is generally reconstructed along the line of David Street and the Street of the Chain, from the Jaffa Gate in the west to the Temple Mount in the east. The only archaeological evidence discovered to date was exposed on the easternmost part of the Street of the Chain, near the Temple Mount.

Additional evidence has come to light that can be attributed to the major north–south streets. As illustrated in the Madaba Map (plate 7), the city's natural topography dictated the construction of the main street (the eastern cardo) from the northern entrance through the Tyropoeon Valley down to the south end of the city at the Siloam Pool. Another street runs straight south from the plaza at the Damascus Gate to the Forum and to the Roman camp in the south (the western cardo). As indicated in the map, and as evidenced in the Byzantine continuation of the cardo in the southern part of the city, the street was flanked by two rows of columns that originally supported the wooden rafters of the roofed sidewalks. Some limestone columns, now in secondary use in the walls of the roofed bazaars in the middle of the Old City — which follow the line of the western cardo — have been identified as columns from the Roman cardo. The eastern cardo appears on the Madaba Map with a colonnade running along one side only. Several stone-paved sections, similar to those uncovered near the Damascus Gate, have been identified as remains of the eastern cardo.[17]

### ARCHED GATEWAYS

Structural remains of Roman arched gateways yield further evidence of city planning. Frequently triple-arched, they could have been incorporated into city walls and thus serve as clear indicators of the city boundaries. Alternatively, they could have been freestanding, either on the city's outskirts or in a more central location.

Fig. 7.3. Reconstruction of the triple-arched gateway incorporated into the Late Roman city wall, leading into the oval plaza. Redrawn by J. Dillon, after: M. Magen, "Recovering Roman Jerusalem," 56.

The most impressive extant remains of Aelia Capitolina are those of a triple-arched gateway opening onto an oval plaza (fig. 7.3). It was exposed in several seasons of excavations beneath the foundations of the Ottoman Damascus Gate, in the northern wall of the Old City.[18] This triple gate had a central entrance with a smaller one flanking either side, indicating the northern starting-point of the two *cardines*.[19] Only the eastern entrance has been preserved in its entirety, indicating that all three entrances were spanned by arches with recessed profiles (fig. 7.4). Of the engaged columns that originally flanked the entrances, all that remains are bases on raised pedestals on either side of the eastern entrance. Fixed above the arch of today's eastern entrance is a fragmentary inscription in Latin, probably in secondary use, which ends "by decree of the decurions of Aelia Capitolina." The gate was mainly constructed with Herodian-style dressed stones that were readily available from the previously destroyed walls. The question remains open as to whether the flanking towers were contemporaneous with the triple-arched gateway or were added shortly before or during the construction of the wall (fig. 7.5). Only a few grooved paving stones from the oval plaza remain in situ (fig. 7.6).

An additional gateway, similar in structure to Aelia Capitolina's

Fig. 7.4. The eastern arch of the Roman gate, located underneath the Ottoman Damascus Gate. Photo H. Bloedhorn.

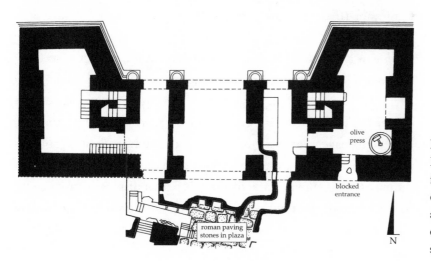

olive press

blocked entrance

roman paving stones in plaza

N

Fig. 7.5. Plan of the Roman arch with the flanking towers. Redrawn by J. Dillon, after: M. Magen, "Recovering Roman Jerusalem," 53.

Fig. 7.6 . Grooved paving stones of street inside the city. Courtesy of the Israel Exploration Society.

northern gate, is located north of the Temple Mount (fig. 7.7). The principal remains known today include the pavement known as the Lithostrotos and part of a triple-arched triumphal gate, the central arch of which is known as the Ecce Homo (fig. 7.8). Christian tradition presents these as the remains of the Antonia fortress, identified incorrectly with the Praetorium, the prison where Jesus's trial took place (Mark 15:1–15). Archaeologists have been able to prove fairly conclusively that these magnificent remains date to the time of Aelia Capitolina (fig. 7.9). Part of the gateway and most of the pavement are today in the Sisters of Zion Convent, while another part of the pavement is in the Chapel of the Condemnation, farther east. Only the central and northern arches of the gateway, built of finely hewn stones with niches cut into the wall of its western façade, have been exposed. The arch might have provided access to the city from the east.[20] The pavement, built of large well-dressed stones, was probably part of a main east–west passageway. Preserved on the eastern side of the exposed pavement is part of a stylobate that originally supported a row of columns. Part of the pavement was laid on vaults (also built at this time) spanning the Strouthion Pool, which before the destruction of the Temple in 70 C.E. lay in the open.

Fig. 7.7. Ecce Homo Arch on the Via Dolorosa, looking west, ca. 1880–1900. Courtesy of the École biblique.

Fig. 7.8. Ecce Homo Arch during excavation, looking east, 1867. Pierotti, *Jerusalem Explored*, plate 13.

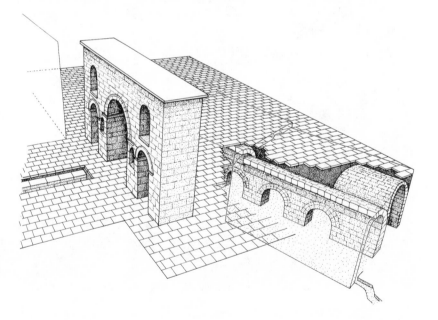

Fig. 7.9 . Reconstruction of the Ecce Homo Arch with the Strouthion Pool. Redrawn by J. Dillon, after: Bahat, *Illustrated Atlas*, 64.

## Necropolis

Unlike the Hasmonean and Herodian period necropolis of Jerusalem, which is very well documented and studied, little attention has been given to Late Roman burials.[21] Other than cist graves, located mostly north of the city, a few caves or burial structures containing a single chamber with troughs or arcosolia can be dated to this period. Most distinct for the second and third centuries C.E., as in other parts of the Roman Empire, are cremation burials either inside burial caves from earlier periods or simple burials dug in the ground.[22] The cremated remains were usually kept in containers, which tended to be ordinary cooking pots. Secondary use of Hellenistic burial complexes for cremation, such as those in the Tomb of the Kings or the Akeldama Tombs, can be associated with the Roman soldiers or pagan citizens of Aelia Capitolina (fig. 7.10).

## Distinctive Finds

Small finds and artifacts of Roman Jerusalem bear hardly any traces of local cultures; the material remains of this period are characterized by features prevalent in the larger Roman world.

Fig. 7.10. Roman tombstone found in the necropolis near St. George's Cathedral. The Latin inscription reads: "Dis Manibus. Lucius Magnius Felix, soldier of the Tenth Legion Fretensis adjutant of the tribunes. He served for 19 years (in the army), he lived for 39 years." Vincent and Abel, *Jérusalem,* II 4, 893, fig. 369.

## POTTERY, ROOF TILES, AND BRICKS

Despite the lack of structural remains — with the exception of stone and pottery pipelines — the presence of the Tenth Roman Legion in Aelia Capitolina can be attested by large numbers of pottery items, roof tiles, and bricks stamped with the name of the Tenth Legion: "L(egio) X Fre(tensis)" (fig. 7.11). These objects were found in excavations conducted in the Citadel and in the Armenian and Jewish Quarters.[23] Recent excavations at Shaikh Badr revealed a full-size army factory for production of pottery and, more importantly, bricks and tiles.[24] The excavated site consisted of several main clusters, including a facility for preparing the clay, a potter's wheel, a drying area for the pottery, a preparation and drying area for the bricks and tiles, and a series of aligned kilns.

Fig. 7.11. Two Roman tiles stamped "L(egio) X Fre(tensis)," in the German Protestant Institute of Archaeology, Jerusalem. Courtesy of the German Protestant Institute of Archaeology, Jerusalem.

## ROMAN STATUARY

The cultural changes introduced by the Romans, particularly after the destruction of the Temple in 70 C.E., can be seen clearly in the rich repertoire of sculpted figural images. The largest assemblage of marble statuary from Aelia Capitolina was found in the Temple Mount excavations. The different types of marble and varied scale of the fragments uncovered — and the reconstructed sculptures, statuettes of gods, and mythological creatures — attest to their belonging to several sculpted works or monuments (figs. 7.12–13).[25] Several fragments of an almost life-size sculpture of a nymph were found in and around one of the three pools of the *frigidarium* in the Roman bathhouse located west of Robinson's Arch (fig. 7.14).[26] In later use her breast was perforated to serve as a fountain.

Fig. 7.12. (Far left) Female statue (goddess?) dedicated by Valeria Aemiliana, from the Temple Mount excavations. The Greek inscription on its base reads: "Valeria Aemiliana set up (the statue) by her vow." Courtesy of E. Mazar, the Temple Mount Publication Project.

Fig. 7.13. (Left, top) Fragment of a putto, originally holding a bow and arrow, from the Temple Mount excavations. Courtesy of E. Mazar, the Temple Mount Publication Project.

Fig. 7.14. (Left, bottom) Fragment of a nymph, from the Temple Mount excavations. Courtesy of E. Mazar, the Temple Mount Publication Project.

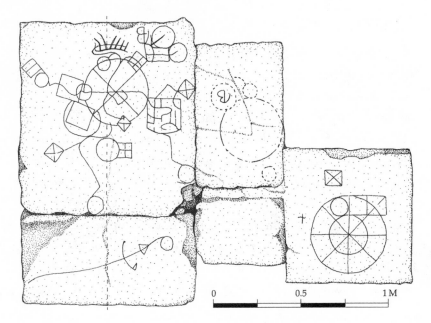

Fig. 7.15. Incised board games on the Strouthion pavement. Redrawn by J. Dillon, after: Vincent and Steve, *Jérusalem*, I, plate 54. See Fig. 6.34 for comparison.

0          0.5          1 M

### BOARD GAMES

One of the main east–west passageways of Aelia Capitolina was most likely part of the eastern forum, which was uncovered in the early 1860s when the Sisters of Zion Convent was built. Designs identified as board games were found incised on some of the paving stones (fig. 7.15). These games, played in the private as well as public sphere, are typical of the Roman and Byzantine periods and attest to soldiers' leisure activities, in Jerusalem and elsewhere in the Roman Empire.[27]

Plate 1. The Old City from the Damascus Gate, looking south along the Tyropoeon Valley, today's Tariq al-Wad. Photo H. Bloedhorn.

Plate 2. Skyline of the Ottoman city wall. Center: the Citadel and Jaffa Gate. Right: the southwestern corner. Below the Citadel: Sultan's Pool (presently dry), used today as an open-air theater. Foreground: the road crossing the Hinnom Valley, leading to Bethlehem and Hebron. Photo H. Bloedhorn.

Plate 3. Bronze Age pottery from the Parker excavations. Vincent, *Jérusalem sous terre*, plate 9.

Plate 4. Burial gifts from Tomb 25 in the Hinnom Valley necropolis. Courtesy of the Israel Museum.

Plate 5. Wall decorated with a colorful fresco in the Palatial Mansion. Courtesy of the Israel Exploration Society.

Plate 6. Mosaic floor decorated with geometric patterns from the living room of a villa in Avigad area F3, in the Wohl Archaeological Museum, Jerusalem. Courtesy of the Israel Exploration Society.

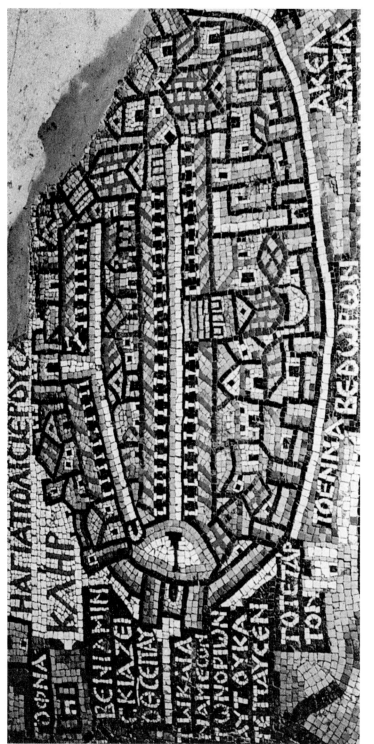

Plate 7. Madaba mosaic map found in the Church of St. George in the city of Madaba in Jordan. Courtesy of the Studium Biblicum Franciscanum.

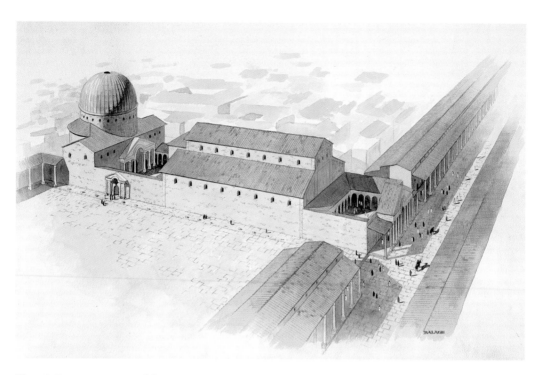

Plate 8. Reconstruction of the Byzantine cardo or main street (right) and the Church of the Holy Sepulchre complex (left). Drawing by B. Balogh; courtesy of the Israel Museum.

Plate 9. Section of the Church of the Holy Sepulchre (right), with the Triportico (center) containing the rock of Golgotha and the Anastasis Rotunda (left). Drawing by B. Balogh; courtesy of the Israel Museum.

Plate 10. Mosaic of Orpheus playing a cithara, in a funerary chapel located northwest of Damascus Gate. Courtesy of the École biblique, aquarelle by H. Vincent.

Plate 11. Mosaics inside the Dome of the Rock. Courtesy of the Institute of Archaeology, Hebrew University Jerusalem.

Plate 12. (Opposite page) The interior and the mihrab of the Dome of the Chain. Photo H. Bloedhorn.

Plate 13. (Above) Mosaic representing Christ on the ceiling of the Chapel of the Calvary. Photo H. Bloedhorn.

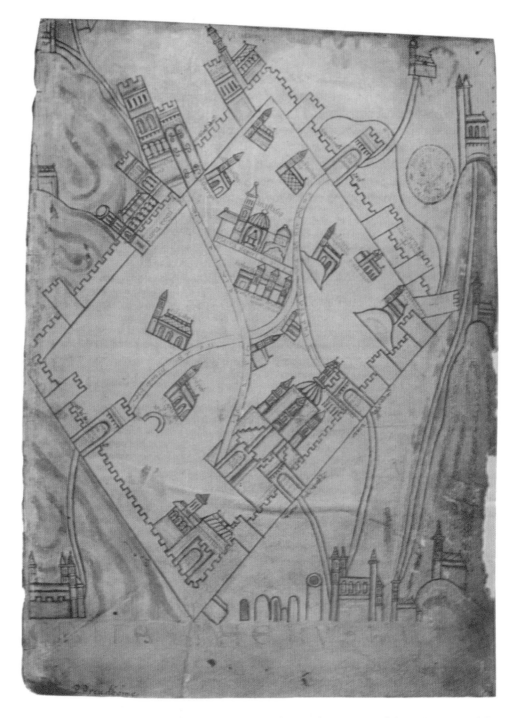

Plate 14. The Cambrai Map, Bibliothèque Municipale, Cambrai, Ms 466 fol. 1r. Courtesy of the Bibliothèque Municipale de Cambrai, France.

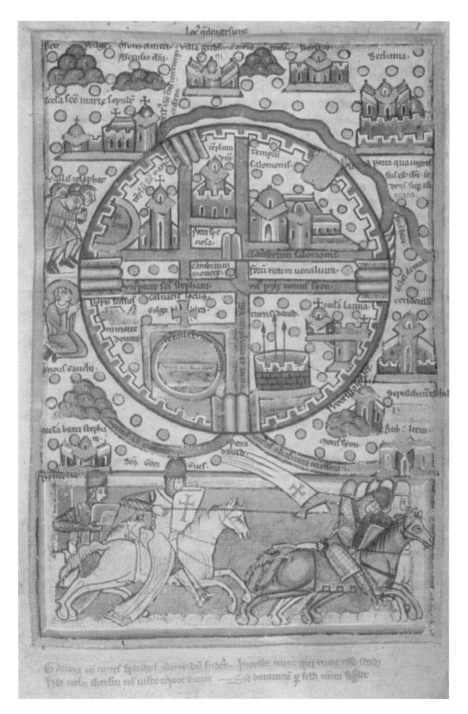

Plate 15. The Hague Map, Koninklijke Bibliotheek, The Hague, Cod. 76 F 5.
Courtesy of the Koninklijke Bibliotheek, The Hague, Netherlands.

Plate 16. Madrasa al-Tankiziya, mihrab with marble panels and mosaic. Courtesy of Carta, Jerusalem.

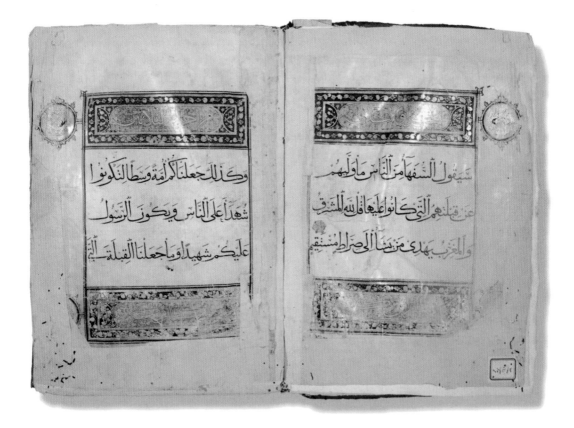

Plate 17. (Opposite page, bottom) Opening pages of Rab'ah of Ibn Qurman,
A.H. 778/ 1376 C.E., in the Islamic Museum, Jerusalem. Courtesy of K. Salameh
(Salameh, *Quran Manuscripts*, 89).

Plate 18. (Above) Dome of the Rock, exterior of the eastern wall, showing
Ottoman marble restoration. Slabs at the bottom are in secondary use.
Photo H. Bloedhorn.

Plate 19 a–b. Dome of the Rock, Ottoman tiles from ca. 1560: detail of a *cuerda seca* tile (19a, top) and a tile painted in underglaze cobalt blue, turquoise, and black (19b, bottom). Courtesy of Al Tajir Trust (Auld and Hillenbrand, *Ottoman Jerusalem*, I, color plate 31 and 33).

Plate 20 a–b. Woman's wedding dress, *thub abu qutba*, from Jerusalem, ca. 1850 (20a, top) and man's *qumbaz* from Jerusalem, ca. 1930 (20b, bottom). Courtesy of Al Tajir Trust (Auld and Hillenbrand, *Ottoman Jerusalem*, I, color plate 13 and 12).

# 8 ✦ The Byzantine Period

On your left is the hillock Golgotha where the Lord was crucified, and about a stone's throw from it is the vault where they laid his body, and he rose again on the third day. By order of the Emperor Constantine there has now been built there a "basilica" — I mean a "place for the Lord" — which has beside it cisterns of remarkable beauty, and beside them a baptistery where children are baptized.

BORDEAUX PILGRIM, *Egeria's Travels to the Holy Land*, 594

## A Christian City

In 313, the Edict of Milan pronounced Christianity one of the legal religions of the Roman Empire. Constantine (306–337 C.E.), ruler of the western part of the empire, defeated his last opponent, Licinius, ruler of the eastern empire, in 324 and became emperor of the entire Roman Empire. In 330, Constantine declared the strategic eastern city of Byzantium as his capital, changing its name to Constantinople. The term "Byzantine" would eventually refer to the eastern Roman Empire and the period of its influence.

Beginning in the fourth century, Jerusalem was transformed from an insignificant Roman town to a major Christian city. The official name remained Aelia, without the pagan designation "Capitolina." Christians emerged from being a persecuted group to become an assertive, dominant force in the city. In 325, Jerusalem rose in stature from a diocese served by a bishop to a metropolis, and in 451 became one of the five patriarchates of the Church, along with the major cities of Alexandria, Antioch, Constantinople, and Rome. Byzantine Palestine in general and Jerusalem in particular served as important centers of Christian pilgrimage and monastic movements. Leading church figures and faithful believers from all over the empire visited the many churches constructed on sites associated with the life, miracles, trial, and crucifixion of Jesus as well as with his disciples and other biblical figures. The churches and holy places, and the traditions with which they are associated, are described in the guidebooks written by pilgrims throughout the Byzantine period.[1]

Church construction and renovation were an ongoing process in the city but were particularly intensive at specific times. As proof of the triumph of Christianity, Jews were allowed to mourn the destruction of the Temple on the Fast of the Ninth of Av while viewing the Temple Mount. The former Temple area, as a structural monument, was intentionally neglected for most of Byzantine rule.[2] During his brief reign (361–363), the emperor Julian the Apostate ordered the rebuilding of the Temple as part of his struggle against Christianity and his revival of paganism throughout the empire. His sudden death, however, put an end to this project. In 614, the Persians invaded the country and took Jerusalem. Christian sources relate that Jews assisted the Persian forces, killing many Christians and damaging or destroying some of the churches and monasteries.[3] Zacharias, Patriarch of Jerusalem, numerous Christians, and the relic known as the True Cross were taken to Persia; local authority was granted to the Christian patriarch Modestus, and some of the ruined churches, including the Holy Sepulchre, were restored.

In 629, the Byzantine emperor Heraclius captured Jerusalem from the Persians. He restored Christian rule and attempted to restore the splendor of Byzantine Jerusalem. In 638, however, Jerusalem surrendered to Caliph Umar I, and was spared the destruction that it had suffered during the Persian invasion.

## The Madaba Map

The Madaba Map is the oldest map of the Holy Land featuring a detailed depiction of Jerusalem in its center (plate 7).[4] It came to light during foundation work undertaken in 1896 for the Greek-Orthodox Church of St. George at the northern end of what was then the small village of Madaba in Jordan. Following the discovery, large fragments of the mosaic pavement (15.7 × 5.6 meters), corresponding in width to the original size of the Byzantine church, were exposed. Each detail represented in the mosaic is oriented to the east, following a convention in practice since the late third millennium[5]

The highlight of the map is clearly the representation of the Holy City of Jerusalem with the protective wall that was erected around 300. Adjacent to the Damascus Gate (on the left), a semicircular plaza with a column in its center gives access to the two main streets stretching from north to south. West of the Byzantine main street lies the Church of the Martyrium and Anastasis ("Resurrection") — today's Church of the Holy Sepulchre — built under Constantine between 325 and 335, followed further south by a side street ending at Jaffa Gate. East of the Byzantine main street lies the Nea Church, dedicated in 543 by Justinian, and at its southern end rises Hagia Sion (Church of Holy Zion), dedicated in 394 and included within the city wall since the mid fifth century C.E. (fig. 8.1). A short side street

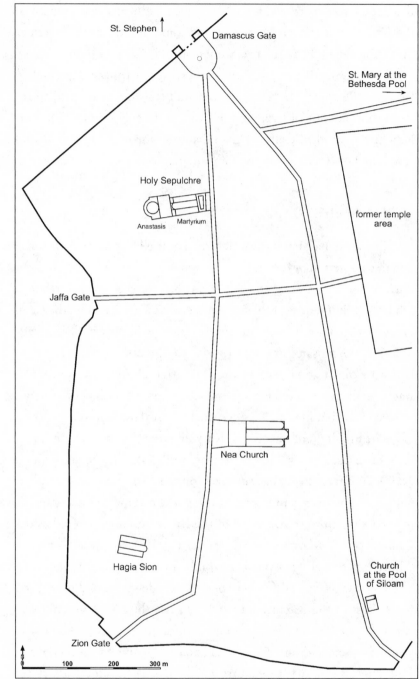

St. Stephen ↑

Damascus Gate

St. Mary at the
Bethesda Pool →

Holy Sepulchre

Anastasis    Martyrium

former temple
area

Jaffa Gate

Nea Church

Hagia Sion

Church
at the Pool
of Siloam

Zion Gate

100    200    300 m

Fig. 8.1. Map indicating locations of the Church of the Holy Sepulchre, the Nea Church, and Hagia Sion along the main artery of the Byzantine city. Drawing by M. Speidel.

branching off to the east, or the secondary side street to St. Stephen's Gate, leads to the Church of St. Mary at the Bethesda Pool (second half of the fifth century). The Temple Mount area, which after 70 remained in ruins, is not represented, nor is the church at the Siloam Pool that would have been located at the southern end of the Ophel. Stylistically, the map may be attributed to the Justinian renaissance and must postdate the Nea Church.

## Fortifications

The nature of the construction and the line of Jerusalem's city wall in the Byzantine period are known from the many remains excavated along its course. Significant sections of the wall and several towers can be traced all around the city — on the Ophel,[6] at the end of the Tyropoeon Valley,[7] and on the southern slope of Mount Zion.[8] Additional sections of the western wall are visible in the Armenian Garden and in the Citadel, and in various areas north of today's Old City wall.[9]

The wall is only about 3 meters thick — thinner than Jerusalem's earlier walls. Judging from the archaeological evidence, the Byzantine wall of Jerusalem can be dated, as a whole, to the late third or early fourth century. The refortification of Jerusalem at this time may be related to the relocation of the Tenth Legion at the end of the third century.

## Sacral Architecture

During the first three centuries following the crucifixion of Jesus, Christianity was a suppressed religion whose adherents congregated in buildings that were not specifically designated for this purpose. Literary sources indicate that the early believers assembled either in private homes (*domus ecclesiae*) or synagogues, rendering impossible the archaeological identification of such early places of Christian assembly.[10] Christian sacred architecture became evident only when Christianity was deemed the legal and official religion of the empire under Constantine the Great. He initiated a building program that placed high priority on Jerusalem and the Holy Land. Initially an emphasis was placed on locations that commemorated events associated with Jesus that are mentioned in the Gospels. Jerusalem was obviously the center of all sites connected with the Passion. Later in the Byzantine period, churches commemorated primarily martyrs, biblical figures, and prophets. After the Councils of Ephesus in 431 C.E. and Chalcedon in 451 C.E., St. Mary, mother of Jesus, became especially important.

Most churches built in the Holy Land and Jerusalem in the Byzantine era are mentioned by the early Church fathers and pilgrims and complement the significant archaeological finds of this period. The continuity of religious structures, which usually replaced each other on the exact same spot, allows us to identify the Byzantine structure even if the remains of this particular period are relatively fragmentary.

Churches can be divided into two categories based on their plans. The majority of churches throughout the Byzantine period are rectangular or basilical in plan; a smaller group was built according to a central plan.[11] The model for the Christian basilica was the multipurpose Roman civic building of the same name, mostly found in public places such as the forum. The reason for adopting the basilical plan is rather obvious. The Christian church, like its predecessor — the Jewish synagogue — had to accommodate worshipers, unlike pagan temples or the First and Second Temples, where only priests were allowed to enter the sanctuary. A large number of basilicas in the Holy Land were built at holy places (*loca sancta*); the majority were, however, simple congregational churches in which Mass was held. Early on, another architectural type evolved, whose plan was more appropriate for commemorative purposes than the basilica. This plan highlighted the center of the structure. This type of church could be either circular, octagonal, square, or cruciform. Unlike the basilica, this design was not based on the orientation of the apse at one end of the building, but rather on the geometrical center, which could emphasize the holy place on or under the floor. These centric churches were also inspired by Roman buildings, secular or religious structures, most importantly monumental tombs (mausolea) of emperors and patricians of Rome.[12]

### FOURTH CENTURY C.E.

According to Eusebius, the desire to translate the new credo architecturally was expressed after the Council of Nicaea in 325 and led to Constantine's decision to build three churches, the Church of the Nativity in Bethlehem, the Church of the Holy Sepulchre in Jerusalem, and the Eleona Church on the Mount of Olives:

> In [Palestine] he discovered three places venerable as the localities of three sacred caves: and these also he adorned with costly structures, paying a fitting tribute of reverence to the scene of the first manifestation of the Saviour's presence; while at the second cavern he hallowed the remembrance of his final ascension from the mountain top; and celebrated his mighty conflict, and the victory which crowned it, at the third. All these places our emperor thus adorned in the hope of proclaiming the symbol of redemption to all mankind; that Cross which has indeed repaid his pious zeal; through which his house and throne alike have prospered, his reign has been confirmed for a lengthened series of years, and the rewards of virtue bestowed on his noble sons, his kindred, and their descendants. (Eusebius, *Oration* IX, 17–18)

The construction process was completed as early as 335. The Church of the Nativity commemorating the birth of Jesus was built in Bethlehem.[13] The Church of the Passion and Resurrection of the Lord (the Martyrium and Anastasis) was built in Jerusalem. Finally, the Eleona Church was erected on the Mount of Olives to mark the spot where Jesus disseminated his teachings amongst his disciples, as well as the site of the Last Supper and Jesus's Ascension. One generation after this construction, around 374, a new place of Ascension, the so-called Imbomon, was established some 70 meters to the north, on the summit of the hill. Around 394, under Emperor Theodosius I, it was decided that the location of the Last Supper was on Mount Zion, and so it was commemorated with the construction of Hagia Sion (the Church of Holy Zion).

### The Church of the Holy Sepulchre

Construction work, fully financed by the imperial coffers, started soon after the Council of Nicaea.[14] The first task was to destroy the pagan temple in the forum to accommodate the building of the Martyrium Basilica and the Anastasis Rotunda (fig. 8.2).[15] The natural slopes of the hill were leveled so that Golgotha itself, the site of the Crucifixion and the nearby sepulchre, would tower over the surrounding area. From the western cardo, which bisected the city from north to south (plate 8), the Holy Sepulchre complex was entered through an entrance hall (*propylon*).[16] Steps led to a narrow courtyard — the first atrium. Three openings led from the atrium to the basilica itself. Four rows of columns divided the basilica into a central nave with four side aisles. At this stage, its apse was oriented to the west, in the direction of the rotunda.[17] Between the basilica and the rotunda at the western end of the complex was an additional courtyard, the Triportico, surrounded on the north, east, and south by porticoes (plate 9). The rock of Golgotha — a bare rock protruding to a height of approximately 5 meters — was included in the southeastern corner of the inner courtyard, surrounded by a metal screen and crowned with a large cross in memory of the Crucifixion. The rock was vener-

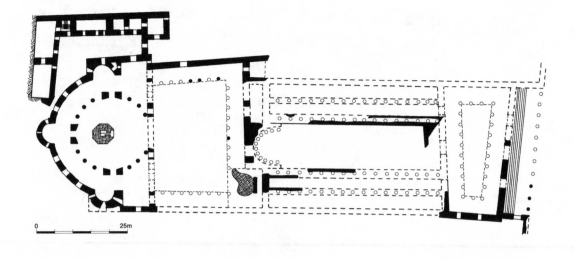

0      25m

ated as the navel of the world, the omphalos. The main part of the church, the Holy Sepulchre itself, stood beyond the inner atrium to the west. The surrounding structure is known as the Anastasis Rotunda because of its circular shape. Structural remains of the atria and basilica were uncovered during excavations conducted in the 1960s.[18] No more than the foundations of the basilica's original church have survived, whereas in the triportico and rotunda, wall sections and several columns still stand up to 11 meters high. The church was dedicated on September 13, 335 C.E.[19]

Fig. 8.2. Plan of the Martyrium Basilica (right) and the Anastasis Rotunda (left). Redrawn by J. Dillon, after: Corbo, *Il Santo Sepolcro*, plate 3.

### The Eleona Church

The Eleona was built on the western slope of the Mount of Olives, near the summit overlooking the Temple Mount.[20] It marked the spot where, according to tradition, Jesus sat with his disciples and where the Last Supper occurred. Although only the foundations were revealed, it is possible to reconstruct the original Constantinian church (fig. 8.3). The atrium in the west was accessed through a peristyle court surrounded by porticoes on four sides. From here, three entrances led to the basilica itself, which was divided by two rows of

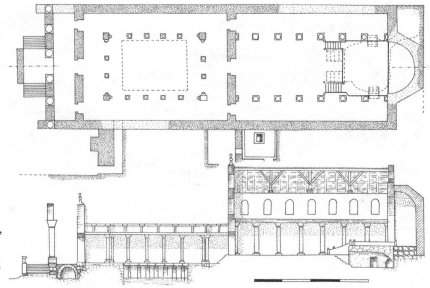

Fig. 8.3. Plan and section of the Eleona Church. Redrawn by J. Dillon, after: Vincent and Abel, *Jérusalem*, II, 1–2, plate 34.

columns into a nave and two aisles. The topography of the site necessitated that steps be built in order to compensate for the difference in height between the outside, the atrium, and the church. The chancel was raised above the venerated cave, to which two flights of stairs were added. One flight was used for ascent and the other for descent, an arrangement that permitted the unfettered procession of worshippers and pilgrims.[21] The apse of the Eleona Church is external, extending outward to the east, beyond the main rectangular structure of the church. Like the Church of the Holy Sepulchre, the Eleona Church represents the incorporation of a holy place, which attracted masses of pilgrims, into a basilica church.

### The Imbomon

The Ascension was initially commemorated in the Eleona. The covered structure was probably unconducive or disturbing to the imagination of pilgrims. Therefore, around 374 C.E., a wealthy pilgrim to Jerusalem named Poemenia supported the construction of a new building. The so-called Imbomon was erected on top of the hill, some 75 meters northeast of the Eleona Church. The newly designed construction featured two concentric rows of columns (fig. 8.4). The remains correspond to the description and drawing by the seventh-century pilgrim Arculf (fig. 8.5). According to tradition the floor in the center remained unpaved so that pilgrims could venerate the footprint of the Lord in the sand. The central part of the dome was open to the sky.[22]

### The Church of Holy Zion (Hagia Sion)

About two decades later (394 C.E.), the tradition of the Last Supper and Passover celebration were also relocated from Eleona to a newly dedicated church on Mount Zion. Soon the Church of Holy Zion (St. Mary on Mount Zion) was recognized as one of the three most important liturgical sites. Excavations exposed only partial remains of the foundations (fig. 10.12); the missing westernmost wall could be reconstructed based on documentation of the church's length in the written sources.[23]

#### FIFTH AND SIXTH CENTURIES C.E.

Church construction accelerated considerably during the fifth century. New buildings were erected to commemorate events and places connected to the Passion of Jesus, such as the grotto of the betrayal.[24] Another marks the site of Jesus's prayer in the garden of Gethsemane; these two buildings are still in place.[25] Two additional churches were built — one next to the Siloam Pool (fig. 8.6), where, according to tradition, Jesus cured the blind man, and the other near the Bethesda Pool, where he healed the paralyzed.[26] Remains of both structures have been uncovered but are no longer preserved.[27]

Other churches for which partial remains have been identified were erected to commemorate various saints: St. John the Baptist on the Mount of Olives[28] and St. Stephen north of the city,[29] St. James (next to the Tomb of the Lord's Brother),[30] St. Isaiah in the Kidron

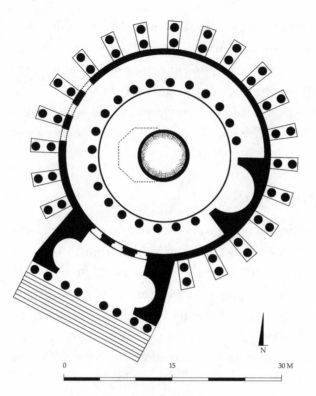

Fig. 8.4. Modified
plan of the Imbomon
following the excava-
tions in the 1960s.
Redrawn by J. Dillon,
after: Wilkinson, *Je-
rusalem as Jesus Knew
It*, 174, fig. 228.

0    15    30 M

N

Fig. 8.5. Plan of the
Imbomon, drawn by
Arculf in the seventh
century. Redrawn by
J. Dillon, after:
Wilkinson, *Jerusalem
Pilgrims*, plate 2 aY.

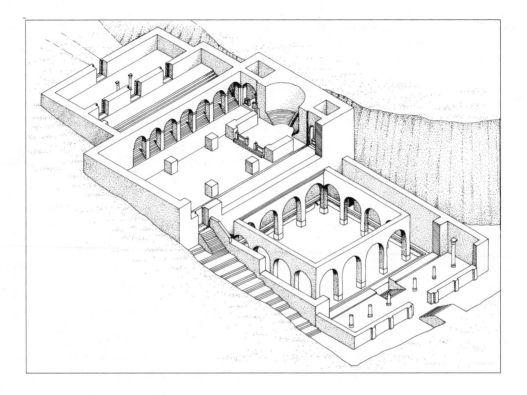

Valley,[31] the Pool of Jeremiah in the Tyropoeon Valley,[32] and St. Procopius[33] above the Hinnom Valley.

Fig. 8.6. Isometric re-
construction of the
church at the Siloam
Pool. Redrawn by J.
Dillon, after: Bahat,
*Illustrated Atlas*, 72.

Following the Councils of Ephesus (431) and Chalcedon (451),
three churches dedicated to Mary were built around the mid fifth
century C.E. Only one of them, located on the road leading to Bethlehem, "where the child moved within her womb," has left partial
remains.[34]

The existence of various ecclesiastical structures in the area
north of the Damascus Gate was established in the early twentieth
century. As a result of the construction of a new major thoroughfare
in this part of the city, additional buildings from the Byzantine period
were exposed, including five chapels or churches, three monasteries,
and four hospices.[35] A hospice for the elderly established by the empress Eudocia can be identified near today's St. Andrew's Church. A

chapel dedicated to St. George and associated with the hospice has been partially uncovered.[36]

### The Nea Church

The Nea Church was built by Justinian and dedicated November 20, 543 (figs. 8.7–8).[37] Damaged either in the Persian invasion of Palestine in 614 or the Arab invasion in 638, it was finally destroyed in the ninth century c.e. The church, whose full name was the New Church of Mary the Mother of God, was described in detail by the contemporary historian Procopius (*Buildings*, V, 6). The first segment of the church was exposed in 1862; later building remains were uncovered in the 1970s and 1980s — the two side apses in the east, the southeastern corner of the basilica, and the basilica's southern retaining wall, a row of vaulted openings spanned by supporting arches (fig. 8.9). In several locations the wall was preserved to a height of 7.5 meters. The vaults, used as a cistern, were built to buttress an enlarged area supporting the church's ancillary buildings. These underground vaults were described rather accurately by Procopius:

> They threw the foundations out as far as the limit of the even ground, and then erected a structure which rose as high as the rock. And when they had raised this up level with the rock they set vaults upon the supporting walls, and joined this substructure to the other foundation of the church. Thus the church is partly based upon living rock, and partly carried in the air by a great extension artificially added to the hill by the Emperor's power. (Procopius, *Buildings*, V, 6)

An inscription found high on the wall of the cistern further corroborates the identification of the structural remains with the Nea Church. It commemorates the construction of the church and explicitly mentions the builder, Emperor Justinian, as well as the year of its dedica-

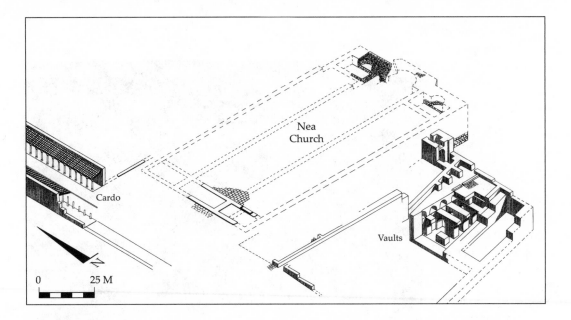

Fig. 8.7. Plan of the Nea Church. Left: the Byzantine cardo; right: an underground vaulted cistern south of the church. The detailed stones at the entrance to the church and in the apses indicate the excavated remains. Redrawn by J. Dillon, after: Bahat, *Illustrated Atlas*, 74–75.

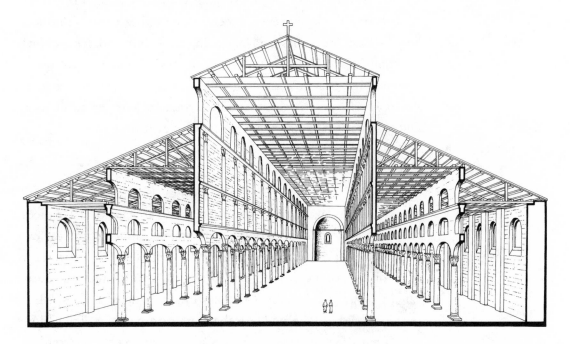

Fig. 8.8. Section through the Nea Church. Redrawn by J. Dillon, after: Ben-Dov, *In the Shadow of the Temple*, 239.

Fig. 8.9. Foundation of the southeastern corner of the Nea Church, some 12 meters below ground level, outside today's Ottoman city wall. Photo H. Bloedhorn.

tion — probably 534–35, according to the excavator's reading: "And this is the work which our most pious emperor Flavius Justinianus carried out with magnificence, under the care and devotion of the most holy Constantinus, priest and hegumen, in the thirteenth (year of the) indiction."[38] The Greek inscription was framed within a *tabula ansata* — a molded, red-painted plaster relief above a large cross, also in relief. As Procopius's description does not fully correspond to the archaeological findings, the plan of the church is somewhat controversial.

### Dwellings

In contrast to the numerous literary and archaeological sources relevant for the reconstruction of monumental architecture, the existing data on private architecture are more limited. On the western slope of the Southeast Hill, part of a north–south street was excavated that was flanked on both sides by domestic structures.[39] Excavations on the Ophel and near the southeastern corner of the Temple Mount also uncovered an impressive level of occupation from the Byzantine period involving several building phases (fig. 8.10).[40] Sev-

eral two-story peristyle houses have been found that were built in the fourth and fifth centuries. Their walls were made of smoothed stones, sometimes plastered and decorated with frescoes and stuccowork, and their roofs were presumably made of wooden beams resting on stone arches set in the middle of the rooms. The floors were either made of beaten earth or paved with stone slabs.

By the end of the Byzantine period, numerous additional houses had been constructed. Some remained preserved. In contrast to the earlier buildings, which were scattered around the area without any order, these later houses were integrated into a municipal master plan. Their configuration consisted of several rooms arranged around a central courtyard, onto which the doors and windows of the rooms opened. The buildings were also two stories high, with rock-cut cellars used for storage and as workshops. Almost every house contained

Fig. 8.10. Large Byzantine house in Mazar area XV, looking northeast. Note the southern retaining wall of the former Temple Mount in the background. Courtesy of E. Mazar, the Temple Mount Publication Project.

some rooms with coarse mosaic floors, some laid in simple geometric and floral patterns, others with Greek biblical inscriptions. As in the earlier phase, the ceilings were made of wooden beams supported by a central stone arch. Some of the roofs were tiled. A complicated system of clay pipes collected rainwater from the roofs and courtyards, feeding it into the central cisterns hewn beneath the buildings. The remains of various industrial installations were found in courtyards and the surrounding rooms, including dyeing and tanning installations and smelting furnaces. Some houses contained the remains of cooking stoves and kitchen utensils; the remains of a lavatory were found concealed in a back courtyard of a house. Other buildings exhibited signs of renovations carried out at various times in the Byzantine period. Some of the buildings on the Ophel were probably destroyed during the Persian invasion of 614 c.e. and never rebuilt; others continued to be used alongside the Umayyad palaces built there in the seventh and eighth centuries c.e. A complete destruction occurred during the earthquake of 749 c.e.[41] In recent years, remains of an additional residential neighborhood were uncovered in proximity to today's Jaffa Gate.[42]

## Necropolis

Byzantine tombs were discovered all around Jerusalem's Old City. Most burial types known from the Hellenistic and Roman periods were maintained; these were simple cist graves as well as caves or burial structures consisting of single or multiple chambers equipped with either troughs or arcosolia. Some were used for individual burials, although extended family or community graves used over several generations remained the rule. One of the most obvious signs of a Byzantine tomb is its placement beside or inside a Byzantine chapel, church, or monastery.

Burial types that are exceptional for the Byzantine era are the large tomb complexes, including rectangular halls known also in other parts of the country, at both Jewish and Christian burial sites.[43] One example is the so-called Tomb of the Prophets on the Mount of

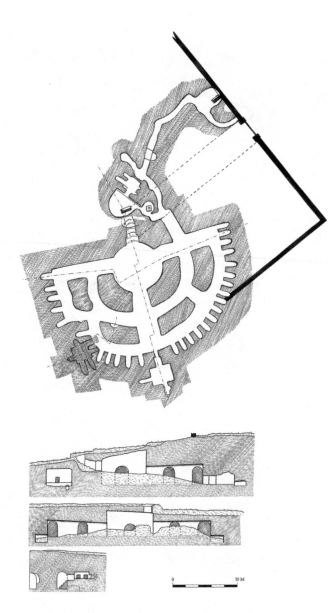

Fig. 8.11. Plan and section of the Tomb of the Prophets on the Mount of Olives. Redrawn by J. Dillon, after: Vincent, "Le tombeau," 75.

Olives, an underground network of chambers and passages with several concentric corridors equipped with loculi (fig. 8.11).[44] Probably dated to the fourth and fifth centuries, this tomb may have functioned as a common burial place for Christian pilgrims who passed away during their stay in Jerusalem. An additional catacomb complex with arcosolia and loculi is located nearby, on the grounds of the Viri

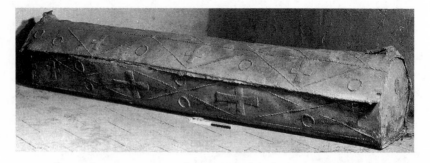

Fig. 8.12. Lead sarcophagus from the second half of the fifth century C.E., found in a mausoleum in the Bet Safafa necropolis, southwest of Jerusalem. Courtesy of the Israel Antiquities Authority.

Galilei monastery.[45] Further concentrations of tombs can be found in the cemetery area north of the city wall, near the Church of St. Stephen,[46] as well as beneath the YMCA,[47] west of the Old City.[48]

Another phenomenon exclusively associated with the Byzantine period is a number of underground caves containing mass burials.[49] These are most likely connected to one or two traumatic events that are recorded in the written sources: the 542 plague or the 614 Persian conquest.[50] Burials of this period are also renowned for the large number of lead coffins found in Jerusalem and elsewhere in the Holy Land (fig. 8.12).

## Distinctive Finds

The Byzantine era is based to a large extent on technical and stylistic innovations introduced during the preceding Roman period. This period is significant foremost for its iconographic themes, often, but not always, recognized by their specifically Christian motifs.

### MOSAICS

Most Byzantine mosaics in Jerusalem were found in the context of Christian church architecture, inside chapels, churches, and monasteries. Some examples of mosaics decorating private dwellings were found in the Jewish Quarter and the southern Temple Mount excava-

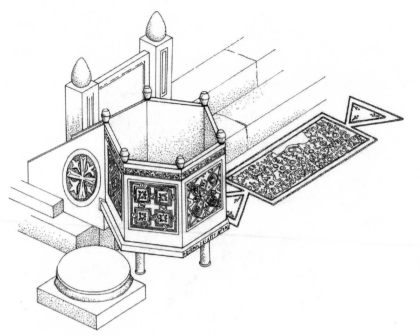

Fig. 8.13. Isometric reconstruction of the ambo in the Church of St. Theodore at Bait Sila, 14 km northwest of Jerusalem. Redrawn by J. Dillon, after: Batz, "Church of St. Theodore," 46, fig. 7.

tions.[51] A few sparsely and simply decorated mosaics exist, although the leading aesthetic concept of Byzantine mosaics is *horror vacui*, exemplified by the filling in of otherwise negative space in the design of a mosaic. In addition to the mosaic carpets containing geometric and floral patterns, landscapes, and hunting scenes with realistic and mythical animals — all of which are characteristic of the Hellenistic tradition — mosaics also depict biblical stories, especially those relating miraculous deliverances and prefigurations of events in the life of Jesus. The cross, the main Christian symbol of identity, served as a decorative motif on mosaic floors, but out of deference for that symbol, its use was forbidden by an edict of the Emperor Theodosius II in 427 C.E.: "We decree specifically that no one shall be permitted to carve or to paint the sign of Christ the Savior upon the floor or the pavement or on the marble slabs placed on the ground."[52] Nevertheless, crosses appear on the mosaic floors of churches as late as the

Fig. 8.14. A reliquary found in the Church of St. Theodore. Courtesy of the Israel Museum.

Fig. 8.15. *Eulogia* ampulla from Asia Minor representing a woman riding a donkey side-saddle (on the reverse side is a depiction of a male rider), found in a Byzantine shop just outside the Jaffa Gate. Courtesy of the Israel Museum.

Fig. 8.16. Lamp with Greek inscription: "The light of Christ shines beautifully for all." Courtesy of the Israel Museum.

Fig. 8.17. Four crosses. The large cross, made of bronze and inset with wood, was found in a Byzantine shop just outside the Jaffa Gate; the three smaller crosses were found in a burial chapel in the Mamilla neighborhood located some 200 meters west of Jaffa Gate. Courtesy of the Israel Museum.

sixth century C.E. Based on a relatively unified artistic and stylistic appearance, attempts have been made to recognize a Jerusalem workshop that served as a regional center for mosaic art.[53]

One of the most remarkable mosaics of the Byzantine period, depicting Orpheus playing a cithara, was uncovered in a funerary chapel located some 215 meters northwest of the Damascus Gate (plate 10). It is now widely believed that the original function of the space was domestic in nature.[54]

### CHURCH FURNISHINGS AND CHRISTIAN IMAGERY

The architectural remains of Byzantine ecclesiastical monuments are further enhanced by excavations that have uncovered valuable information regarding early church furnishings and decorations, including numerous examples of chancel screens, altars, ambos, and reliquaries (figs. 8.13–14).[55]

Typical Christian images and symbols appear on pilgrim flasks, oil lamps, bread stamps, and censers, as well as on hanging lamps and suspended ornaments (figs. 8.15–16). Distinct Christian imagery includes the Christogram, fish and crosses, and representative scenes of the Annunciation, Madonna and Child, the Adoration of the Magi, and depictions of the sacred horseman (fig. 8.17).[56] Objects and souvenirs associated with Christian pilgrimage continued to be produced and used beyond the Byzantine period.

# 9 ✦ The Early Islamic Period

Among provincial towns none is larger than Jerusalem, and many
capitals are in fact smaller . . . The buildings of the Holy City are of
stone, and you will find nowhere finer or more solid constructions . . . Provisions are most excellent here, the markets are clean,
the mosque is of the largest, and nowhere are Holy Places more numerous . . . In Jerusalem are all manner of learned men and doctors,
and for this reason the hearts of men of intelligence yearn towards
her. All the year round, never are her streets empty of strangers.

AL-MUQADDASI, *Description of Syria*, 165–67

## Muslim al-Quds

Caliph Umar I conquered Jerusalem (al-Quds, in Arabic) around
A.H. 16–17/637–638 C.E. without causing havoc or imposing destruction.[1] Within a few years he succeeded in defeating the two exhausted

superpowers, Persia and the Byzantine Empire.[2] Umar I intentionally avoided incurring damage on Jerusalem because of its special role
for adherents of the new religion of Islam. The site of the Jewish
Temple in Jerusalem was also Muhammad's destination during his
legendary night journey from Mecca on his steed al-Burak, and it is
the site from which the Prophet ascended the seven heavens into the
presence of the Almighty. Umar I built a mosque on top of the Temple Mount platform, which the Arabs renamed at first al-Jami al-Aqsa
and after the Crusader period the Haram al-Sharif (the Noble Sanctuary) (fig. 9.1).[3]

Jerusalem became increasingly important after the Umayyad caliphs came to power around A.H. 40/660 C.E., although it never assumed the role of capital during this phase of the city's history.[4]

The first Islamic architectural masterpiece on the Haram, the
Dome of the Rock — Qubbat al-Sakhra — was built by a later caliph of
the Umayyad Dynasty, Abd al-Malik (A.H. 65–86/685–705 C.E.), who
employed Byzantine architects and craftsmen in the region. His reasons for this architectural undertaking were of a political, economic,
and religious nature. A rival caliph challenged his authority over
Mecca; as the birthplace of Muhammad, this city attracted large reve-
nues from pilgrims, many of whom came from Abd al-Malik's do-
minions. A shrine in Jerusalem would enhance the political importance of the city and also serve as an alternative to pilgrimage to
Mecca. Moreover, the presence of so many handsome local churches
motivated the caliph to surpass the glory of Christian spaces. The
Dome of the Rock was an admirable instrument for this purpose.[5]

The nearby Aqsa Mosque was the work of Abd al-Malik's son,
Caliph Walid I (A.H. 86–96/705–715 C.E.); nothing remains of the
original structure, except parts of the southern wall and the orientation of the building. After the Abbasid Dynasty acceded to the throne,
the capital of the Arab empire was transferred to Baghdad in A.H.
145/762 C.E. Conditions in Palestine now took a turn for the worse,
with Jerusalem being the first to suffer.

Fig. 9.1. Aerial view of the Haram al-Sharif taken in the 1940s, looking north. Courtesy of the Israel Antiquities Authority.

Conversions to Islam under the Umayyad and succeeding Abbasid dynasties increased, although Christians and Jews were allowed to reside in the city and control their own communal affairs. Soon after the Arab conquest, the Gaonim, who constituted the supreme Jewish religious authority in the Holy Land, moved their seat from Tiberias to Jerusalem, where it remained until the eleventh century C.E. Monks and pilgrims encountered little interference from the Muslim administration. The problems of the Jerusalem Christian community were largely internal, caused by the widening breach between the Eastern (Orthodox) and Western (Latin) churches. With Jerusalem now under Arab dominion, it was severed from the premier Latin patriarchate of Rome and the principal eastern patriarchate of Constantinople.

In the ensuing century, under Fatimid rule, Jerusalem was to experience both a high and a low point.[6] This new dynasty (claiming descent from Fatima, daughter of Muhammad) conquered Egypt in A.H. 359/969 C.E. and established the new capital in Cairo. A few years later, under Caliph al-Aziz (A.H. 365–386/976–996 C.E.), Fatimid rule was extended to Palestine and Syria. During the reign of al-Aziz, Christians and Jews in Jerusalem enjoyed considerable freedom. Under his successor, al-Hakim (A.H. 386–411/996–1021 C.E.) — known as "the mad caliph" — Jerusalem suffered havoc.[7] The Martyrium Basilica was destroyed in A.H. 400/1009 C.E., along with four other churches located in other parts of the empire.[8] Shortly after, al-Hakim authorized the reconstruction of the destroyed houses of worship and pilgrimages were resumed. The dome of the Anastasis Rotunda underwent repairs; the Martyrium Basilica, however, was never rebuilt.[9] The next fifty years were comparatively uneventful — barring three earthquakes, one of which gravely damaged the Dome of the Rock (A.H. 425/1033 C.E.).[10]

The Seljuks, an outlying branch of the Turks, converted to Islam at the end of the tenth century while serving as mercenaries for the Muslim rulers of Persia and northwest India. Like their earlier counterparts, they soon overthrew their overlords, and in A.H. 447/1055 C.E. established their capital in Baghdad. In A.H. 464/1071 C.E., they overran most of Syria and Palestine, and held Jerusalem for the next twenty-five years.

The Seljuks pillaged Jerusalem and reestablished a policy of persecuting Christians and Jews. Their maltreatment of Christians, stopping of pilgrimage, and abuse of those pilgrims who succeeded in arriving in Jerusalem gave additional prompting to the counteroffensive of the Christian world — the First Crusade. Shortly before this happened, the Fatimids reestablished their authority in Jerusalem — but the fervent armies coming from Europe were already on their way.

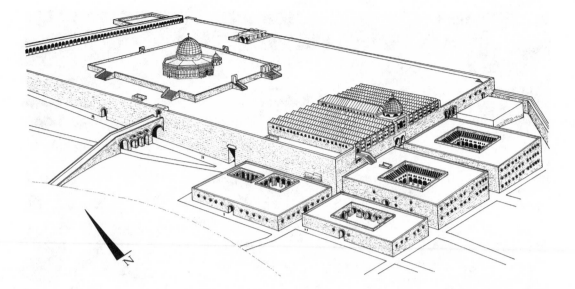

## The Haram al-Sharif—the Noble Sanctuary

Since the destruction of the Jewish Temple in 70 C.E., the entire area of the former Temple Mount remained in ruins—with the exception of two columns supporting the statues of Jupiter and Emperor Hadrian.[11] In the Late Roman and Byzantine periods, the Temple Mount was mainly used as a stone quarry. When Caliph Umar I and his forces entered the city around A.H. 16–17/637–38 C.E., no immediate changes were introduced. Several years later, after the establishment of the Umayyad Dynasty and the nomination of Mu'awiya as caliph (A.H. 40/660–61 C.E.), the Muslim population initiated work on their own house of worship (fig. 9.2).[12] The increasing tension vis-à-vis the Christian population encouraged them to erect a monument that could compete with the existing Church of the Holy Sepulchre.[13]

The damaged sections of the enclosure wall needed to be repaired and reconstructed, and renovations were carried out in the tunnels leading up from the Huldah Gates toward the top of the platform. The platform could be accessed via two entrances in the

Fig. 9.2. Reconstruction of the Haram al-Sharif in the Umayyad period. Redrawn by J. Dillon, after: Bahat, *Illustrated Atlas*, 82–83.

Fig. 9.3. The Golden
Gate. Photo R.
Schick.

southern wall, four in the western wall, two in the northern wall, and one in the eastern wall. The newly built Golden Gate or Gate of Mercy was most likely built in place of an earlier entrance (fig. 9.3). The internal and external architectural decoration, which is similar to ornamentation added on top of the Herodian Huldah Gate, confirms the Umayyad date of construction (figs. 9.4–5).

## Religious Architecture

Around 680 C.E., on the pilgrimage of Bishop Arculf to Jerusalem, Adomnan described a rudimentary place of worship located somewhere at the southern end of the platform:

Fig. 9.4. Detailed architrave and cornice of the southwestern corner of the Golden Gate. Photo H. Bloedhorn.

Fig. 9.5. An Umayyad decorative addition to the western Huldah Gate. Photo H. Bloedhorn.

Moreover near the [city-]wall on the east, in that famous place where once stood the magnificent Temple, the Saracens have now built an oblong house of prayer which they pieced together with upright planks and large beams over some ruined remains. This they attend, and it is said that this building can hold three thousand people.[14] (Adomnan, 226–227)

At this point, the sanctuary in the center had not yet been built.[15] Exactly when and for what reason the rock began to be venerated is not clear. The contemporary sources do not offer an explanation; there is no mention of the legend of the Prophet's night journey, the sacrifice of Isaac, the tradition of the omphalos of the world, or the gate to Paradise accounts that would later be associated with the rock. Al-Yaqubi reports (A.H. 261/874 C.E.) that Abd al-Malik intended to create an Umayyad alternative to the pilgrimage to Mecca; according to al-Muqaddasi (A.H. 375/985 C.E.), the caliph was interested foremost in creating an architectural masterpiece that would eclipse the Christian buildings in the city. A structural analysis of the Dome of the Rock illustrates this intention well.

### THE DOME OF THE ROCK — QUBBAT AL-SAKHRA

An elevated platform with stairways and arcades (*mawazin*) supporting the Dome of the Rock was created to compensate for the gradually ascending terrain, from the margins toward the center (fig. 9.6).[16] This upper Muslim platform could be reached from the lower Herodian platform by different staircases. A building with an octagonal plan was erected on top of this upper surface, each side measuring 20.6 meters long and 12.1 meters high (figs. 9.7–8). Entry was through any of the four entrances, on the western, northern, eastern, and southern sides.[17] A small prayer niche (*mihrab*) is located east of the southern entrance. There are seven arches in each of the eight walls of the octagon; the five central arches all have windows whereas the two side

arches are blind niches. The interior space is divided into three areas by means of an intermediate octagon with archways supported by corner pillars, with two columns between each pillar.[18] The visible rock in the center of the building is surrounded by a ring of archways composed of four pillars, with three columns between each pillar (fig. 9.9).[19] A high drum supporting the dome rises above this ring. The wonderful architectural design of the Dome of the Rock is exemplified in that the diameter of the dome is equal to its height, thereby creating a perfect interior space. Moreover, the length of each of the eight sides of the octagon is identical to this diameter. The diameter of the dome is 20.4 meters, and its total height from the rock to the top of the dome is 35.4 meters.[20]

The high cylindrical drum contributes to the raised appearance of the dome that rests upon it. This is even more striking when we

Fig. 9.6. Dome of the Rock, looking northeast, 1910. Courtesy of the École biblique.

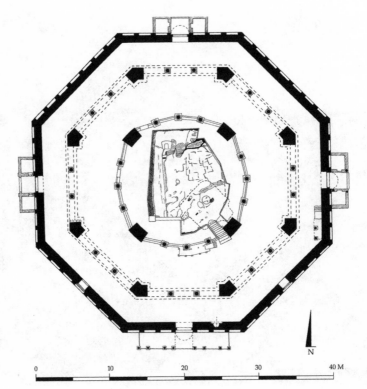

Fig. 9.7 . Plan of the Dome of the Rock. Redrawn by J. Dillon, after: Cresswell, *Early Muslim Architecture*, I, fig. 21.

0    10    20    30    40 M

N

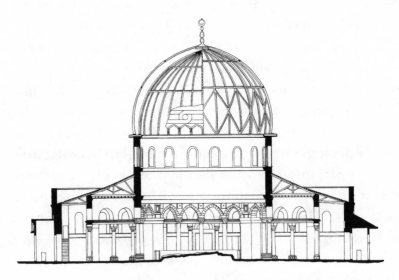

Fig. 9.8. Section of the Dome of the Rock. Redrawn by J. Dillon, after: Cresswell, *Early Muslim Architecture*, I, fig. 20.

compare the external appearance of the Dome of the Rock, notable for its lightness, with the famous earlier domed structure — the Hagia Sophia in Constantinople, whose immense dome is supported by a series of half- and quarter-domes, and appears from its exterior to be very heavy. It may be noted that the dome of Hagia Sophia is made of solid stone while the Dome of the Rock is made of wood, much lighter by nature. The high drum also contributes to the building's light appearance. The Dome of the Rock is actually composed of two separate domes, one on the inside and the other on the outside, with enough room in between for a man to pass through for maintenance purposes. This construction creates an insulation space between the domes and also distributes the dome's weight.[21]

The Umayyads, imperial patrons of a range of religious and secular buildings in Greater Syria, employed Byzantine architects and

Fig. 9.9. The rock inside the Dome of the Rock, ca. 1924. Courtesy of the École biblique.

artisans to build this magnificent centralized building located between two older rotundas in Jerusalem — the Anastasis, on the western extremity of the city on a slightly higher site, and the Imbomon,
on the Mount of Olives.[22] Byzantine mosaic workshops were also
responsible for the interior decoration of the Dome of the Rock.[23] A
240-meter-long inscription runs along the lowest mosaic panel of
both sides of the intermediate octagon (plate 11). The dedication
begins on its outer side at the height of the mihrab and runs clock-
wise; it continues, counter-clockwise, along the inside of the octagon,
recording that the Dome of the Rock was built by Caliph Abd al-
Malik and completed in A.H. 72 (691–692 C.E.).[24]

The decoration of the walls and ceilings of the Dome of the Rock
were as carefully conceived by the architects as the structural components of the shrine. The lower sections of the walls and piers are
covered with marble slabs (fig. 9.10). Mosaics cover the soffits and
spandrels of the two arcades, the upper sections of the piers, as well as
the drums — all told, a surface of about 280 square meters. Representations consist of a seemingly endless variety of shapes harmoniously
and repetitively distributed over all the surfaces without ever repeat-
ing the exact same design twice. Conforming to Islamic religious principles, depictions of human figures and animals are usually avoided.
The countless combinations of vegetal motifs with stylized trees, gar-
lands, and scrolls are borrowed from the vocabulary of Byzantine
churches and join palmettes, wings, and composite flowers taken from
the world of Persian artistry.

Just as the choice of decorative elements in the building was meaningful, so was the choice of the building's location. The rock in the
center of the structure was purposefully intended to recall the spot
where the Temple of Solomon was believed to have stood. Accord-
ingly, sacrifices in the Jewish Temple would have been performed in
this location, thus marking the place where the salvation at the End of
Days would ultimately begin. This concept was appropriated and pre-

Fig. 9.10. Marble carvings inside the Dome of the Rock. Courtesy of the Israel Antiquities Authority.

served in the Islamic tradition. The End of Days continued to be envisioned as a Paradise, and therefore this central location inside the Dome of the Rock is decorated with mosaics of palm trees, lavish tendrils, and wings. Tendrils with fruit also appear on the lower sides of the arches in the exterior arcade as well as on the architraves of the pillars and on the frieze of the exterior walls beneath the windows (the latter is not a mosaic, however, but is represented by gilded grills). This luxuriant ornamentation is reminiscent of Solomon's Temple (1 Kgs 6:29–35), and was also to appear in the Jewish Temple at the End of Days (Ezra 41:17–25).[25]

Despite several renovations in later periods, the sanctuary preserves intact the original Umayyad period design concepts regarding the use of space, solutions for construction problems and proportions, as well as most of its internal decor. The original exterior mosaic decoration was replaced with blue faience tiles under Suleiman the Magnificent in the mid sixteenth century.

## THE DOME OF THE CHAIN — QUBBAT AL-SILSILA

Close to the eastern entrance to the Dome of the Rock is the Dome of the Chain.[26] This is a small building, reminiscent of the Dome of the Rock, and many have suggested that it served as a model for it (fig. 9.11). This explanation, however, is unfounded; in terms of plan and elevation, the differences are considerable. Unlike the Dome of the Rock, this building is open in all directions and consists of two concentric rows of columns topped by a dome, which originally had small openings.

Column capitals and bases in the Dome of the Chain are not uniform; like examples in the Dome of the Rock, they came from other pre-Islamic buildings. Aside from the addition of the mihrab, no other structural changes were introduced into the building's plan (plate 12).[27] The location of the mihrab in the center of the monumental platform has been compared to the central location of the omphalos inside the Martyrium of the Church of the Holy Sepulchre, suggesting that the monument indicated the center of the Muslim shrine in the city. A recently discovered manuscript suggests that the Dome of the Chain was also built by Abd al-Malik.[28]

## THE AQSA MOSQUE — AL-JAMI AL-AQSA

Mention was made earlier of a rudimentary construction on top of the platform that predated the building of the Dome of the Rock.[29] Papyri written between A.H. 90 and 93/708 and 711 C.E. found in the Egyptian village of Kom Ishqau, or ancient Aphroditopolis, record that a relatively large number of artisans were sent to Jerusalem with building materials to build a mosque and a palace, thus indicating the approximate date of construction.[30] The text seems to refer to the Aqsa Mosque, and possibly to the palaces located further south, because the Dome of the Rock was already standing at this time.[31] Based on a survey during the renovation in the 1930s, the plan of the original stone building could be reconstructed (fig. 9.12).[32] It was built

Fig. 9.11. Dome of the Chain, looking southwest, ca. 1880–1900. Courtesy of the École biblique.

over the cavities in the southern area of the Haram, and for this purpose the southern Herodian enclosure wall had to be repaired. It was a quadrangular structure, with a wide and elevated nave in the center and a clerestory for lighting. There were seven aisles on both sides of the central nave, each with an entrance from the courtyard of the platform (fig. 9.13). The entire building measured 103.5 × 50.8 meters.[33]

As a result of the earthquake of A.H. 132/749 C.E., the Aqsa Mosque collapsed almost entirely, excluding the area of the mihrab. Caliph al-Mansur gave orders to rebuild the mosque on a larger scale (now 103.5 × 70 meters), and a dome was erected in front of the mihrab (fig. 9.14). It is interesting to note that the caliph had to sell the gold and silver fittings of the doors to finance this project. When Caliph al-Mahdi

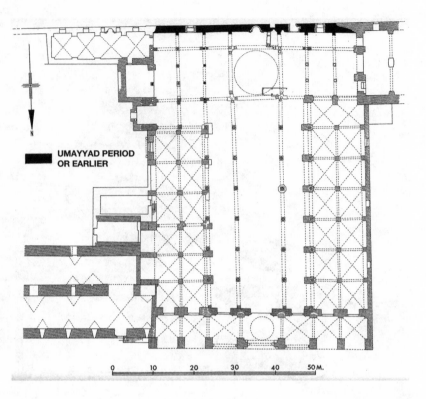

**UMAYYAD PERIOD
OR EARLIER**

N

0    10    20    30    40    50 M.

Fig. 9.12. Plan of the
Aqsa Mosque. Re-
drawn by J. Dillon, af-
ter: Cresswell, *Early
Muslim Architecture*, I,
fig. 446.

visited al-Quds in A.H. 164–165/780 C.E., he prayed in this newly
rebuilt mosque. In A.H. 425/1033 C.E., the building was again seriously
damaged by an earthquake. The Fatimid ruler Caliph al-Zahir repaired it, albeit on a smaller scale. The plan of the mosque was similar
to the one that exists today, although hardly anything has remained of
that building. Only seven aisles have survived; the square area below the
dome is most likely the only area that still exists from the Fatimid structure, although fragments of earlier periods can be found there as well.[34]

## Secular Architecture

At the foot of the southern wall and southwestern corner of the
Haram al-Sharif, a complex of Umayyad buildings was partially excavated (fig. 9.15).[35] The presence of a Governor's House (Dar al-

Fig. 9.13. The Aqsa Mosque with Ayyubid porch, looking southeast, British Mandate period. Courtesy of the École biblique.

Imara) near a mosque is common for the Early Islamic period in other parts of the Muslim world as well.[36] These structures included residences, administrative buildings, storerooms, baths, and installations for craftsmen, and were meant to be used for secular purposes.

The complex consisted of at least six buildings planned in conjunction with the monumental platform. A bridge connected the roof of Building II with the Aqsa Mosque, spanning the street running along the southern wall and enabling direct access from the roof of the building into the mosque. Construction of the complex probably began during the reign of Abd al-Malik, but work continued into that of Walid I. Buildings II and III were similar in plan, with rooms arranged around an open courtyard, partly paved with stone and partly planted with flowers and trees; covered porticoes surrounded the open central space (fig. 9.16).[37] The foundations of the interior and exterior walls were massive and set deeply into the ground, often reaching 9 meters

Fig. 9.14. The dome and the mihrab at the southern end of the Aqsa Mosque, 1930. Courtesy of the École biblique.

below floor level. The roofs were flat timber beams supported by arches. The windows were placed high above the floor (about 4 meters). A well-designed sewage system constructed of clay pipes was discovered in one of the buildings. The pipes were installed vertically in grooves carved in the walls, indicating the existence of an upper level. The floor plans of Buildings II and III were adapted from the Roman-Byzantine fortress plan and resemble those of many other Umayyad mansions and palaces. In contrast to other contemporary buildings in Palestine, Transjordan, and Syria, the two buildings in Jerusalem lack corner towers.[38] Such towers were defensive in purpose and would have been superfluous inside a walled city such as Jerusalem. Building II had three gates — northern, eastern, and western — each of which was located in the center of its wall.[39] Most walls

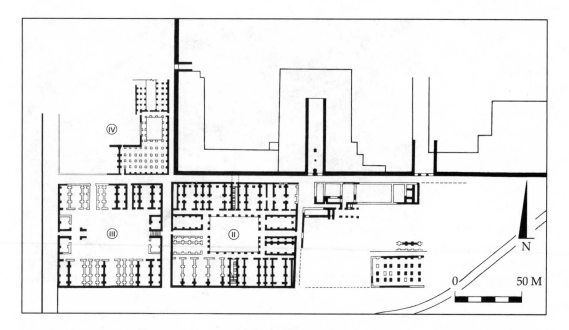

were plastered on the inside; some were decorated with polychrome frescoes bearing geometric and floral designs. The simplicity of the wall decoration and of the gates is distinct from what is known about other Umayyad palaces outside Jerusalem and may be due to the sanctity of the city.

In addition to Buildings II and III, four only partially excavated buildings border the western and southern walls of the Haram. The northern Building IV included an earlier bathhouse with its furnaces still in place. Despite its fragmentary state, the original size of the *caldarium* can be reconstructed as covering an area of more than 1000 square meters.[40]

Late in the Umayyad period (A.H. 132/749 C.E.), a great earthquake destroyed the palace and adjacent structures; they were rebuilt in the subsequent Abbasid period; then during the Fatimid period, Building II was completely modified and Building IV renovated. Towards the end of the eleventh century the by then mostly dilapidated buildings were converted into a huge quarry, an excellent source of high-quality building stone. The area south of Building IV was used

Fig. 9.15. Plan of Buildings II–IV south of the Haram al-Sharif. The addition of the western side of Building III bordering the cardo is based on excavations conducted in 1948 (compare fig. 9.2). Redrawn by J. Dillon, after: Bahat, "Physical Infrastructure," 71; corrections by K. Bieberstein and H. Bloedhorn.

Fig. 9.16. The courtyard and northern wing of Building II, bordering the southern wall of the Haram al-Sharif. Photo H. Bloedhorn.

as a cemetery, suggesting that the glamorous complex that once stood here was entirely forgotten.[41]

### Distinctive Finds

The principles of classic Islamic artistic creativity were already evident in Jerusalem from the beginning of the Early Islamic period. In addition to Hellenistic, Roman, and Byzantine artistic traditions previously established in Palestine, newly imported influences from Coptic, Sassanian, and Persian art gave birth to a unique school of Islamic art that developed in the Umayyad period.

Early Islamic art is notable for the wealth of materials used and for its ornamentation, primarily as architectural decoration. The principal materials used were marble, glass tesserae, metal, and wood. The variety of colors, accompanied by many gold highlights, is one of the characteristics that distinguish Jerusalem's architecture from contemporary buildings elsewhere.

### STONE AND WOOD CARVINGS

Unlike most decorative techniques used in the Early Islamic period, which were derivatives or continuations of pre-Islamic traditions, some of the wood and stone carvings were unique creations of the Umayyad period.

A series of carved marble panels from the end of the seventh century has been preserved in different locations inside the Dome of the Rock—along the interior walls, around the corner pillars of the intermediate octagon, around the pillars of the central ring, and in one or two areas of the drum supporting the dome. The floral and architectural motifs, consisting of rosettes, half-palmettes, and continuous arcades of trees, integrate themselves into the global decorative scheme of the building while preserving a particular theme for each subsection. Most of the design, which is made with the *champlevé* technique, is on the surface level, with the background shallowly etched out.[42]

Fig. 9.17. Decorated wooden console in the Aqsa Mosque. Courtesy of the Israel Antiquities Authority.

Even more fortunate is the preservation of a group of carved wood panels, constituting the only surviving element of the original Umayyad period Aqsa Mosque (fig. 9.17).[43] These woodcarvings were used to embellish the supporting end of the mosque's roof beams. The decorative theme is in relief, with additional details lightly incised or carved out. Like the marble panels, the wood panels were originally polychrome. Although the compositions are very similar and integrate themselves harmoniously into the general iconographic and decorative scheme, there is virtually no repetition of design from one panel to the next.

Fig. 9.18. Metal plate above the southern entrance of the Dome of the Rock. Courtesy of the Israel Exploration Society.

## CALLIGRAPHY

Jerusalem exhibits inscriptions from various subperiods of the Early Islamic period. Some of the examples can be dated and therefore allow us to trace the development of ornamental Arabic script from its inception in the Umayyad period through the middle of the Fatimid period.

The earliest Umayyad inscription is found on both sides of the arcade of the intermediate octagon of the Dome of the Rock. The letters of this mosaic inscription are made of tesserae backed with gold leaf placed against a green background. The straight baseline from which the thin and strictly angular letters sprout is characteristic of Kufic script.

Additional contemporary inscriptions decorated metal plates set above two of the four entrances to the Dome of the Rock (fig. 9.18).[44] Two metal plate inscriptions have the date of Abbasid caliph al-Ma'mun on them. The date of Abd al-Malik is preserved in the mosaic inscription around the octagon.

The most beautiful Fatimid inscription is another mosaic found on the arch in front of the dome of the Aqsa Mosque. The inscription consists of two complete lines and can be dated to about A.H. 426/1035 C.E. The flourishes at the end of the letters and the ornamentation along their upper extremities are characteristic of the so-called "flowering Kufic" script (fig. 9.19).

Beyond the informative aspect of the inscriptions, these early examples of calligraphy are documents of a newly and rapidly evolving artistic creation within Islam.

Fig. 9.19. Kufic inscription from the Dome of the Rock. Van Berchem, *Matériaux pour un Corpus inscriptionum Arabicarum*, III, plate 12.

# 10 ✦ The Crusader and Ayyubid Periods

The entry to Jerusalem is on the west side next to the Tower of David. Beneath in the city is the Sepulchre of the Lord, and outside it is the centre of the world. From there to the north is the Prison of the Lord, and next to it is where he was bound and flogged, crowned and stripped, and where his clothes were shared out. Mount Calvary: under it is Golgotha, where the blood of the Lord fell through the rent rock. Beyond this mount is a place where St. Helena found the Cross of the Lord.

*Ottobonian Guide*, chapter 2

## A European-Oriental Metropolis

The end of the eleventh century in Europe ushered in the epic movement of the European Crusades for the recovery of the Tomb of Christ from the "infidels." The First Crusade, led by Godfrey of Bouillon, reached the walls of Jerusalem after a march of several years across southeastern Europe, Asia Minor, and Syria. On Shaban 22, A.H. 492/ July 15, 1099 C.E., the Crusaders stormed the city, and in the ensuing carnage the Muslim population was slaughtered and Jews were burnt in their synagogues. The conquering knights divided the city's houses and palaces among themselves. Godfrey assumed the title "Protector of the Holy Sepulchre," and his successor, Baldwin I, crowned himself king of Jerusalem.[1]

For the thousand years that followed Jerusalem's destruction by Titus in 70, the city was considered a provincial outpost. With the rise of the Crusader Kingdom, it again assumed the status of capital. The feudal system served as the model for the Crusader administration. The Church, which inspired the movement in the name of the Christian religion, owned the land; the knights were responsible for the fighting, and the merchants, mostly from Italy, supplied the fleets. Later, additional powers were granted to the three military orders — the Templars, the Hospitallers, and the Teutonic Knights. The Latin patriarch was the local representative of the pope, whose power rivaled that of the king.

The Crusaders first confiscated the property abandoned by the Muslims and made no changes to the city's appearance. Only in subsequent years did they begin large-scale construction, primarily of churches. Here and there the Crusaders dismantled older buildings. On the Haram al-Sharif, they converted the Dome of the Rock and the Aqsa Mosque into churches.

A distinctive feature of Crusader Jerusalem was its cosmopolitanism; the population was composed, on the one hand, of members of the Oriental Christian communities (Armenian, Georgian, Greek, Syrian) and, on the other, of the Franks, the newcomers from Europe. Among the latter were English, French, German, Hungarian, Italian, Portuguese, and Spanish.

Salah al-Din (A.H. 533–90/1138–93 C.E.), founder of the Ayyubid Dynasty, was raised and educated in Damascus, which at the time was the main center of Moslem learning and a center of Moslem culture. Salah al-Din succeeded his uncle as vizier of Egypt and soon extended his rule over Syria. After the battle at Hittin on Rabi' II 25, A.H. 583/ July 4, 1187 C.E., he controlled, either by conquest or negotiation, all of the territory that encompassed the Kingdom of Jerusalem.

In contrast to the Crusaders' actions in the city eighty-eight years earlier, Salah al-Din treated the Christian inhabitants with the utmost chivalry and generosity. He reassumed possession of the Haram al-Sharif, with the Dome of the Rock and the Aqsa Mosque, which he purified with rose water and restored to their former state, but he left most of the churches untouched, except those adjacent to the northern and western enclosure walls of the Haram. As a result of the treaty between Frederic II and Salah al-Din in A.H. 627/1229 C.E., the Crusaders were allowed to continue to live in Jerusalem for ten years. They stayed until A.H. 642/1244 C.E., when the Khwarezmian Turks occupied the city. Christian rule in Jerusalem at this time ceased until the British occupation in 1917. The Crusader Kingdom maintained itself on the Mediterranean coast until A.H. 690/1291 C.E., with its capital in Acre.

## Fortifications and Gates

Two major fortification projects are known to have taken place in the eleventh century (A.H. 425/1033 C.E. and A.H. 455–56/1063 C.E.). Just a year before the arrival of the Crusaders in Jerusalem, the Fatimids made repairs after recapturing the city from the Seljuks. Most of the written evidence on the city's defenses built under Seljuk and Fatimid rule is contained in the Frankish sources describing the conquest of Jerusalem in A.H. 492/1099 C.E. After the conquest, the Crusaders made two major repairs to the walls (in A.H. 510/1116 C.E. and A.H. 573/1177 C.E.).[2] After Salah al-Din captured the city (A.H. 583/1187 C.E.), an additional phase of repair is recorded.[3] The Ayyubid sultan al-Malik al-Mu'azzam Isa's repair in the early thirteenth

century (A.H. 599–609/1202–12 C.E.) is better known from archaeological finds than from historical sources. "Ironically, it was al-
Mu'azzam himself who subsequently, in March 1219, destroyed the
walls of Jerusalem, leaving them in ruins until they were rebuilt by
the Ottoman sultan Sulaiman the Magnificent . . . [A.H. 944–948/
1537–41 C.E.]. This destruction was extensive, involving the dismantling of towers and sections of both the main wall and the forewall.
The Citadel, however, remained intact."[4]

Several well-preserved sections of the forewall built (or restored)
under Seljuk rule (A.H. 466–92/1073–98 C.E.) were uncovered in the
northern and western sections of the Old City wall.[5] Approximately
4.5 meters wide, it was constructed directly above the rock-cut scarp
of the moat and was preserved to a maximum height of 5 meters. It is
constructed from roughly shaped fieldstones and, like the main wall,
has prominent towers set on projections in the rock-cut scarp. The
moat, or fosse, was probably constructed at the same time as the
forewall and served as a source of building stones for both walls. The
northern moat, approximately 19 meters wide and 7 meters deep, is
still visible at a number of points.[6] The only place where a fairly
extensive stretch of the main Crusader wall can be seen together with
its forewall is north of David's Gate, where it is preserved in places up
to eleven or twelve courses with an average width of 3 meters.[7]

### THE TOWER OF DAVID AND THE CITADEL

When the Crusader troops broke into the city through the northern wall on Shaban 22, A.H. 492/July 15, 1099 C.E., the Muslim and
Jewish inhabitants fled to the Tower of David (figs. 10.1–2). This
tower was built on top of the Herodian podium, which had once been
the base of one of three towers of the Citadel of Jerusalem built by
King Herod in the first century B.C.E. According to the written sources,
the tower was simply built into the city wall.[8] As of 1120, Godfrey of
Bouillon used the tower as his residence; it also served as a strong-

Fig. 10.1. Aerial view of the Citadel, looking southeast. Photo H. Bloedhorn.

hold and as one of the chief centers of civic administration. Its traditional connection with King David gave it a special significance in Frankish eyes that transformed it into a symbol of Frankish sovereignty in Jerusalem.[9]

In the second half of the twelfth century, the permanent population of Jerusalem continued to grow and was augmented by merchants and masses of pilgrims who entered the city through David's Gate. It is therefore hardly surprising that the need was felt for new administrative buildings, including a new royal palace and a larger citadel. The rebuilding of the citadel and the new palace constituted a major project in Jerusalem around 1120, just prior to the rebuilding of the Church of the Holy Sepulchre in the 1140s. Archaeological remains of this well-fortified courtyard complex, surrounded by its own curtain wall and forewall and flanked by several towers, were uncovered during different excavation campaigns.[10] Following its destruction by al-Nasir Da'ud of al-Karak in 1239, the Citadel was rebuilt under Mamluk and Ottoman rule to take on its present form.[11] Today's Citadel is probably very similar to the expanded Citadel of the later twelfth century.

### GATES

Crusader Jerusalem had five major gates and several minor gates or posterns (perhaps as many as eight).[12] The principal gates were David's Gate in the west (modern Jaffa Gate), St. Stephen's Gate in the north (modern Damascus Gate), the Gate of Jehoshaphat (mod-

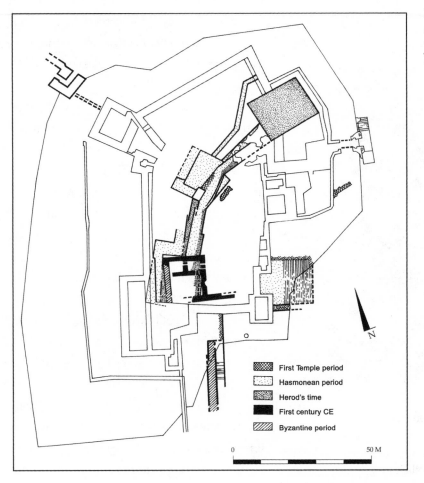

Fig. 10.2. Plan of the Citadel. Redrawn by J. Dillon, after: Geva, "First Wall," 724.

First Temple period

Hasmonean period

Herod's time

First century CE

Byzantine period

0                    50 M

ern Lions' or St. Stephen's Gate), the Golden Gate or the Gate of Mercy in the east, and Mount Zion Gate (modern Zion Gate) in the south. As in other walled towns, the gates of Jerusalem were closed from sunset to sunrise.[13] In most cases, possibly in all, they were protected by gate towers with indirect entrance passages.

## Streets, Quarters, and Marketplaces

The network of streets laid in the Byzantine period continued to exist throughout the Crusader period (figs. 10.3–4).[14] The impressive pavements of the main streets had deteriorated, but were refurbished in the Early Islamic and Crusader periods. This process became evident from the archaeological excavations conducted at the former Byzantine cardo and elsewhere in the city.[15]

Fig. 10.3. One of the thoroughfares of the triple-lane Crusader suq southeast of the Holy Sepulchre, looking north, 1936. Courtesy of the École biblique.

The principal thoroughfares were no wider than 5 meters; the narrow and often steep streets made vehicular transport difficult, and most of the time impossible. David Street, the main east–west artery, and the ancient Byzantine main street, the principal north–south artery, are often steep and in some places stepped. Most traffic inside the city walls was therefore pedestrian. Goods were transported on small, two-wheeled handcarts, similar to the ones in use today.

The network of streets divided Crusader Jerusalem into a number of quarters.[16] The Patriarch's Quarter, which was administered by the patriarchate, was autonomous in the Crusader city. It was virtually identical to the present-day Christian Quarter. The northeastern quarter was inhabited by Jews (who still retained the name *Judaria* or *Juvrie*) until they were massacred or evicted during the Crusader

Fig. 10.4. Inscription "Anna" in the triple-lane Crusader suq, indicating its ownership by the Church of St. Anne. Photo H. Bloedhorn.

conquest of the city; it was then occupied by Eastern Christians who hailed from beyond the Jordan River, from the area around al-Karak.[17] The Armenians occupied the southwestern quarter. The southeastern part of the city was occupied by Germans, and there seem to have been other communities located in other parts of the city—Provençals, Hungarians, and Greeks, for example. One should be wary of suggesting that there was a rigid division of the city quarters along ethnic lines, however. For example, it is not at all certain that there were any German residents on Germans' Street except in the German Hospice itself, and the same is true for other supposedly ethnic divisions such as the Spanish Street in the north of the city.[18]

Jerusalem was not a major commercial center like Acre and Tyre, but with a growing population and with the great influx of pilgrims arriving in the city, the need grew to supply them with food, clothing, religious articles, keepsakes, and a variety of other commodities. In order to cater to this trade, Frankish merchants and craftsmen inhabited the old bazaars. The open fields on the outskirts of the city, but within the walls, were occupied by open markets selling grain, pigs, and cattle. Nearby were the workshops of the tanners and the butchers' stalls. Market streets, halls, and squares in the heart of the city were reserved for foodstuffs and manufactured items.[19]

Unlike most Roman and Byzantine shops, of which only partial fragments have survived, the remains of Crusader market structures are very well preserved. Some are still in use today. These market structures could be barrel-vaulted passageways or individual rows of shops with groin-vaulted bays facing the streets. Some of the shops were large enough for work and storage areas. The occasional existence of upper levels suggests that shop owners may have lived on the premises as well.[20]

### Military Orders

Three military orders concentrated their forces in Jerusalem. The Templars converted the Aqsa Mosque and the southern part of the Haram into their living quarters and used the subterranean areas as stables.[21] Those well-preserved structures are still referred to as Solomon's Stables (fig. 6.9). The Hospitallers were based south of the Holy Sepulchre, where the order's living quarters and hospitals were located.[22] The name Muristan, today applied to the relatively recent marketplace (constructed shortly after 1900) adjacent to the Holy Sepulchre, is actually a corruption of the Persian word *bimeristan* (hospital).[23] The Teutonic Knights, who in the twelfth century were merely a branch of the Hospitallers, had their headquarters in the modern-day Jewish Quarter.[24] Another order, the Lepers of St. Lazar, was located outside the city, near the present-day New Gate.[25]

### Churches, Chapels, and Monasteries

After the Crusaders conquered the city, they soon embarked on a major church-building program, which reached its peak some fifty years later, with the dedication of the new Church of the Holy Sepulchre. The architectural variety among these buildings is impressive, consisting of a mixture of local and long-established forms as well as more innovative styles imported from Europe. Among the many

churches of Jerusalem were those that, through association with
Christ, the Virgin Mary, the Apostles, or other holy personages, came
to be held in particularly high regard. Most of these traditions originated in the Byzantine period. Some others, like the Templum Domini
(the Dome of the Rock), achieved their status as important Christian
holy sites only under Crusader rule. In contrast to the coastal cities,
Jerusalem's architectural program consisted mainly of churches, monasteries, and establishments of the orders.[26] Based on their differences
in organization, tradition, and architectural style, they can be divided
into four groups: those belonging to the Augustinian Order; the Benedictine Order; the Secular Orders; and, finally, the Armenians.[27]

The first group includes the four chapters of the four principal
churches in Jerusalem; the Church of the Holy Sepulchre and the
Templum Domini within the city's boundaries; St. Mary on Mount
Zion, and the Church of the Ascension on the Mount of Olives.

### THE HOLY SEPULCHRE

As early as A.H. 411/1020 C.E., Caliph al-Hakim returned the
church with its confiscated goods to the Jerusalemites. Mass was
temporarily held in the ruins of the building since funds for reconstruction were not yet available.[28] Under al-Hakim's successor az-
Zahir, a treaty between the Fatimids and the Byzantines was signed,
allowing Emperor Constantine VIII to rebuild the ruined church.[29]
The treaty was renewed under Romanus III Argyrus, but it was not
until Constantine IX Monomachus that renovation began in 1033,
albeit on a limited scale; the work was completed in 1048.[30] The
Martyrium Basilica proper was never rebuilt. The focus of the project
was the reconstruction of the Anastasis Rotunda. In order to create
an enclosed house of worship, its eastern side was closed with an apse
(fig. 10.5).[31] The rock of Golgotha in the southeastern corner of the
Triportico remained intact. Three additional chapels were added
south of the rotunda. When the Crusaders arrived on the scene in

Fig. 10.5. The eleventh-century restorations in the Holy Sepulchre; northern section of the former eastern apse of the rotunda. Photo H. Bloedhorn.

1099, the rotunda, the chapels, and Golgotha were all that remained of the grand Constantinian church complex.

In 1114, Patriarch Arculf installed a chapter of Augustinian canons and built a monastery with a cloister on the rubble of the former Martyrium Basilica.[32] The construction of the church itself did not get under way until well into the twelfth century (figs. 10.6–7).[33] Since it was the ultimate pilgrimage church (fig. 10.8), the Franks chose to rebuild it based on the model of the great Romanesque pilgrimage churches in Europe.[34] Only the choir with the ambulatory was built, however.[35] Its design allowed large numbers of pilgrims to move freely about the church without disturbing the canons' services in the choir, and gave access to different chapels in the transept and ambulatory so that several Masses could be held simultaneously. Now, for the first time, Golgotha and Calvary were included in the church rather than being located in its courtyard. The façade was decorated with columns, archivolts, and cornices uniformly produced in Crusader workshops (figs. 10.9–10). The walls inside and outside the building were covered with paintings or mosaics, of which only one has survived (plate 13). The new church was dedicated on July 15, 1149, fifty years after the conquest of the city.

When Salah al-Din took the city in A.H. 583/1187 C.E., he ignored the demands of some of the emirs to destroy the church. He realized that it was the sanctity of the site, not the building, that attracted the veneration of Christians.[36] Other than the interior (wall paintings, mosaics, liturgical furniture — and the *aedicula*, which was destroyed by the great fire of October 12, 1808), the current structure largely reflects the original medieval state of the church.

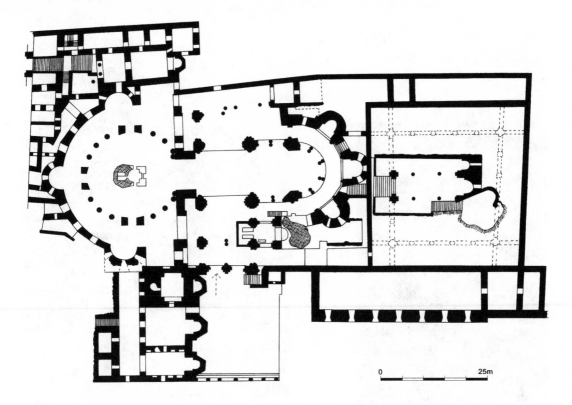

Fig. 10.6. Plan of the Crusader Holy Sepulchre. Redrawn by J. Dillon, after: Corbo, *Il Santo Sepolcro*, plate 6.

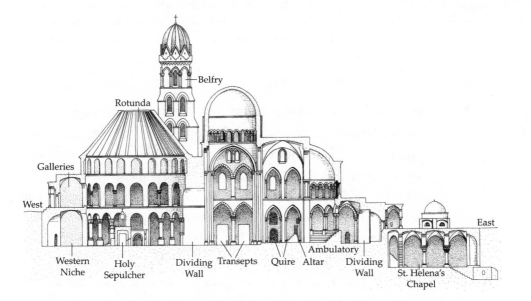

Fig. 10.7. Section of the Crusader Holy Sepulchre. Redrawn by J. Dillon, after: Bahat, *Illustrated Atlas*, 94–95.

Fig. 10.8. Pilgrim's crosses next to the stairway leading down to the Chapel of St. Helena. Photo H. Bloedhorn.

Fig. 10.9. Twin portal of the Crusader entrance to the Holy Sepulchre with the original lintels still in situ, ca. 1880–1900. Courtesy of the École biblique.

### THE TEMPLUM DOMINI

The Templum Domini was one of the prominent features on medieval maps of the city.[37] It was depicted on the royal seals of the kings of Jerusalem alongside the Church of the Holy Sepulchre and the Tower of David and is described in detail in most of the itineraria. The Franks identified the Umayyad shrine on the former Temple Mount with the biblical Temple; thus able to justify leaving this remarkable Muslim building intact after the conquest, they transformed it into a church dedicated to St. Mary. Certain alterations were necessary to lend the building a Christian character and to protect it from the growing numbers of pilgrims and their increasing desire to obtain holy relics. This work commenced around 1114 and continued for several years. Changes included covering the rock with marble slabs, enclosing it in an iron grille, and placing a great cross on the dome, which in the tenth century had been plated with gilded brass (fig. 10.11). This was perhaps an intentional measure taken by the Franks together with the rebuilding of the Holy Sepulchre to restore the balance between the two religious foci in the city, the Haram al-Sharif and the Holy Sepulchre. A degree of parity seems to have been achieved by enhancing the latter and lessening somewhat the visual impact of the former.

From 1112, Augustinian canons were installed in the Church of St. Mary. Not long thereafter they were housed in an abbey built on the northern part of the platform. Almost nothing is known of the conventual buildings of the canons.

In A.H. 583/1187 C.E., following the Ayyubid conquest, the Dome of the Rock reverted to Muslim use. The gold-plated cross was lowered from the top and the dome was regilded. The altar and marble slabs were removed from over the rock and the frescoes were effaced. The iron grille remained in place until the middle of the twentieth century.

Fig. 10.10. Cornice outside the Chapel of the Franks. Photo H. Bloedhorn.

Fig. 10.11. The Crusader period iron grill inside the Dome of the Rock, ca. 1880–1900; replaced in the 1960s by a wooden screen. Courtesy of the École biblique.

## ST. MARY ON MOUNT ZION

Another important church in Crusader Jerusalem was St. Mary on Mount Zion.[38] This church with its abbey marked the traditional site of the home of St. Mary and some of the central events in the Gospels, notably the Last Supper and Pentecost. The church was apparently rebuilt by the Franks in the first decades of the twelfth century, incorporating the foundations of the former Byzantine church Hagia Sion

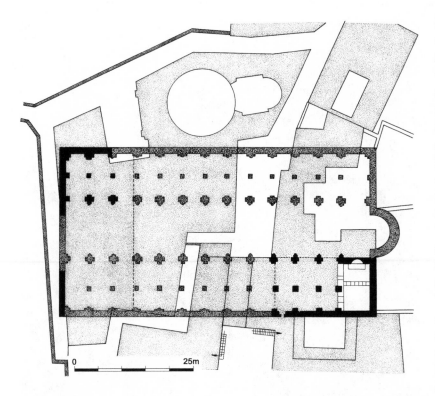

0        25m

Fig. 10.12. Plan of the church of St. Mary on Mount Zion. The walls and pillars marked in black still exist; the hatched ones are reconstructed. The broken line in the west indicates the western extent of the original Byzantine church. The Cenacle is in the southeastern corner on the second floor, above the traditional Tomb of David. The round church to the north is the Benedictine Church of the Dormition Abbey consecrated in 1910. Drawing by K. Bieberstein.

(fig. 10.12). The triapsidal basilica was enlarged to the west (by ca. 14 meters) and was now the second-largest church in twelfth-century Jerusalem.

In 1187, Salah al-Din gave the church to the Oriental Christians. Shortly after, in 1219, it was destroyed by the Ayyubids. When the Crusaders were allowed to resettle in Jerusalem in 1229, they set about to rebuild the church. All that remains standing of this former building, which had a central nave flanked by four side aisles, is the southeast corner, including its pillars and columns; the foundations of the northwest corner and western wall are preserved underneath the modern abbey. The ground level of the southeast corner of the church houses the traditional Tomb of King David; the upper level contains the Cenacle, the traditional room of the Last Supper (figs. 10.13–14).[39]

Fig. 10.13. Inside the Cenacle, looking northwest, 1908. Courtesy of the École biblique.

### THE CHURCH OF THE ASCENSION

The original Byzantine church, circular in plan, was destroyed sometime during the tenth or eleventh century. Immediately after the conquest of the city, the Crusaders built a small open aedicula on the Mount of Olives, described by Abbot Daniel in 1106.[40] After 1130, a new octagonal chapel (8 meters in diameter) was erected on top of the rock on which, according to tradition, the footprint of Christ was preserved.[41] The aedicula was decorated on its exterior with marble imposts and capitals (fig. 10.15).[42] The surrounding courtyard — possibly including a portico — was also octagonal (37.8 meters in diameter). The design has been compared to that of the Dome of the Rock, and it seems that this newly erected building was an imitation of the Umayyad structure. At the end of the fifteenth century, the octagonal courtyard was reduced on its eastern and southeastern sides; later, a new cupola was placed on top of the aedicula.

## ST. ANNE

The Benedictine complexes in the city were just as important as the four Augustinian ones. These, too, perpetuated traditions established in pre-Crusader times. The architectural similarities between Benedictine and Augustinian constructions are evident, in large basilicas with a central nave, two side aisles, and a transeptal dome.

The earliest among these edifices is St. Anne, located immediately west of the Lions' Gate or the Gate of Jehoshaphat (fig. 10.16).[43] The associated Benedictine convent, founded at the beginning of Frankish rule, became one of the wealthiest and most important ecclesiastical establishments in the city. Built south of the former Byzantine church of St. Mary of the Piscina Probatica and dedicated to St. Anne, mother

Fig. 10.14. Southern pillar with two buttresses; the right one pointing toward the nave of the former church of St. Mary on Mount Zion, the left one pointing toward the southern aisle. Photo H. Bloedhorn.

Fig. 10.15. The Church of the Ascension, ca. 1880–1900. Courtesy of the École biblique.

of the Virgin Mary, the basilica marked the place traditionally held to be where Anne and Joachim lived. A church or chapel must have existed on the site before the new basilica was constructed in the 1140s. St. Anne is a fairly standard Romanesque triapsidal basilica, apart from the inscribed transept and the cupola at the junction of the nave and transept (figs. 10.17–18). The façade of the church has a central hood-arched door and a second door on the south. The upper window of two above the main door is nearly as large as the door; above it is a shallow gable. The crypt of the church, originally a cave, is traditionally identified as the birthplace of the Virgin Mary. The belfry in the southwest corner was one of the most imposing features of the church in the Crusader period. The upper level of this massive struc-

Fig. 10.16. St. Anne, looking northeast, British Mandate period. Courtesy of the École biblique.

ture, somewhat taller than the church, had large, hood-arched double windows and, like the belfry of the Church of the Holy Sepulchre, was supported by buttresses.

Part of the aesthetic quality of this church lies in its simplicity, reinforced by the absence of remains of the mosaics and frescoes that originally covered its walls. The architectural sculpture is very simple; there is remarkably little of it. In A.H. 588/1192 C.E., the church was converted into the Madrasa al-Salahiya, a school for teaching Islamic theology and religious law. In 1856, after the Crimean War, the Ottoman sultan presented it to Napoleon III and the interior was renovated and cleared of later additions.

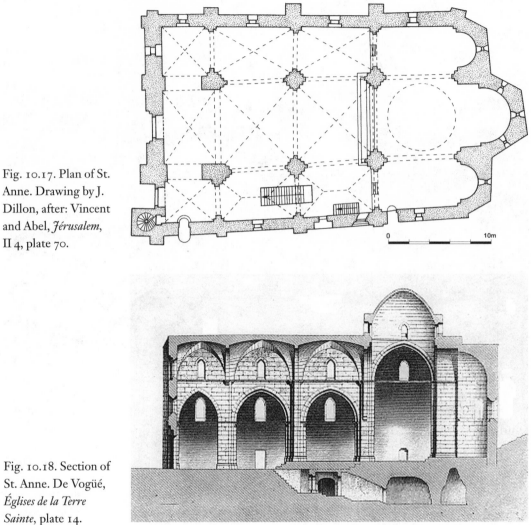

Fig. 10.17. Plan of St. Anne. Drawing by J. Dillon, after: Vincent and Abel, *Jérusalem*, II 4, plate 70.

Fig. 10.18. Section of St. Anne. De Vogüé, *Églises de la Terre Sainte*, plate 14.

## ST. MARY LATINA AND ST. MARY MAJOR

Two churches of St. Mary, very similar in plan, were founded south of the Holy Sepulchre. Partial remains of these churches survived until the end of the nineteenth century.

The original St. Mary Latina probably dates from the time of Charlemagne and was later reconstructed by merchants from Amalfi (some time before 1080).[44] Around the mid twelfth century, the Crusaders established a new triapsidal basilica (40 × 23 meters) with a belfry in the southwest and the main entrance in the north, the nave and aisles each consisting of four groin-vaulted bays. The northern portal with its symbolic representations of the twelve months and the cloister to the south can still be seen today. The ruins of the entire architectural complex were still visible in the mid nineteenth century. Today, the Lutheran Church of the Redeemer is a copy of the original Crusader building.

St. Mary Major, dedicated in 1080 and rebuilt by the Crusaders, was very similar (35 × 21 meters), indeed almost identical to St. Mary Latina, in particular with respect to its architectural decoration (fig. 10.19).[45] It, too, had a large northern portal and a belfry in the southwest and probably also direct access to the hospital located next to its western wall. Unfortunately, following the discovery of the building's remains around 1900, no excavations were carried out. Its foundations were covered up and are now buried underneath the Greek Bazaar.

Fig. 10.19. Corinthian capital from the church of St. Mary Major. Courtesy of the Israel Antiquities Authority.

Fig. 10.20. Northern part of the cloister of St. Mary Magdalene, during excavation in the 1980s. Courtesy of the Israel Exploration Society.

### ST. MARY MAGDALENE

This church was located near today's Herod's Gate.[46] In 1118, the former Coptic church (ninth century C.E.) was replaced by a building in Late Romanesque style, with a nave with two side aisles and an adjacent cloister. As early as 1138, the church was returned to the Coptic community. After A.H. 583/1187 C.E., the Christian community was expelled from the northern quarter of the city and their churches were converted to Muslim use. St. Mary Magdalene was rededicated as the Madrasa al-Mamuniya in A.H. 593/1197 C.E. By 1500, the building lay in ruins. In 1887, the remains were cleared to make way for a new school building. A small section of the cloister was excavated in the early 1980s (fig. 10.20).[47]

### THE CHURCH AT THE TOMB OF ST. MARY

The church at the Tomb of the Virgin Mary is situated at the bottom of the Kidron Valley (Jehoshaphat Valley), next to Gethsemane (fig. 10.21).[48] The origins of the church go back to the mid fifth

Bonfils

314 *Tombeau de la Vierge et grotte de l'agonie*

century. A description that includes a map by the pilgrim Arculf from around 680 provides documentation. The earlier church was destroyed, probably in the early ninth century.

It was supposedly Godfrey of Bouillon who, in 1099–1100, dedicated a monastery on the site of the tomb of St. Mary. Construction was only begun in 1112, however, under the abbot Hugh. The monastery became one of the most affluent ecclesiastical establishments, possessing vast estates in the Holy Land. It was also used as the private monastery of the Lower Lorraine kings.

The tomb chamber was decorated with typical twelfth-century sculptures and frescoes representing the Dormition and Assumption of the Virgin. The stairway to the south was enlarged to make room

Fig. 10.21. Entrance to the Tomb of the Virgin Mary near Gethsemane, ca. 1880–1900. Courtesy of the École biblique.

for a new Romanesque entrance façade. Lady Morphia in 1126–27 and Queen Melissende in 1160, both members of the Lower Lorraine royal family, were buried in the niches of this stairway. After Salah al-Din occupied the city in 1187, the abbey was destroyed, except for the tomb itself, and the stones were used for repairing the city walls. During modern construction work in 1935, the monastery underwent partial archaeological investigation.

An additional Crusader church dedicated to the Holy Savior was built in the nearby Garden of Gethsemane. This church survived only until the fourteenth century.[49]

### CHURCHES OF THE SECULAR ORDERS

The development of the churches of the secular orders was less homogenous. The first order of Crusaders was the Templars, founded in 1118–19 by Hugh of Payens and charged with protection of the pilgrimage routes. Upon arrival in the city, the order was housed in one of the wings of the Royal Palace (Templum Salomonis). After the royal residence transferred to the Citadel in 1120, the Templars occupied the entire complex. The Jami al-Nisa next to the Aqsa Mosque testifies to the Crusader building activities.[50]

The Leper's Hospital antedates the Crusader period. Early plans from around 1130 indicate that the hospital was located northwest of the city. To date, no archaeological remains have been recovered.

The Hospitallers, too, existed prior to the Crusader period. The late Byzantine Church of St. John, south of the Holy Sepulchre, was built according to a small trefoil plan.[51] The Crusader church was erected on top of the walls of the earlier building. It became the conventual church of the Order of the Hospitallers of St. John. The associated hospital was located east of the church.[52] Another basilica, dedicated to St. John the Evangelist, is located in Tariq al-Wad.[53] Both buildings are preserved to this day.

The Germans in Jerusalem owned at least two churches. St.

Mary Alemannorum (St. Mary of the Germans), located on the Street of the Germans, was a small triapsidal basilica built around 1143 c.e.[54] It was flanked on one side by a hospital and on the other by a hospice. The church of St. Thomas Alemannorum (St. Thomas of the Germans) was located north of the Armenian Cathedral of St. James. Both are partially preserved.[55]

### THE ARMENIAN CHURCHES

All Armenian churches in Jerusalem dating to the Crusader period are still preserved. The Armenian Cathedral of St. James was built in the mid twelfth century on a site in the Armenian Quarter of the city.[56] It has been identified as the place where the head of St. James the Elder was buried after he was beheaded by Herod Agrippa I (Acts 12:2). Other churches in the Armenian Quarter include St. James Intercisus (or St. James the Persian).[57] The small church of St. Toros (St. Theodore) is similar in plan to St. James Intercisus, being also a single-aisled church.[58]

## Royal Palaces

After the conquest of Jerusalem, and especially the occupation of the Haram al-Sharif by Tancred, Godfrey of Bouillon bought the entire Haram area for 700 pieces of silver and settled in the complex of the Aqsa Mosque, which was now called the Templum Salomonis.

When Baldwin I assumed power in 1104, he neglected the palace and allowed parts of the lead roof and stones to be reused in other buildings (as we are informed by Fulcher of Chartres) — such as in some of the capitals in the newly rebuilt Church of the Holy Sepulchre.

When the order of the Knights Templars was founded in 1118–19, Baldwin II allowed them to settle in the southern part of the Templum Salomonis, which was subsequently restored. The order expanded after 1128, when additional buildings were added around the Templum Salomonis. The Jami al-Nisa is the only one that has survived. Al-Idrisi (1154), John of Würzburg (after 1160), and Theoderich (before 1170) have furnished us with detailed descriptions of the Templum Salomonis (fig. 10.22).

As of 1120, the kings resided in another part of the city before the new palace was built near the Citadel in 1170.[59] Maps from the Crusader period show the palace in two different locations. The Uppsala Map, for example, locates the "aula regis" (the Royal Palace) northeast of the Holy Sepulchre.[60] The Copenhagen Map locates the "habitatio regis et prophetarum" (the House of the King and the Prophets) at the intersection of two main streets.[61] Since it is unlikely to have two palaces in such a short span of time, we can assume that one or both maps are wrong. Felix Fabri's description of Jerusalem from 1483 places the king's residence just west of the Holy Sepulchre. He writes in his *Evagatorium* (123b):

> After this we came out of the courtyard and passed through a door on the left-hand side of it as you look towards the church into a garden planted with orange-trees and pomegranates, from which garden we went up into a great house with many rooms . . . it is a great and stately house, containing a very great number of vaulted chambers. It adjoins the western side of the Church of the Holy Sepulchre . . . this house was once the dwelling of the Kings of Jerusalem, who dwelt there that they might always be near to the most holy sepulchre of our Lord.

The royal family moved their residence once more, this time to the western end of the city, next to the Tower of David (south of today's Citadel). The construction of the palace was probably completed around 1160. Although John of Würzburg does not mention it, Theoderich later remarks (*Libellus* I, 4):

Fig. 10.22. Drawing of The Hague Map of Crusader Jerusalem. Röhricht, "Karten und Pläne" [1], plate 4.

The Tower of David is incomparably strong, made of squared blocks of enormous size. It is next to the south gate by which the road goes towards Bethlehem, and its site is next to the newly built dwelling and palace, which is heavily defended with ditches and barbicans, and is now the property of the King of Jerusalem.

The "curia regis" reproduced on the Cambrai Map should only be viewed as a symbolic representation of the palace (fig. 10.23). Archaeological remains, uncovered in today's Armenian Garden and in the courtyard of the police station, are reduced to two groin-vaulted rooms and two barrel-vaulted halls revealing typical Crusader-style masonry.

### Ayyubid Building Initiatives

The Ayyubids' rule, initiated in A.H. 583/1187 C.E., was short-lived. Their goal to turn Jerusalem into a Muslim city was primarily visible on top of the Haram al-Sharif. During the fifteen years of Crusader rule (A.H. 625–40/1229–44 C.E.), Islamic building initiatives were interrupted, so that only about two dozen Ayyubid period buildings can be documented.[62] Converted Crusader structures, re-used building segments and architectural details, and imitations of Crusader-style architecture make it difficult at times to separate the different phases of construction and use.

As early as A.H. 587/1191 C.E., Salah al-Din initiated the repair of the partially destroyed city wall. In the northwest, the wall was rebuilt to both sides of the Tancred Tower or Qasr Jallut. Additional repairs by Sultan al-Malik al-Mu'azzam Isa, carried out in the southern section of the wall, are documented by inscriptions that are dated to A.H. 599–609/1202–12 C.E. A new gate (Bab al-Niya), located at the end of the main street, was erected in conjunction with those repairs, replacing the not very long-lasting, earlier entrance (fig. 10.24).[63]

When the new Muslim rulers took over the city, no buildings were

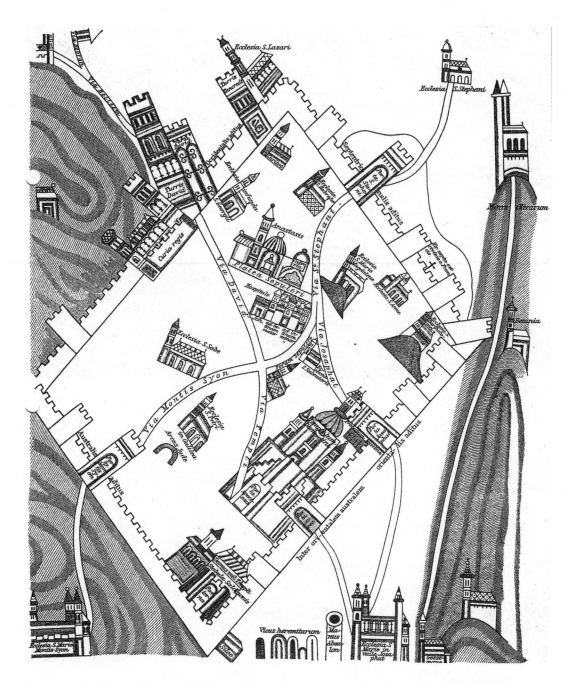

Fig. 10.23. Drawing of the Cambrai Map of Crusader Jerusalem. Röhricht, "Karten und Pläne" [2], plate 1.

Fig. 10.24. Ayyubid Bab al-Niya at the southern end of the main street. Photo H. Bloedhorn.

destroyed, except on the Haram al-Sharif. The Christian population was forced to leave the Haram al-Sharif, and all their buildings bordering the enclosure walls' northern and western sides — including churches — were Islamicized. Initially, all Christian building elements within and around the Dome of the Rock[64] and al-Aqsa Mosque[65] were eliminated so as to reclaim the monuments as Islamic. The structures of the Templars next to al-Aqsa were transformed into mosques (Jami al-Nisa and Jami al-Mughariba)[66] and various smaller buildings were erected around the Dome of the Rock, such as the Qubbat al-Miraj,[67] Qubbat Sulaiman,[68] and Qubbat Nahawiya.[69] The northern portico of the Haram al-Sharif was built during the Ayyubid period,[70] and the gates Bab al-Atm,[71] Bab Hitta,[72] Bab al-Silsila, and Bab al-Sakina were also rebuilt (fig. 10.25).[73]

Within the city itself, the former Benedictine convent of St. Anne was immediately transformed into the Madrasa Salahiya.[74] The

Khanqah al-Salahiya was established as a gathering place for Sufis within various parts of the
Latin patriarchate north of the Holy Sepulchre
(A.H. 585/1189 C.E.).[75] The Jamil al-Afdal (A.H.
589/1193 C.E.) was consecrated within the northern part of the Johannite Hospice, south of the
Holy Sepulchre.[76] Although the minarets of both
buildings are located along the same axis as the
dome of the Holy Sepulchre rotunda, they exceed
it in height. Madrasa al-Mu'azzamiya was endowed at the beginning of the thirteenth century,
in A.H. 606/1209 C.E.[77] Madrasa al-Badriya followed in A.H. 610/1213–14 C.E.[78]

Several cemeteries attest to the Ayyubid presence in the city. These include the cemeteries to
the left and right of the Golden Gate, the Sahira
cemetery north of Herod's Gate, and the Mamilla
cemetery in the upper part of the Hinnom Valley
west of the Jaffa Gate. Among the more noteworthy burial monuments is the Qubbah al-
Qaymuriyah, a funerary structure located some 1 km northwest of the
Jaffa Gate. It was built by the al-Qaimari family around 1250 and
mentioned by Mujir al-Din. The main body of the *qubbah* (domed
mausoleum) is a cube with a shallow domed roof. The undecorated
entrance is in the north wall; the south, east, and west outer walls are
divided in the middle by projections with oblong window-openings.
The drum has four broader window-openings. Inside, on the left, are
the original bases of the five tombs. A slightly pointed arch is inscribed on the south, east, and west walls; in the angles between the
arches are squinch-arches crowned by three concentric moldings. The
springers of the arches on the walls extend to form small engaged
columns. Between the top of the columns and the frieze are capitals
with acanthus leaves or volutes. In the south wall is a small mihrab.[79]

Fig. 10.25. Ayyubid Bab al-Sakina (left) and
Bab al-Silsila (right) with Crusader spolia.
Photo H. Bloedhorn.

### Distinctive Finds

Crusader sculpture and monumental painting, with their unique synthesis of Byzantine, western European, and Levantine styles and iconography, have left numerous remains throughout the Holy Land.[80] Among examples of manuscript illumination originating in Crusader Jerusalem, a few of the works produced in the scriptorium of the Church of the Holy Sepulchre have survived.[81] Despite the eclectic nature of Crusader art and architecture, a local variation crystallized in Jerusalem. As for the Ayyubid city, most of it is no longer preserved, and in several cases little has remained beyond the epigraphic evidence.[82]

Fig. 10.26. Fragment of a Crusader frieze from the Muristan, depicting an archer during a hunt with his dog beside him. Courtesy of the Israel Antiquities Authority.

Fig. 10.27. A Crusader voussoir from the Muristan, showing a saint. Courtesy of the École biblique.

Fig. 10.28. Minbar of Nur al-Din in the Aqsa Mosque, ca. 1880–1900 (destroyed by arson in 1969). Courtesy of the École biblique.

## ARCHITECTURAL SCULPTURE

Unlike Crusader architecture in Jerusalem, which was heavily influenced by the Romanesque style that flourished in southern France and southern Italy, the Crusader city's architectural and ornamental sculpture was based on a local vocabulary of style and technique. Most likely, a Jerusalem workshop produced the numerous examples still standing on and around the Haram al-Sharif, including panels,

lintels, abaci, and capitals that distinguish themselves by their sche-
matization of decorative elements and their sparse use of figurative
images (figs. 10.26–27).[83]

### MAPS

The form of representation from which we can perhaps learn the
most is the map. Fourteen maps of Frankish Jerusalem are known
today.[84] Eleven are round maps and the remaining three are quadrilateral. The most important of the latter is the twelfth-century
Cambrai Map, featuring a realistic representation of the city's layout
and some of its principal buildings (plate 14). The round maps of
Jerusalem, such as the so-called The Hague Map (plate 15), are distinctive, signifying the high regard in which the city was held. Rather
than being naive representations of the city containing little factual
data, these maps are highly useful sources of information for the
medieval city.

### MINBAR OF NUR AL-DIN

An elaborate pulpit (minbar) was ordered by Nur al-Din (A.H.
564/1168–69 C.E.), intended to be placed in the Aqsa Mosque when
he conquered Jerusalem (fig. 10.28). It was first used in the Great
Mosque of Aleppo and was eventually brought to Jerusalem after the
death of Nur al-Din, at Salah al-Din's request. The minbar remained
in the Aqsa Mosque until it was destroyed by an Australian fanatic in
1969. The minbar of Nur al-Din played a key role in the Counter-
Crusade in Jerusalem.[85]

# 11  ✦  The Mamluk Period

[The Gate of the Cotton Merchants is] a large [Haram] gate that was just built and recently opened. There are ten steps down (inside). On each side there are platforms, and the length of each of them is seven and two-thirds pics. The construction of the gate is perfect: its height is eight pics and its width is five. Its arch is of double facing and made of stone which is sculpted and colored. Its inscription is gilt and incised into the stone. Its two portals are covered with plates of gilt and inscribed copper.

AL-ʿUMARI, MASALIK AL-ABSAR 161–62

## A City between Cairo and Damascus

The Ayyubids, rulers of Egypt and Syria since A.H. 567/1171 C.E., were succeeded by the Mamluks (a name from Arabic meaning "slaves") in A.H. 648/1250 C.E.[1] The Mamluks ruled for over two and a half centuries, until the Ottoman conquest in A.H. 923/1517 C.E. The Bahri Mamluks, originally Qipchaqs from the Mongols' Golden Horde on the Volga, were based on the island of Rhoda in Cairo; the Burji Mamluks were Circassians by origin and were stationed in the Citadel of Cairo.

The Mamluks' defeat of the Mongol army in A.H. 658/1260 C.E. at 'Ain Jalut in the Jezreel Valley in northern Palestine was the decisive event in the history of Jerusalem in this period. This battle and the expulsion of the Mongols to lands beyond the Euphrates enabled the Mamluks to extend their sovereignty to Palestine, henceforth a part of Greater Syria. From this point on, a series of governors served in Jerusalem until the end of Mamluk rule.

Although Jerusalem retained its importance as a Muslim sacred place, it played a relatively minor political role in the larger regional context. Whether by choice or by compulsion, the city's governors usually joined the more widespread factional disputes and uprisings. Neither its diminished political status nor its location off the main routes prevented an impressive list of visitors from coming to Jerusalem throughout the duration of Mamluk rule.

For the first time since the reign of Salah al-Din, the city remained in the hands of Muslims without interruption. With the fall of Acre to al-Malik al-Ashraf Khalil in A.H. 690/1291 C.E., the Mamluks succeeded in expelling the Crusaders from the Holy Land. That Jerusalem was no longer a target of European aggression provided the inhabitants with a new kind of stability, and there was, therefore, no apparent reason to refortify the city with new walls (fig. 11.1). In comparison to Ayyubid rule, the Mamluk state as a whole was stronger, better controlled, and much more centralized, despite the internal rivalry and strife that manifested in numerous attempts by amirs stationed in the principal cities of Syria to assert their independence.

In the early years of Mamluk rule, according to al-Qalqashandi (d. A.H. 821/1418 C.E.), Jerusalem functioned as a governorate under the jurisdiction of the viceroy of Damascus. Later (after A.H. 800/1398

Fig. 11.1. Map showing concentration of Mamluk monuments around the Haram. Redrawn by M. Speidel, afer: Burgoyne, *Mamluk Jerusalem,* 35, fig. 2.

C.E., when Egypt and Syria were not in conflict), Jerusalem officials were appointed by the sultan in Cairo. We know the names and dates of several key individuals (mostly amirs but also many judges[2]) recorded by historians of the Mamluk period.[3] Often the rulers of Jerusalem were given the title of viceroy or, alternatively, supervisor of the "Two Sacred Harams" — Jerusalem and Hebron. During the reign of Sultan al-Nasir Muhammad (A.H. 693–741/ 1293–1341 C.E.), the two positions were filled by the same person, a practice often followed thereafter.

The reign of Sultan al-Ashraf Qaytbay (A.H. 872–901/1468–1496 C.E.) is notable for the number of fine buildings he and his amirs

erected, although this era marked the onset of the close of the Mamluk Empire. The year A.H. 923/1517 C.E. marked the final demise of
the state and its incorporation into the Ottoman Empire.

## The Haram al-Sharif—The Noble Sanctuary

Epigraphic and literary documents indicate that from the earliest
days of Islam the maintenance and embellishment of the Haram al-
Sharif had been a royal preserve. Most Muslim rulers invested in
repairing and decorating the complex as a whole and, more particularly, its two main monuments, the Dome of the Rock and the
Aqsa Mosque. The most impressive new construction undertaken on
top of the esplanade during the Mamluk era can be attributed to the
last decades before Ottoman rule. Sultan al-Ashraf Qaytbay reestablished the sultanate after a period of political tumult and economic
decline. His reign was characterized by a great revival of the arts, in
which architecture was characterized by elegance and harmony rather
than size.

The main entrance to the Haram al-Sharif, the Bab al-Silsila, is
one means of access to the Dome of the Rock platform from the
west.[4] One encounters wide stone steps crowned with a triple-arched
arcade, the southwestern *qanatir* (fig. 11.2).[5] The still-visible steps
and colonnade were built under Sultan Qaytbay in place of an earlier
narrow-vaulted stairway.

The fountain (*sabil*) of Sultan Qaytbay is located on the western
side of the Haram esplanade not far from Madrasa al-Ashrafiya, which
was also sponsored by Qaytbay (fig. 11.3).[6] Made entirely of stone, the
fountain's elongated and graceful form is a result of several building
components placed one on top of the other. The structure is supported by a raised prayer platform with a freestanding mihrab whose
base consists of a simple room (4.60 × 4.80 meters and 7.65 meters
high) illuminated by large grilled windows and a relatively small entrance. Various transitions are apparent in the structure—from the

Fig. 11.2. Southwest qanatir of the Dome of the Rock terrace, looking west. Photo R. Schick.

square base to the round, high drum that ultimately merges with the dome itself. The structure is crowned with a pointed dome decorated with arabesque stone carvings. This is the only notable dome of this kind that has survived outside Cairo. It is 13.28 meters high, with a base consisting primarily of *ablaq* construction of alternating red- and cream-colored stones. The inscriptions on the fountain's exterior refer to the three main stages of construction. An earlier structure was built by Sultan Inal (ca. A.H. 854/1450 C.E.), replaced in A.H. 887/1482 C.E. by the present construction of Sultan Qaytbay. This was later restored in A.H. 1300/1883 C.E. under the Ottoman sultan 'Abd al-Hamid. The latter restoration and subsequent transformations, however, have left the original design of Qaytbay relatively intact.

## Religious Institutions

A substantial number of *ribats* (hospices for pilgrims), were built under Ayyubid rule and a few additional ones were established during the Mamluk period.[7] The earliest Mamluk religious institution,

Fig. 11.3. Sabil Qayt-
bay, looking north-
east. Courtesy of
Michael Burgoyne
(Burgoyne, *Mamluk
Jerusalem*, color plate
30).

Ribat 'Ala al-Din (A.H. 666/1267–68 C.E.), is located on the northern side of Tariq Bab al-Nazir.[8] The use of the building as a hospice for pilgrims is one of the main factors that justified its proximity to the Haram al-Sharif.

Ribat al-Mansuri was built a few years later (A.H. 681/1282–83 C.E.) by Sultan al-Mansur Qala'un.[9] Established for the use of pilgrims visiting the Holy City, it subsisted on income from rents from urban and agricultural properties in the region. The hospice is located on the southern side of Tariq Bab al-Nazir Street, which leads toward Bab al-Nazir on the western wall of the Haram. The entrance to the hospice is 30 meters from the gate. The building is composed of vaulted rooms of various sizes enclosing a rectangular courtyard aligned east–west with the street. The building's arched portal leads into a vestibule giving access to the courtyard on the west and a large rectangular hall on the east.

The earliest Mamluk building abutting the Haram wall is Ribat al-Amir of Kurt al-Mansuri (A.H. 693/1293–94 C.E.), next to the Bab al-Hadid.[10] Here, the rock surface is below the level of the Haram, which in some ways determined the choice of location for the construction as well as the narrowness of the building's layout. Excavations conducted outside the southwestern corner of the Haram have shown that when Titus caused the walls of the Temple area to collapse in 70, the fallen masonry piled up at the base of the ruins until the Umayyad reconstruction of the Haram walls. By then, the accumulated debris next to Bab al-Hadid may have risen almost to the level of the Haram esplanade, and it was on this strip of raised surface that Ribat of Kurt al-Mansuri was built.

Nine ribats mentioned in Haram documents have left no physical trace, nor are they mentioned by Mujir al-Din (A.H. 860–928/1456–1522 C.E.).[11] The only one listed by him, Ribat al-Maridini (before A.H. 763/1361 C.E.), can be identified some 15 meters north of Ribat al-Awhadiya in Tariq Bab Hitta.[12] Other than the pointed-arched portal that incorporates the remains of an earlier building, its architectural style is rather simple. The earlier ribats share a common ornate architectural style that would soon be replaced by more elaborate buildings with particularly ornate entrance portals.

The earliest madrasas in Jerusalem were also built by the Ayyubids. Not until more than a century after their introduction, however, were madrasas constructed immediately next to the Haram's boundaries, primarily on its north and west. Most of these edifices were the result of individual patronage; the spiritual significance of these building initiatives is expressed in the contemporary Fada'il and Muthir literature.

Khanqah al-Dawadariya (fig. 11.4) was erected against the northern border of the Haram, east of Tariq Bab al-Atm. A foundation inscription above the door identifies the Sufi *khanqah* and dates it to A.H. 694/late 1295 C.E. or to A.H. 696 /1297 C.E., according to Mujir al-Din.[13] Its founder, Amir Alam al-Din Sanjar al-Dawadari (b. A.H. 628/1230–31 C.E.), possessed enormous administrative powers in the Mamluk Syrian territories. The amir died in A.H. 700/1300 C.E. in a battle against the Mongols.

The Dawadariya is set within the urban fabric, sharing most of its northern and eastern walls with neighboring buildings; its southern wall is incorporated into the Haram portico. The rock surface right next to Bab al-Atm is almost at the same level as the Haram esplanade, while further east it slopes steeply downward. Prior to construction, the site was leveled by the erection of two long vaulted tunnels located west of a large water reservoir, Birkat Bani Isra'il. Given the structural relationship between the vaults and Bab Hitta, the latter must be from the Umayyad period, while the tunnels' date must be slightly earlier. Since the floor level of the khanqah is higher than the top part of the vaults, we can assume that a different structure occupied the site previously. This earlier structure may have been "the places of prayer" of the Sufis in Fatimid times, which, according to Nasir-i Khusraw, existed approximately in this location. This traditional association of the site was commemorated with the

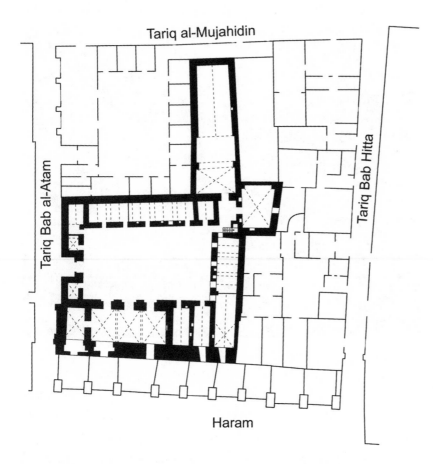

Tariq al-Mujahidin

Tariq Bab al-Atam

Tariq Bab Hitta

Haram

Fig. 11.4. Plan, Khan-qah al-Dawadariya. Redrawn by M. Spei-del, after: Burgoyne, *Mamluk Jerusalem,* 155, fig. 8.2.

establishment of the Khanqah al-Dawadariya for thirty Sufis and their followers.

The building's most striking feature is its ornate entrance portal, one of the main characteristics of Mamluk architecture. The door-way's recess is 3 meters wide and 2 meters deep, with stone benches flanking the entryway. It is crowned with twin vaults resting on three tiers of *muqarnas* (stalactite squinches) and on twin trefoil arches built into the portal arch (fig. 11.5). The entrance is made of red and white ablaq masonry topped with a pointed arch. The design was clearly influenced by a series of contemporary portals built in Damascus, and may even prove to have been made by the Damascene craftsman 'Ali ibn Salama.

Fig. 11.5. Vault of entrance portal from below, Khanqah al-Dawadariya. Photo R. Schick.

Inside, the Dawadariya is constructed around a large rectangular courtyard with vaulted cells to its north, east, and west; an upper story of halls was added at a later date. The lower cells can be accessed through doorways with pointed arches. A large classroom crowned by three cross-vaulted halls of equal size dominates the southern end of the courtyard. A small vestibule in the northeastern corner encloses the stairs leading up to the roof and also provides access to annexes located to its east and north. The smaller eastern annex has an irregular plan and is capped by a cross-vault. The northern annex, which extends along the adjacent Madrasa al-Sallamiya, consists of a long barrel-vaulted hall preceded by a courtyard. The classroom is the main area on the first level; its courtyard's façade has symmetrical arched niches for its door and two windows, which are framed with ablaq masonry. The central niche for the doorway is decorated with a tympanum enclosing a disc. Inside, the hall is subdivided into three vaulted bays with two transverse arches. The building currently houses Madrasa al-Bakriya. Numerous additional madrasas were built

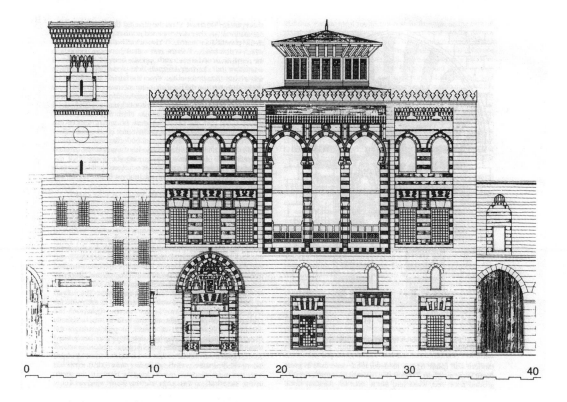

during the course of Mamluk rule, including such noteworthy examples as Madrasa al-Jawiliya, al-Tankiziya, al-Sallamiya, al-Manjakiya, al-Baladiya, al-Subaybiya, al-Ghadiriya, and al-Hasaniya.[14]

Madrasa al-Ashrafiya (A.H. 887/1480–81 C.E.), located north of the main Haram gate Bab al-Silsila, rests partly on the roof of the Baladiya and partly on an assembly hall that incorporates three arched openings of the Haram portico.[15] The Ashrafiya was built in typical Egyptian style, by a team headed by a Coptic architect commissioned by the sultan from Egypt. The builders made use of expensive materials, such as timber for roofs and windows and marble slabs for floors and walls.

The entrance, which can be accessed directly from the Haram, is clearly one of the most harmonious Mamluk architectural features in Jerusalem (fig. 11.6). It incorporates all the typical elements in as-

Fig. 11.6. Restored east elevation, al-Ashrafiya. Drawing by A. Walls (Burgoyne, *Mamluk Jerusalem*, 599, fig. 63.6).

tonishing equilibrium — the recessed portal, stone benches on either side of the entrance, ablaq, muqarnas, inscriptions, geometric patterns, a three-lobed arch, voussoirs with ornamental carvings, and polychrome ceramic incrustations.

Although the Ashrafiya was partially destroyed during earthquakes it can still be reconstructed as the height of Mamluk architectural achievements on the Haram. It was the only madrasa to be built on the border of the Haram expressly for a sultan and was clearly the most ornate of all. In the words of Mujir al-Din (*Histoire de Jérusalem*, 387–88), the circumstances of its construction were as follows:

> The amir Hassan al-Zahari built the earlier al-Malik al-Zahri Khushqaddam Madrasa. When this prince died, he asked al-Malik al-Ashraf Qaytbay to receive it. The governor accepted it and gave his name to the madrasa, and appointed a supervisor, Sufi devotees, and lawyers, paying them salaries. Some time after this, in 880 [1475 C.E.], al-Malik al-Ashraf Qayt Bay came to Jerusalem, and did not like the building. Likewise, in 884 [1479 C.E.] he sent one of his servants with an order to destroy the structure and expand it, and add more buildings to it. They began to dig the excavations of the present madrasa building on Shawan 14, 885 [October 19, 1480 C.E.]. The architects began work, and actual construction began in 887 [1482 C.E.]. They covered the roof with lead plates, similar to al-Aqsa Mosque. In any event, the most impressive thing about this building is its location in the Noble Sanctuary. The madrasa is the third jewel there: the first is the Dome of the Rock, the second is al-Aqsa Mosque, and the third is this madrasa.

Only royalty was entitled to build on top of the Haram esplanade; the structure of the Zawiya al-Fakhriya built by the judge Fakhr al-Din al-Muhammad on the southwestern extremity was an exception.[16] This was probably justified by its being hidden behind the enormous Crusader and Ayyubid halls used during the Mamluk period as the Women's Mosque and the Maghribi Mosque. Given their size and proximity to the Haram walls, it may be assumed that the converted halls were considered to be at the Haram border at the time. This exception would therefore not have been viewed as going against the established convention.

## Mosques, Mihrabs, and Minarets

Besides the Aqsa Mosque, only two other mosques were built in Jerusalem during the Mamluk period.[17] One was located within the Citadel next to Jaffa Gate (Bab al-Khalil), at the western end of the city. Traces of reconstruction by the Crusaders and partial dismantling by the Ayyubids are visible, as are repairs made in the Citadel during the reign of Sultan al-Nasir Muhammad when the mosque (or *jami*, a congregational mosque for Friday prayer) was added, primarily to enable the garrison to attend weekly prayers without having to leave the fortified area.[18] The other mosque is the Masjid al-Mansuri (*masjid, place of worship*). Both mosques are simple vaulted halls with a mihrab in the *qibla* wall that marks the direction of Mecca.

Mihrabs and minarets are clear indicators of Islamic architecture. Mihrabs, usually in the shape of semicircular arched niches, can be found in some of the foundations in Jerusalem. Among the twelve surviving madrasas and khanqahs located adjacent to the northern border of the Haram, only one, the Is'ardiya, has a mihrab. In contrast, all the madrasas and khanqahs near the western border have mihrabs. Given the presence of the archetype qibla of the Aqsa Mosque, institutions located adjacent to the northern border of the Haram required no further indication of the direction of Mecca.

Among the most famous minarets in Jerusalem from the Mamluk period are those that served the Aqsa Mosque. Their function in general was not only to indicate the location of houses of worship, but also to make a statement of supremacy over the non-Muslim populations in the city.

Most minarets in Jerusalem are square stone towers of the Syrian type. One of them, located on the northwestern corner of the Haram, is the Minaret al-Ghawanima (fig. 11.7).[19] Built almost completely of stone (A.H. 697/1298 C.E.), apart from a wooden canopy over the muezzin's gallery, it represents one of the sturdiest and highest constructions in the Old City of Jerusalem. Its solid structure has survived several earthquakes. The tower's robust edifice is countered by a certain elegance in its decoration. The minaret is dug into the natural bedrock and is partitioned into several levels by stone molding and muqarnas galleries. The first two lower levels are wider and directly touch the bedrock, forming the tower's substructure. Four additional levels, including the muezzin's gallery, are topped by a circular drum and bulbous dome. The stairway is visible from the outside up to the first two levels, but continues then inside until it reaches the muezzin's gallery.

Only one year after the Minaret al-Ghawanima was built, the so-called Bab al-Silsila Minaret was erected on the western border of the Haram, adjacent to the main entrance to the esplanade.[20] Toward the early sixteenth century, Mujir al-Din wrote that the Bab al-Silsila Minaret was to be reserved for the best muezzins in Jerusalem.[21] From this tower came the first call to prayer, and only afterwards would the voices of muezzins from other minarets be heard. Built entirely out of stone according to the traditional Syrian square tower model, this minaret probably replaced an earlier Umayyad one. The inscriptions indicate that this restoration was carried out in the days of Sultan al-Nasir Muhammad, apparently by Amir Tankiz, the Mamluk governor of Syria, at the same time he built Madrasa al-Tankiziya.

The intensity of construction next to the Haram borders diminished visibly over the following years. The next two decades record only one building project — the cylindrical minaret near Bab al-Asbat, erected in A.H. 769/1367-68 C.E. (fig. 11.8).[22] The present slender

Fig. 11.7. East façade, al-Manjakiya, and the Bab al-Ghawanima Minaret. Courtesy of A. Duncan and Al Tajir Trust (Burgoyne, *Mamluk Jerusalem*, color plate 16).

Fig. 11.8. From left to right, looking southwest: Bab al-Asbat Minaret, al-Aqsa Mosque, Dome of the Chain, Dome of the Rock, dome of the Hurva synagogue (late Ottoman period). Courtesy of the École biblique.

tower, elegantly and beautifully proportioned, built against the westernmost portico of the esplanade's northern border, overlooks the Haram and the Bethesda Pool. The cylindrical stone shaft, probably of Ottoman date, sits on a rectangular Mamluk base that rests on top of a triangulated transition zone. The shaft narrows above the level of the muezzin's gallery and terminates with a bulbous dome. This upper section of the minaret was reconstructed after the 1927 earthquake, rendering a harmonious mélange of the various stages of construction.

## Commercial and Domestic Construction

Most Mamluk commercial and domestic construction was linked to the establishment of religious institutions. The upkeep of Madrasa al-Tankiziya, for instance, was partially financed by income from the large commercial center known as Suq al-Qattanin (Market of the

Cotton Workers).[23] Reconstructed to replace an older building in A.H. 737/1336–37 C.E. by Tankiz, governor of Syria for Sultan al-Malik al-Nasir Muhammad, it was defined as one of the finest bazaars in Greater Syria. The market street begins at the monumental gate Bab al-Qattanin on the western border of the Haram, extends westward into the city, and ends at Tariq al-Wad. The elongated vaulted space is dramatically lit by skylight openings. The street is bordered by lodgings, two bathhouses, shops, a small market, and a caravansary.

Bab al-Qattanin is the grandest of the Haram gates, built into the west portico of the esplanade (fig. 11.9). It lies beneath an impressive muqarnas vault. Its trefoil arch is set within a significantly larger recess, which is crowned by a semi-dome supported by marvelous muqarnas pendentives and surrounded by a slightly pointed arch of alternating red- and cream-colored ablaq construction.

Several of the main markets are monuments containing Crusader architectural elements in secondary use. Suq al-Qattanin appears to be built on top of the remains of a Crusader market (fig. 11.10). The Wakala, a warehouse founded by Sultan Barquq (A.H. 788/1386–87 C.E.) where state taxes were collected, incorporates sections of a Crusader market on the northern end of Tariq Bab al-Silsila.

Northwest of the Citadel, beyond the city walls, a caravansary known as Khan al-Zahir was established under Sultan Baybars in A.H. 662/1263 C.E. The Bab al-Id, which was transported from the palace of the Fatimid caliphs in Cairo to Jerusalem, served as the fortification's main entrance. Baybars provided an imam for the mosque and installed an oven and a mill within the caravansary. Near the gate, food was distributed to the poor and their shoes could be repaired. Other than an inscription, now in the Islamic Museum on the Haram, no additional traces of the caravansary can be identified.[24]

Two impressive structures from the Mamluk period incorporating magnificent residences were built northwest of the Citadel, at some distance from the Haram but still providing a clear view of it. Clusters of domestic structures near the Haram's border frequently

Fig. 11.9. Bab al-Qattanin, looking west. Photo H. Bloedhorn.

Fig. 11.10. Suq al-Qattanin, looking east. Photo K. Bieberstein.

included a loggia for taking advantage of the view. With the limited availability of space for new building activity near the esplanade in the fourteenth century C.E., ingenious devices were contrived to give a sense of closeness to the Haram.

The Dar al-Sitt Tunshuq is located on the traditional Christian site of the Hospital of Queen Helena, mother of the Byzantine emperor Constantine.[25] It is the only surviving grand palace of Mamluk Jerusalem, approximating in scale and opulence the palaces built for high-ranking amirs in Cairo. The ground here rises some 10 meters above the Haram's esplanade, which can be accessed via three monumental portals opening onto a horse stable (fig. 11.11). The main living and reception rooms of the palace were located on the upper level. The most impressive part was a formal reception area with a magnificent view overlooking the Haram to the east. It was originally designed for the otherwise unknown Lady Tunshuq al-Muzaffariya. On the same street, opposite the palace lies her tomb, Turbat al-Sitt Tunshuq.[26] Her palace and tomb represent the last important

Fig. 11.11. Entrance portal, al-Tankiziya, 1905–1910. Courtesy of the École biblique.

Mamluk buildings to have been established away from the Haram's border.

## Mausolea

The mauloseum (*turba*) was another noteworthy building type of the period. Built in the center of the city, half a dozen still stand today. Tomb chambers are incorporated in many of the religious buildings; in some cases they form independent entities. Although burial next to the Haram has been practiced since early Islamic times, no graves can be found within the Haram precinct proper. Shaddad ibn Aws was buried in the Golden Gate cemetery in the seventh century C.E., which to this day is the main Muslim cemetery of the city. No burials are attested until after the conquest by Salah al-Din. The growing significance of burial near the Haram in the thirteenth century C.E. can be associated with the dominant role of eschatological traditions

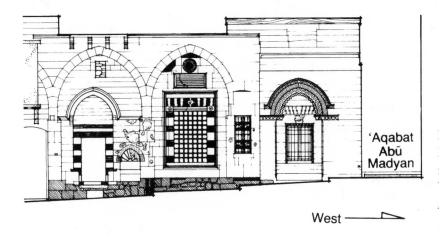

'Aqabat
Abū
Madyan

West ⟶

Fig. 11.12. Turba of
Barka Khan, northern
façade. Drawing by A.
Walls (Burgoyne,
*Mamluk Jerusalem,*
113, fig. 2.4).

identifying Jerusalem as the place of the Last Judgment. Objections
voiced by several religious leaders such as Ibn Taymiya against the
erection of funerary structures were obviously ignored by many during the Mamluk period. The earliest funerary structure to be erected
on Tariq Bab al-Silsila, the main street leading to the Haram, is
Turbat Barka Khan, built in the mid thirteenth century C.E. (fig.
11.12).[27] The earliest to be erected immediately next to the Haram,
Turbat al-Malik al-Awhad, dates to the end of the same century.
From this time onward, eight additional tombs were built against the
northern and western borders of the Haram, and six additional ones
along Tariq Bab al-Silsila. The bodies of some amirs who died elsewhere were brought to Jerusalem for burial. Most of the funerary
structures have domed chambers. The cenotaph (*tabut*), a rectangular stone or marble chest-like structure, slightly elevated on a low
plinth, marks the location of the underground grave chamber and is
the only distinguishing piece of furniture in the chamber. Additional
notable examples include the Turbat al-Awhadiya and the dome
tomb of Tashtamur al-'Ala' I.[28]

## Distinctive Finds

The minor arts from Mamluk Jerusalem, like the architectural corpus, illustrate the impact of artistic trends of contemporary Cairo and Damascus. Other than wall mosaics and glasswork, this era is noteworthy for its beautiful manuscripts, elegant calligraphy, masterful metalwork, and numerous ceramic types.[29]

### WALL MOSAICS

Mosaics of colored and gilded glass, colored paste, turquoise faience, and mother-of-pearl, as well as colored stone and marble, embellish some of the above-mentioned Mamluk buildings. The most impressive wall mosaic is located in Madrasa al-Tankiziya.[30] Its mihrab is covered with narrow strips of polychrome marble, flanked by reused Crusader columns with capitals, clearly analogous to certain features of Umayyad wall mosaics in the Dome of the Rock, in particular with its mother-of-pearl inlay (plate 16). It appears that this late-emerging art drew its inspiration from the seventh-century mosaics in the Dome of the Rock. Historical sources indicate that restorations of the wall mosaics were carried out during the Mamluk period in both the Dome of the Rock and the Dome of the Chain. Although Syria and Egypt have similar types of wall mosaics, Jerusalem appears to have been the home of a genuine Palestinian school that lasted for centuries.

### MANUSCRIPTS

Mostly from the late fourteenth century, the so-called "Haram documents," were discovered during the course of repairs and reorganization of the Islamic Museum and its holdings in the 1970s. The texts, written primarily in Arabic, some in Persian, provide much information on the history of Palestine and Jerusalem in particular under Mamluk rule.[31] Some of them were written on parchment, and

others on paper. In addition to the qur'anic manuscripts the documents include legal decrees, petitions, property and land registra-
tions, marriage contracts, title deeds, wills, and so on. The art of
Qur'an illumination consists of calligraphy, plant and geometric designs, and coloring. Most of the Mamluk period manuscripts are written in *thuluth* or *muhaqqaq* and are decorated with geometrical or
floral motifs, including arabesques, fan palmettes, and lotus flowers.
The predominant colors during this period are blue and gold.[32] The
tradition of bookbinding was already well established at the beginning
of the Mamluk period. Most Qur'an manuscripts featured a central
oval medallion with scalloped edges on the front and back covers, with
delicate floral and geometric patterns, along with additional partial
medallions in the corners.[33] A double page of a fourteenth-century
document (Rab'ah of Ibn Qurman) presents the Surat al-Fatiha (the
first chapter of the Qur'an) written in thuluth script. The text is bordered on the top and bottom by golden panels, reading Fatihat al-
kitab (the Opener) and seven verses in the upper panel and "Only the
pure may touch it" and "Praise to god, Lord of the Two Worlds" on
the bottom (plate 17).[34]

# 12 ✦ The Ottoman Period

When he [Sultan Suleiman] became an independent king the
Prophet appeared to him in a blessed night and told him, " . . . You
should spend these spoils on embellishing Mecca and Medina, and
for the fortification of the citadel of Jerusalem, in order to repulse
the unbelievers, when they attempt to take possession of Jerusalem
during the reigns of your followers. You should also embellish its
Sanctuary with a water-basin . . . and also embellish the Rock of Al-
lah and rebuild Jerusalem."

EVLIYA ÇELEBI, *Seyahat-namé*, fol. 91

## City of Pilgrimage

In A.H. 857/1453 C.E., the Ottoman ruler Mehmed the Con-
queror took over Constantinople and the last territories of Byzantium. Additional regions to the south and east, including the Levant

and Egypt, were subsequently conquered by his successors. To the Ottomans, Syria, Palestine, Egypt, and Arabia were provinces of a much larger empire whose center of gravity lay in Anatolia and the Balkans. These provinces were a source of revenue, manpower, and raw materials, yet in all other respects played a secondary role. They were governed by appointees from Istanbul, where the metropolitan court and administration spoke Turkish and adopted Persian culture. Although Palestine continued to be ruled by Muslims holding a deep respect for Arab culture, their first loyalty was to the Turkish sultan in Istanbul.[1] The new rulers' building initiatives in Jerusalem clearly reflect this significant change.

In the generation after the Ottoman conquest of Jerusalem in A.H. 922/1516 C.E., the city sank to the status of a minor provincial town.[2] Most of the important Ottoman contributions to Jerusalem's architectural heritage can be linked directly to the rule of Suleiman the Magnificent between A.H. 926 and 974/1520 and 1566 C.E. The flourishing economy that had characterized most of Mamluk rule in the city gave way to stagnation and decline. Jerusalem turned inwards, resting on past glories while its current interests were maintained by a few leading local Arab families, who dominated the religious and administrative affairs of the waqfs or endowments of its many pious institutions.

In spite of dramatic political changes under the Ottomans, Jerusalem continued to attract large numbers of pilgrims. In the sixteenth century, Nasir al-Din Rumi described the itinerary of the Muslim pilgrims visiting the holy places in Jerusalem. One of the most famous guides to the holy places of Mecca, Medina, and Jerusalem, known as the Dala'il al-Khairat, was compiled by the Berber mystic al-Jazuli (d. A.H. 869/1465 C.E.). In addition to prayers for the Prophet and other spiritually meaningful texts, his illustrated itineraries, which include detailed views of the three holy cities and a list of religious sites to be visited by pilgrims, became very popular in Ottoman times and were circulated widely. Perhaps not surprisingly, the itinerary for Muslim

Jerusalem was similar in many ways to the Via Dolorosa followed by Christian pilgrims.

## Fortifications

The most important building projects by Suleiman the Magnificent in Jerusalem include the city's fortifications — the rebuilding of the walls and repair of the Citadel. The city wall was meant to protect Jerusalem's inhabitants, but it was also meant to keep the Holy City apart.

### CITY WALLS

Among the first tasks undertaken by Suleiman was the reconstruction of the conquered city's wall (plate 2).[3] Completed in four years (A.H. 944–47/1537–40 C.E.), the goal of its construction was to supply the Holy City with a modern defensive system to partially replace and reinforce the medieval enclosure, and to enlarge it to the size of the rectangular area we see today (fig. 2.3). The wall enclosure took the shape of an irregular quadrilateral and included thirty-five square towers and several crenellated gates whose openings were mostly Roman — and even earlier. Some sixteen inscriptions over the main gates record the dates of the wall's reconstruction and feature hymns that praise the sultan.[4]

The city walls were intended to defend Muslims and their holy shrines from the Christian enemy.[5] Despite its inland position, Jerusalem was vulnerable to attacks from the sea, as much as any coastal town of Syria and Palestine — such as Tartous, Tripoli, Sidon, Acre, Jaffa, or Gaza. In addition to protecting Jerusalem's inhabitants from potential European invaders and Bedouin incursions, the wall was meant to visually emphasize the Ottomans' presence and political strength in the eyes of the locals and to symbolically mark Jerusalem's religious role of being the third holiest city in Islam, as well as to

physically separate the Holy City from the rest of the world.[6] The Jerusalem city wall, one of the most complete of its kind from the sixteenth century to have survived intact, is unusual also because the Ottomans built very few fortifications and rarely invested in efforts comparable to those in Jerusalem.

Fig. 12.1. Damascus Gate, looking south-west. Photo B. St. Laurent.

The gates are among the wall's most impressive features. The largest and best known is the Damascus, or Nablus, Gate (Bab al-'Amud, or Gate of the Column), located to the north (fig. 12.1). Its façade is crowned with pinnacled battlements and decorated with floral and geometric reliefs.

A similar set-up exists at the Zion Gate (Bab Nabi Da'ud) on the south, the Jaffa Gate (Bab al-Khalil) on the west, and the Lions' Gate (Bab al-Asbat or Bab al-Sitt Maryam) on the east (fig. 12.2). In terms of style, the gates indicate continuity as well as a certain revival of Crusader and Ayyubid elements in their conception, meant more as a façade to intimidate those approaching the town from outside than as a triumphal entrance.

Fig. 12.2. Lions' Gate, looking west, ca. 1880–1900. Courtesy of the École biblique.

### THE CITADEL

The Citadel is one of the most significant landmarks in the city (fig. 12.3). Its location at the western entrance to the city, immediately south of the Jaffa Gate, was determined by the earlier fortifications as an area where defensive strength was greatly needed.[7]

The Citadel as we know it today is primarily the fourteenth-century Mamluk fortress, but it also incorporates several earlier ele-

ments and later Ottoman additions. The structure has an irregular rectangular plan located south and west of Herod's tower along the existing city wall. Three of its sides are almost straight, and the fourth, the south side, zigzags, most likely following the course of an earlier fortification. The Citadel's curtain walls connect four large towers at each of its four corners, and a fifth tower near the midpoint of its eastern side, enclosing a central courtyard. It furthermore includes two outworks, one on the eastern side and the other on the west. The entire structure is encircled by a moat.

Fig. 12.3. Citadel, looking northeast. Photo H. Bloedhorn.

The main access to the Citadel's interior is through its modern-day eastern entrance (fig. 12.4). A double flight of steps leads to an outer gateway that ultimately connects with the entrance itself. Above the vaulted portal, an inscription in Arabic marks the restoration of the citadel by the Ottoman sultan Suleiman in A.H. 938/1531–32 C.E. The wooden bridge that replaced the original drawbridge spans the

Fig. 12.4. Citadel,
eastern entrance.
Gröber, *Palästina*,
plate 10.

outer moat and gives access to the barbican. From there one passes
through the main entrance over another bridge, this one made of
stone, spanning the inner moat.

One of the main functions of the Citadel was to garrison the military forces that guarded against internal unrest and outside threats. It
also served as an armory for the manufacture of cannons. In addition
to its military role, the Citadel served other secondary functions, including that of a prison. The complex also included luxurious residential quarters for the imam and the muezzin. A Friday mosque — the
only one in Jerusalem apart from al-Aqsa Mosque — was also built on
the grounds of the Citadel. As a result, soldiers did not have to leave
their posts for Friday prayers.

The main difference between the Jerusalem Citadel and Ottoman citadels in other cities, such as Cairo, Damascus, or Aleppo, was
that the one in Jerusalem did not have an administrative and residential compound for the city's ruling elite. Apparently, the *saray* (palace)
in the Jawiliya compound (the modern-day ʻUmariya Madrasa, in the
area in the northwestern corner of the Haram al-Sharif), fulfilled this
function.

Among the most important changes in the Citadel under Ottoman rule is the addition of the so-called Summer Mosque, an open-air building surrounded by a low wall to the west and north and barbican battlements to the south and east. An inscription in Turkish above the lintel of the doorway dates the repair of the Summer Mosque by the *agha* (commander) of the Janissaries, the Khassaki 'Ali Agha, to A.H. 1151/1738 C.E. (fig. 12.5).[8]

A remarkable testimony to Ottoman construction is the mosque's minaret, consisting of a cylindrical stone shaft divided into three stories by molded stringcourses. A square stone-built base with rounded edges supports the cylindrical shaft. A door at the southern end leads to an interior spiral staircase that climbs to the gallery of the *muezzin* (caller to prayer).

An inscription on the base commemorates the restoration of the minaret by Muhammad Pasha during the reign of Sultan Muhammad IV in A.H. 1065/1655 C.E.[9] Additional construction work that

Fig. 12.5. Citadel, inscription mentioning the repair of the Summer Mosque by Khassaki 'Ali Agha. Courtesy of Al Tajir Trust (Auld and Hillenbrand, *Ottoman Jerusalem*, I, plate 32,13).

can be identified with the rule of Sultan Suleiman, based partially on the presence of inscriptions and partially on related building elements, are the moat, the glacis, and the western terrace.[10]

The Citadel was run-down by the end of the nineteenth century, as testified by travelers' accounts and contemporary photographs. The building officially ceased to be a military stronghold on December 11, 1917, when General Allenby proclaimed the British occupation of Jerusalem.

## Water Installations

Immediately after addressing Jerusalem's security concerns, the Ottomans worked on the city's water supply system, to ensure the availability of water for the inhabitants' daily and religious needs.[11] Nevertheless, a severe drought in A.H. 1277/1860 C.E. left the channels dry and led to endemic disease that swept through Jerusalem.[12]

### AQUEDUCTS

Construction and restoration of aqueducts and channels to convey water to Jerusalem had been revived in the 1530s. According to some literary accounts, this activity was necessary despite restoration work that had been carried out by Qaytbay in the late fifteenth century.[13] Two earlier reservoirs at Solomon's Pools south of Bethlehem were supplemented by a third pool; all were named after their patron.[14] Birkat al-Sultan (named after the Mamluk sultan Barquq), located immediately beyond the city walls, southwest of Bab al-Khalil, was repaired and a small fountain with two troughs to provide water for animals was built.[15] New and older channels directed water from this pool toward the city. Joseph ha-Cohen, a Jewish resident of Jerusalem in A.H. 944/1537 C.E., stated that "they also extended the tunnel into the town lest the people thirst for water."[16] Five additional fountains, all of a very similar design and fed by the newly restored channels, were erected in the name of the sultan, near the Haram. Work on the water channels most likely continued throughout the 1540s and 1550s.

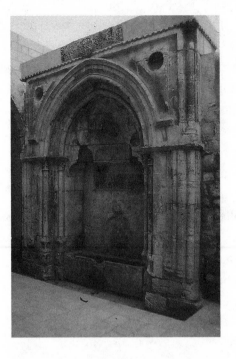

Fig. 12.6. Sabil in Tariq al-Wad with Herodian sarcophagus, simple style. Photo H. Bloedhorn.

Fig. 12.7. Sabil Bab al-Nazir with Crusader spoils, elaborate style, 1908. Courtesy of the École biblique.

## FOUNTAINS

Thirteen fountains (*sabil*) from the Ottoman period have been preserved in Jerusalem. Of the nine attributed to Sultan Suleiman, six are still standing. Their concentration on the Haram platform indicates unequivocally that they not only fulfilled a secular purpose, but also a religious one. Water ablutions are required to precede each of the five daily prayers that Muslims perform. The majority of the fountains (eight) date to the sixteenth century C.E., while the remaining five were built over the following three centuries. Structurally, we can distinguish between a simple and a more elaborate style (figs. 12.6–7). The simple style, with a recessed niche surmounted by a pointed arch enclosed within a rectangular stone panel, is represented by six examples, all constructed by Sultan Suleiman. Most of the panels appear to be attached to a wall, and therefore this type is sometimes referred to as the "walled niche sabil," or *çeşme*.[17]

Other than those of Qasim Pasha, a windowless eight-sided structure with a marble panel niche in each face, all the fountains were of the more elaborate type, having four sides surmounted by a small, shallow dome. This style has been referred to as "the four-sided sabil," the design of which facilitated the distribution of water to passersby coming from various directions.[18]

Water for the fountains came from either a branch of the Qanat al-Sabil tunnel or rainwater collected in the Haram cisterns. Some of the sabils were built directly over one of these cisterns, such as Sabil Bab al-Maghariba and Sabil Sha'lan; others were assigned a certain sum of money by a donor to buy water, especially in the summer, when water had to be transported.

### HAMMAMS

For most of the Ottoman period, six public bathhouses were in use in the city: Hammam al-'Ain, Hammam al-Shifa', Hammam al-Batrak, Hammam al-Sultan, Hammam al-Sayida Maryam, and Hammam al-Jamal.[19] Whereas Hammam al-'Ain and Hammam al-Shifa' in Suq al-Qattanin were originally built in the Mamluk period, at least two of the others were built or renovated next to or in the same location as one of the earlier bathhouses (fig. 12.8).[20] The names of these hammams changed rather frequently.

The Jerusalem hammams belonged to a charitable endowment, at least during the early Ottoman period. During the nineteenth century, however, there was a tendency for ownership to be transferred to a family endowment.[21]

The main room in the hammam was always the dressing room, equipped with a stone basin and a fountain in its center (fig. 12.9). This feature at Hammam al-Batrak had a typical octagonal shape and a circular pool on top.[22] Stone benches along the walls of the dressing

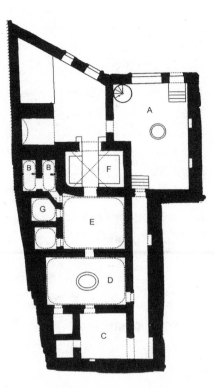

N

0 1 5 10m

Fig. 12.8. Hammam al-Sayyida Maryam, plan. Courtesy of Al Tajir Trust (Auld and Hillenbrand, *Ottoman Jerusalem*, I, 522, fig. 33.1).

Fig. 12.9. Hammam al-Sayyida Maryam, summer dressing room. Courtesy of Al Tajir Trust (Auld and Hillenbrand, *Ottoman Jerusalem*, I, 524, plate 33.5).

room were covered with soft furnishings, such as cushions.[23] Sometimes a second, usually smaller and sometimes heated dressing room
existed in the mountainous regions of Palestine and was used for
changing during the cold winters. Earlier hammams usually had both
warm and hot rooms. In later bathhouses, however, the warm washing room was not a standard feature. The exact arrangement in the
Ottoman period is not known. The hot room was clearly the main
washing room, surrounded by several small chambers that branched
off of it. The furnace was located behind the hot room, and a duct
carrying the steam passed beneath the floor of the heated rooms and
was expelled from a chimney on the far side of the heated dressing
room. Brass or copper cauldrons were built above the furnace to heat
the reservoir of water.

The significance of the hammam, in Jerusalem and in the rest of
the Arab and Islamic world, is of a religious nature. Washing the body
is an essential obligation for Muslims; head, hands, and feet have to
be washed before prayer, and, as a result, places for ablutions are
found near all major mosques. Furthermore, anyone in a state of
"unseemliness" has to purify himself or herself.[24]

In Jerusalem, as elsewhere in the Middle East, the hammam represented an important feature of civilized living in the city. It would
have been inconceivable for Jerusalem not to have a number of functioning hammams. When Western influence had taken hold their
number was reduced, so that by the end of the Ottoman period — the
beginning of the twentieth century — only four hammams were still
functioning.

### The Haram al-Sharif—The Noble Sanctuary

The modifications on the Haram esplanade under Ottoman rule
were both visually and politically significant and were undoubtedly
intricately linked to each other. Most notable were the replacement
of the exterior decoration of the Dome of the Rock and various
privately endowed and initiated building programs.

## THE DOME OF THE ROCK — QUBBAT AL-SAKHRA

Initial repair work in the Dome of the Rock was conducted in A.H. 935/1529 C.E., focusing only on the stained glass windows around the drum. A few years later, the existing Umayyad glass mosaics on the exterior of the drum and the octagonal ambulatory below it were replaced with tiles, and the lower parts of the octagon were revetted with marble (plate 18).[25] In A.H. 969/1561–62 C.E., Qubbat al-Silsila, east of the Dome of the Rock, was retiled.[26] Additional repairs were carried out, focusing on the lead work of both the Dome of the Rock and the Aqsa Mosque. After completing the exterior of the Dome of the Rock, the doors were repaired (A.H. 972/1564–65 C.E.), and soon after that, two windows were reopened (A.H. 1006/1597–98 C.E.).[27]

### SMALL CELLS

The largest concentration of new buildings was located against the western and northern sides of the upper esplanade in the form of fourteen small, two-storied cells (*khalwa*), only some of which have foundation inscriptions.[28] The practice of building structures against the side of the upper platform of the Haram al-Sharif began as early as the Ayyubid period. Frederick Catherwood, who visited the city in 1833, writes that there were "apartments . . . appropriated to the poorer classes of Mahomedan pilgrims, who are lodged and fed gratuitously from the funds of the mosque."[29] In other words, even in the latter years of the Ottoman Empire, these cells still provided for those who made pilgrimage to the city.

## A Charitable Institution

The Takiyat Khassaki Sultan in Jerusalem was the largest charitable institution in Palestine at the time (fig. 12.10).[30] The endowment for its construction was made possible by the founder's intimate relationship with the sultan.[31] The large size of the complex and the resources it would have required for its daily maintenance are

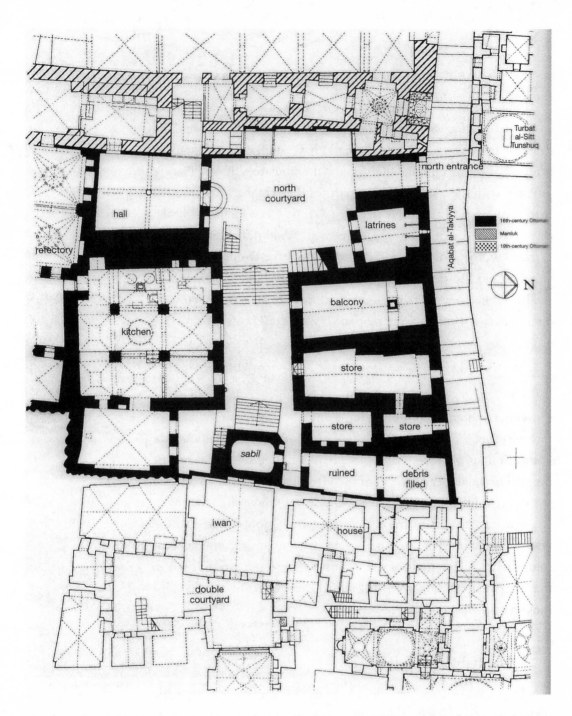

Fig. 12.10. Khassaki Sultan complex, plan. Courtesy of Al Tajir Trust (Auld and Hillenbrand, *Ottoman Jerusalem*, I, 572, fig. 35.1).

impressive. One imperial document states that the complex consumed half of the city's total water supply.[32] It appears that in order to meet the requirements of the complex and the city, an additional water channel had to be built; Khassaki Sultan Hürrem covered the cost herself.

The complex was built partially in and around the large Mamluk Dar al-Sitt Tunshuq.[33] The main components of this "Flourishing Edifice" (*'Imara al-'Amira*) were a *khan* (inn), accommodations for a Sufi community, a refectory, a mosque, a bakery, probably a bathhouse, a soup kitchen that distributed two free meals daily to the poor and to the Sufi residents, and a charitable foundation composed of a public water fountain and an elementary school for learning the Qur'an (*sabil kuttab*).

### Religious Architecture

The Ottomans initiated the construction of numerous mosques in Jerusalem, including Masjid al-Qaimari, Masjid al-Hamra' (ca. A.H. 939/1532–33 C.E.), Masjid al-'Imara al-'Amira al-Khassaki Sultan, and Masjid al-Zawiya al-Qadiriya (A.H. 1043/1633 C.E.). The religious focus was obviously the omnipresence of the Haram al-Sharif, which housed the Aqsa Mosque and the Dome of the Rock.

In addition to mosques, Ottoman Jerusalem saw the construction of several minarets. During the sixteenth and seventeenth centuries, five new minarets were built, including the minaret of al-Nabi Da'ud (A.H. 930/1524 C.E.), the minaret of al-Jami' al-Maulawiya (before A.H. 995/1586–87 C.E.), and the minaret of the Citadel (A.H. 938/1532 C.E.). Shortly after the conversion of the Cenacle into a mosque, the minaret of al-Nabi Da'ud was erected. Two Mamluk minarets may have been restored or completely rebuilt — the minaret of Bab al-Asbat (A.H. 769/1369–70 C.E.)[34] and the minaret of al-Zawiya al-Fakhriya (A.H. 745/1345 C.E.).[35] Among the new minarets, those of al-Nabi Da'ud and the Citadel are both built on top of roofs.

Several noteworthy synagogues were established during Ottoman rule, including the Yohanan Ben Zakkai Synagogue (1606), the Prophet Elijah Synagogue (1625), the Beth El Synagogue (1737), Or ha-Chaim (1742), the Hurva Synagogue (1864), and Tiferet Yisrael (1872).[36]

Since the mid-nineteenth century onward, European communities were granted permission to establish new churches in the city. These include Christ Church (1849), the Holy Trinity Church (1872), the Church of the Redeemer (1898), St. George's Cathedral (1898), St. Stephen (1900), and the Dormition Abbey (1910).[37]

## Cemeteries

A large number of mausoleum and tomb (*maqam*) structures were erected during the Ottoman period; most no longer exist today. We know the names of about fifty renowned personages who were buried within the city walls. Architecturally, these tombs are very diverse, ranging from separate mausolea to ordinary burial structures. Mausolea from the period are mostly crowned with domes. Their interiors contain places of prayer, often including mihrabs. Some tombs are merely simple rooms or open spaces, while others are composed of two or three buildings. The tomb proper is generally located in the center of the room, but sometimes it can be found in the courtyard or outside.

In addition to these intramural burial structures, three main cemeteries existed outside the city walls — the Bab al-Rahma cemetery, the Bab al-Sahira cemetery, and the Mamilla cemetery.[38]

## Distinctive Finds

Among the decorative arts, calligraphy maintained an important position. Manuscripts and dedicated albums were often illustrated with miniatures, an art form influenced by the Persian and Byzantine traditions. The Ottoman Empire was noted for the quality of its gold and silver jewelry and other precious items. This period is also known for magnificent carpets and textiles. One could purchase a variety of luxury items in Jerusalem; however, the city is not associated with any significant locally produced objects.

### TILES

Unlike the structural components of the Dome of the Rock that have kept their original Umayyad period composition, its exterior was significantly modified. When Sultan Suleiman came to rule in A.H. 926/1520 C.E., polychrome tiles replaced the original glass mosaics. The effect of this new colorful composition stands in contrast to the relative sobriety of Ottoman architecture and makes a clear statement about the new rulers, who were not only masters of the Haram but of the entire city. The tile industry was brought to Turkey from Persia, probably by craftsmen from Tabriz in northwestern Iran. The transition from the traditional Persian *cuerda seca* technique (outlines drawn on the surface of the tile to prevent the colored glazes from mingling) to underglaze decoration (applied before the tiles are glazed) occurred some time in the mid fifteenth century, although during the first half of the sixteenth century several imperial buildings were still decorated in the traditional technique. Both techniques were used simultaneously for tiles on the Dome of the Rock (plate 19).

### COSTUMES

Other than travelers' accounts and early photographs, our knowledge about Ottoman clothing derives from garments that have been preserved dating from the second half of the nineteenth century and the first half of the twentieth. Other than the many itinerants, the city's population, in addition to native residents, largely consisted of Turks representing the Ottoman government in Istanbul and Europeans who came to the region for the long or short term as missionaries, tourists, or bureaucrats. The ethnic, religious, and social complexity of Jerusalem's population does not allow us to examine here all the different types of clothing worn in the city. Select examples of the typical local female and male dress provide us with only a partial glimpse of the various styles, fabrics, and colors.[39]

Women in the central region of Palestine usually wore a white cotton, sometimes embroidered, undergarment. The garment worn over it was a long dress (*thub*) with a round neck opening. The sleeves were usually long and pointed. For additional fullness of the dress, the skirt sometimes had extra panels added down the sides. A wedding dress (*thub abu qutba*) from Jerusalem that dates to ca. 1850 includes pieces of green and red silk, with sleeves of gold silk (plate 20a). It is decorated with the characteristic central panel (*qabba*) and is only sparingly embroidered with scalloped silk in red, green, and yellow. Silk tassels hang from the neckline cord.

Men throughout the Arab world wore basically the same attire, consisting of a long cotton or wool tunic or shirt (*thub*) reaching the knees as well as baggy cotton trousers (*shirwal* or *libas*) reaching between the knee and ankle. They also wore a long coat of plain or striped fabric (*qumbaz*) that was wrapped and tied in the front. The color and type of the fabric indicated the religious or class identity of the wearer. A qumbaz from Jerusalem, dating ca. 1930, is made of white silk with red and yellow stripes. The neck opening is decorated with an ochre-colored silk braid (plate 20b).

Just as those garments have brought together the local and foreign cultures passing through and residing or settling in Jerusalem, the material culture of this place has always represented a complex fusion of local and external elements. In addition to creating a link between local and foreign currents, between eastern and western civilizations, the surviving material remains from the city and vicinity establish a concrete connection between Jerusalem's past and present.

# Epilogue

The archaeological remains described in this volume, spanning some five thousand years of civilization, represent but a small fraction of Jerusalem's glorious past. This partial yet significant window into the city's rich history clearly reflects the spotty nature of the field of archaeology. No one discipline — history, archaeology, epigraphy, numismatics, art history, and more — presumes to capture the full scope of Jerusalem's heritage.

Beyond the inherent limitations of archaeology and other fields, we have chosen to provide our readers with a representative selection of the city's material remains as well as relevant scholarly literature for those wishing to pursue further study. Additional discoveries and newly published studies and reports will undoubtedly require a re-evaluation of the archaeological information presented in this volume. Nevertheless, we feel hopeful that this book will encourage our readership to continue its investigation of the city's past; we see this as only the beginning of a process to uncover Jerusalem's thousand faces.

Jerusalem is a complex city. The political and religious turmoil among its inhabitants, as well as the ongoing construction to maintain a modern urban center, have placed innumerable obstacles and constraints on the archaeologist and historian wishing to expose and preserve the city's historical legacy for the three monotheistic religions. Yet, despite these drawbacks, the incessant activity to achieve this goal has left its mark in uncovering the city's past.

The relationship between Judaism, Christianity, and Islam to Jerusalem is enmeshed in the city's history. Thus, any information that sheds light on the emergence and development of each cultural and religious group is invaluable. We would be pleased if the systematic presentation of the archaeological finds in this volume furnishes our readers with a clear and reliable picture of the historical continuity within the city and its significance for the three religions in the various periods.

# Appendix I
# Jerusalem Chronology

| | |
|---|---|
| **7000–4000** B.C.E. | **Neolithic Period** |
| **4000–3300** | **Chalcolithic Period** |
| **3300–2200** | **Early Bronze Age** |
| 3150–2850 | EB I |
| 2850–2650 | EB II |
| 2650–2350 | EB III |
| 2350–2200 | EB IV |
| **2200–1550** | **Middle Bronze Age** |
| 2200–2000 | MB I |
| 2000–1800 | MB IIA |
| 1800–1550 | MB IIB |
| **1550–1200** | **Late Bronze Age** |
| 1550–1400 | LB I |
| 1400–1300 | LB IIA |
| 1300–1200 | LB IIB |
| **1200–586** | **Iron Age** |
| 1200–1150 | IA IA |
| 1150–1000 | IA IB |
| 1000–900 | IA IIA |
| 900–700 | IA IIB |
| 700–586 | IA IIC |

| | |
|---|---|
| **586–539** | **Babylonian and Persian Periods** |
| 586–539 | Babylonian Period |
| 539–332 | Persian Period |
| **332 B.C.E.–70 C.E.** | **Hellenistic Period** |
| 332–167 B.C.E. | Early Hellenistic Period |
| 167–37 B.C.E. | Hasmonean Period (Middle Hellenistic) |
| 37 B.C.E.–70 C.E. | Herodian Period (Late Hellenistic) |
| **70–324** | **Roman Period** |
| **324–638** | **Byzantine Period** |
| **635/38–1099** | **Early Islamic Period** |
| 635/38–750 | Umayyad Period |
| 750–969 | Abbasid Period |
| 969–1070 | Fatimid Period |
| 1070–1099 | Seljuk Period |
| **1099–1260** | **Crusader and Ayyubid Periods** |
| 1099–1187 | Crusader Period I |
| 1187–1229 | Ayyubid Period I |
| 1229–1244 | Crusader Period II |
| 1244–1291 | Ayyubid Period II |
| **1291–1516** | **Mamluk and Ottoman Periods** |
| 1291–1382 | Early Mamluk Period (The Bahrits) |
| 1382–1516 | Late Mamluk Period (The Burjits) |
| 1516–1917 | Ottoman Period |

# Appendix II
## Major Excavations in Jerusalem

| Year | Director/s | Institution | Location |
|------|-----------|-------------|----------|
| 1864 | C. W. Wilson | Ordnance Survey of Jerusalem | Old City |
| 1867–70 | C. Warren and C. W. Wilson | Palestine Exploration Fund | Enclosure walls of Haram al-Sharif, Ophel |
| 1881 | H. Guthe | Deutscher Palästina-Verein | Southeast Hill, eastern slope |
| 1894–97 | F. J. Bliss and A. C. Dickie | Palestine Exploration Fund | Southeast Hill, Southwest Hill, Mount of Olives |
| 1909–11 | M. B. Parker (with the assistance of H. Vincent) | M. B. Parker | Southeast Hill, Gihon, Siloam Tunnel |
| 1913–14, 1923–24 | R. Weill | Rothschild Foundation | Southeast Hill, southern end |
| 1923–25 | R. A. S. Macalister and J. G. Duncan | Palestine Exploration Fund | Southeast Hill, eastern slope |
| 1925–28, 1940 | L. A. Mayer and E. L. Sukenik | Jewish Palestine Exploration Society and Hebrew University of Jerusalem | North of the Old City, the so-called Third Wall |

| Year | Director/s | Institution | Location |
|------|-----------|-------------|----------|
| 1927–29 | J. W. Crowfoot and G. M. FitzGerald | Palestine Exploration Fund | Southeast Hill, western slope |
| 1934–40 | C. N. Johns | Department of Antiquities of Palestine | Citadel |
| 1937–38 | R. W. Hamilton | Department of Antiquities of Palestine | Areas between the Damascus Gate and Herod's Gate |
| 1961–67 | K. M. Kenyon | British School of Archaeology | South of Haram al-Sharif, Southeast Hill, Southwest Hill, eastern slope |
| 1964–66 | J. Hennessy | British School of Archaeology | Outside Damascus Gate |
| 1968–69 | R. Amiran and A. Eitan | Israel Department of Antiquities and Museums | Citadel |
| 1968–78 | B. Mazar | Hebrew University of Jerusalem | South of Haram al-Sharif |
| 1969–82 | N. Avigad | Hebrew University of Jerusalem | Jewish Quarter |
| 1973–78 | M. Broshi | Israel Department of Antiquities and Museums | West and south of the city wall |
| 1975, 1979–80, 1988–89 | G. Barkay | Israel Department of Antiquities and Museums | Ketef Hinnom |
| 1979–84 | M. Magen | Israel Department of Antiquities and Museums | Inside Damascus Gate |
| 1985–87 | Y. Shiloh | Hebrew University of Jerusalem | Southeast Hill, eastern slope |
| 1980–88 | R. Sivan and G. Solar | Israel Department of Antiquities and Museums | Citadel |
| 1986–87 | B. and E. Mazar | Hebrew University of Jerusalem | South of Haram al-Sharif |

| Year | Director/s | Institution | Location |
|------|-----------|-------------|----------|
| 1989–92 | A. M. Maeir, R. Reich, and E. Shukron | Israel Department of Antiquities and Museums / Israel Antiquities Authority | Outside Jaffa Gate |
| 1991–92 | D. Amit and S. Wolff | Israel Antiquities Authority | Morasha neighborhood |
| Since 1995 | R. Reich and E. Shukron | Israel Antiquities Authority | Southeast Hill, Gihon, and water system |

Note: This list follows Geva, "Twenty-five Years of Excavations," 1–28. It does not include unpublished excavations.

# Notes

Note: Page numbers of English summaries of Hebrew texts are indicated with an asterisk.

## Chapter 1. Introduction

1. On Jerusalem in the eyes of the earliest chroniclers, visitors, and pilgrims, see Peters, *Jerusalem: The Holy City*. His comparative literary and religious studies of the three monotheistic religions as reflected in the historical reality of Jerusalem are most valuable, and have yet to be paralleled in the field of archaeology; see Peters, *Children of Abraham; Jerusalem and Mecca; Monotheists.*
2. Feldman, "Josephus," 901–21, 1189–97.
3. Silberman, *Digging for God and Country.*
4. For recent publications on the history of the research, see Silberman, *Digging for God and Country;* Tubb and Chapman, *Archaeology and the Bible,* 9–36; Moorey, *Century of Biblical Archaeology;* regarding the work of foreign archaeologists and archaeological institutes, see King, Davies, Benoit, Weippert, and Mazar, in Drinkard et al., *Benchmarks in Time and Culture,* 15–108; for the history of excavations, see Kenyon, *Digging Up Jerusalem* 1–35; for a systematic overview and summary of the excavations, see Geva, *Ancient Jerusalem Revealed,* 359–64.
5. Smith and Hitchcock, *Life.*

6. See chapter 6. Robinson, *Biblical Researches* I–III; Robinson, *Later Biblical Researches*, 465–67.

7. Goren, "Titus Tobler's Legacy," 57–62, with earlier literature.

8. Tobler, *Lustreise*.

9. Tobler, *Grundriss*.

10. Tobler, *Golgatha; Siloahquelle; Denkblätter; Topographie* I–II; *Dritte Wanderung;* "Analekten," 250–55, 273–79 (about Jerusalem).

11. Tobler, *Bibliographia*.

12. Schick was German, born in Bitz, in the former Kingdom of Württemberg. Strobel, *Conrad Schick;* Goren, *For Jerusalem's Sake;* Goren, "Undoubtedly, the best connoisseur," 105–128.

13. Schick, "Aqueducts at Siloam," 88–91; *Beit el Makdas; Stiftshütte*.

14. On Félix de Saulcy: Musée d'Art et d'Essay, Palais de Tokyo, *Félix de Saulcy;* his travel reports: *Voyage autour de la Mer Morte* [= *Narrative of a Journey round the Dead Sea*]; *Voyage en Terre Sainte; Jérusalem*.

15. de Saulcy, *Voyage autour de la Mer Morte* II, 219–28 [= *Narrative of a Journey round the Dead Sea* II, 134–46].

16. On the history of British archaeological work in Jerusalem between 1865 and 1967 see Gibson, "British Archaeological Work."

17. Watson, *Life of Major-General Sir Charles William Wilson*.

18. Ibid., 116–17, 215.

19. Wilson, *Ordnance Survey of Jerusalem*.

20. Williams, *Life of General Sir Charles Warren*.

21. Wilson and Warren, *Recovery of Jerusalem*, 238–56.

22. Ibid.

23. Elath, "Claude Reignier Conder," 21–41.

24. Warren and Conder, *Survey of Western Palestine: Jerusalem*.

25. Clermont-Ganneau, "Une stèle du Temple de Jérusalem," 214–34, 290–96; idem, "La stèle de Dheban," 184–207, 357–86; Dearman, *Studies in the Mesha Inscription*.

26. Clermont-Ganneau, *Archaeological Researches;* idem, *Recueil d'archéologie orientale;* idem, *Études*.

27. Goren, "Scientific Organizations," 153–65; idem, "Undoubtedly, the best connoisseur," 105–28. For a survey on the history of the German Institute of Archaeology see Hübner, "Protestant Institute."

28. Guthe, *Ausgrabungen bei Jerusalem*.

29. Bliss and Dickie, *Excavations at Jerusalem*. The new excavations are still unpublished.

30. Silberman, "In Search of Solomon's Lost Treasures," 30–41.

31. The École biblique et archéologique française was established in 1890 as the École pratique d'études bibliques. See Trimbur, "École biblique."

32. Vincent, *Jérusalem sous terre* [= *Underground Jerusalem*]; idem, "Les récentes fouilles d'Ophel" [1], 566–91; idem, "Les récentes fouilles d'Ophel" [2], 86–111, 424–53, 544–74.

33. Weill, *La cité de David.*

34. Ibid., 99–100, 186–90; last mentioned by Kloppenborg-Verbin, "Dating Theodotos," 243–280.

35. Weill, *La cité de David* II.

36. Macalister and Duncan, *Excavations of the Hill of Ophel;* and Thomas, "Success and Failure of R. A. S. Macalister," 33–36.

37. Crowfoot and Fitzgerald, *Excavations in the Tyropoeon Valley;* idem, "Ophel Again," 66–104.

38. Sukenik and Mayer, *Third Wall;* idem, "New Section of the Third Wall," 145–51. On the history of excavations conducted by Jewish scholars before the establishment of the State of Israel and after, see Reich, "Israel Exploration Society."

39. C. N. Johns, "Jerusalem: Ancient Street Levels," 97–100; Hamilton, "Street Levels in the Tyropoeon Valley" [1], 105–10; idem, "Street Levels in the Tyropoeon Valley" [2] 34–40; idem, "Excavations against the North Wall of Jerusalem," 1–26; idem, C. N. Johns, "Excavations at the Citadel," 127–31; idem, "The Citadel," 121–90.

40. See Kenyon's popular books: *Jerusalem: Excavating 3000 Years; Digging Up Jerusalem;* see also the first five final reports: Tushingham, *Excavations in Jerusalem* I; Franken and Steiner, *Excavations in Jerusalem* II; Steiner, *Excavations in Jerusalem* III; Eshel et al., *Excavations in Jerusalem* IV; Prag, *Excavations in Jerusalem* V.

41. See Seligman, "Antiquities Authority."

42. See the popular book: Avigad, *Discovering Jerusalem;* as well as the first three final reports that have appeared recently: Geva, *Jewish Quarter Excavations* I–III; Gutfeld, *Jewish Quarter Excavations* V.

43. See the popular books: B. Mazar, *Mountain of the Lord;* and Ben-Dov, *In the Shadow of the Temple;* see also the first four final reports: E. and B. Mazar, *Excavations in the South of the Temple Mount;* E. Mazar, *Temple Mount Excavations in Jerusalem* II–IV.

44. Amiran and Eitan, "Excavations in the Courtyard of the Citadel," 9–17.

45. Geva, "Excavations in the Citadel," 55–71.

46. Sivan and Solar, "Excavations in the Jerusalem Citadel," 168–76.

47. See the short report by Re'em, "Excavations in the Citadel 2000–2001," 7–15.

48. Broshi, "Along Jerusalem's Walls," 11–17.

49. Bahat and Broshi, "Jerusalem, Old City," 171–72.

50. Shiloh, *City of David* I; Ariel, *City of David* II; De Groot and Ariel, *City of*

*David* III; idem, *City of David* IV; idem, *City of David* V; Ariel, *City of David* VI; De Groot and Bernick-Greenberg, *City of David* VII a and VII b.

51. See their last report: Reich and Shukron, "The History of the Gihon Spring," 211–23.

52. See n. 70 in chapter 6 and discussion of the Madaba Map in chapter 8.

53. See n. 5 in chapter 4.

54. See discussion of churches from the fifth and sixth centuries in chapter 8.

55. de Vogüé, *Églises.*

56. Vincent and Abel, *Jérusalem nouvelle* II, 1–4.

57. Pringle, *Churches* I–IV.

58. See Vernoit, "Islamic Archaeology," 1.

59. Creswell, *Early Muslim Architecture*; Burgoyne, *Mamluk Jerusalem* (1987); Meinecke, *Mamlukische Architektur.*

60. Hawari, *Ayyubid Architecture.*

61. Auld and Hillenbrand, *Ottoman Jerusalem* I–II; Korn, *Ayyubidische Architektur.*

62. Cotton et al., *Corpus Inscriptionum I.1* and Cotton et al., *Corpus Inscriptionum I.2*; and van Berchem, *Corpus Inscriptionum Arabicarum.*

## Chapter 2. Natural and Built City Limits

1. The following publications are useful resources for studying the society, economy, and ecology of ancient Palestine and the Near East in general: Levy, *Archaeology of Society in the Holy Land*; Pastor, *Land and Economy in Ancient Palestine*; Issar and Zohar, *Climate Change*; and Hillel, *Natural History of the Bible.* However, the neglect of Jerusalem in this literature is astonishing. Contextual archaeological approaches are most widely used for the prehistoric periods, somewhat less for the Bronze and Iron Ages, and more rarely for the classical and postclassical periods. Furthermore, Jerusalem is only rarely considered independent of its larger regional context. In contrast to most recent excavations carried out in other parts of Israel and Jordan, field projects in Jerusalem have adopted a very traditional approach, only marginally going beyond conventional stratigraphical methods. Even in publications such as those of De Groot and Ariel, *City of David* III, 105–48; idem, *City of David* IV, 298–317; and Tushingham, *Excavations in Jerusalem* I, 252–56, scientific studies are relegated to the appendices without being evaluated or integrated into the general archaeological report. The first and only study so far countering this deficiency was conducted by R. Reich (archaeologist) and G. Bar (paleozoologist). Their analysis is devoted to a Herodian period dump. See Bouchnik et al., "Animal Bone Remains," 71–80 (Hebrew;

English summary, 50*); idem, "More Bones from the City Dump, 175–185 (40*–41*); idem, "Faunal Remains, 109–22 (16*); Reich and Bar-Oz, "The Jerusalem City Dump," 83–98 (14*–15*); Weiss et al., "A Dump Near the Temple?," 99–107 (15*). The aim of their pioneering work is to determine the diet of Jerusalem's inhabitants between the Iron Age and the Early Roman period.

2. Regarding the location: Dalman, *Jerusalem;* Simons, *Jerusalem in the Old Testament,* 6–26; Mare, *Archaeology,* 21–23.

3. See Dalman, *Jerusalem,* 21–151.

4. Archaeologists usually calculate 250 inhabitants per hectare (or per 2.5 acres), which corresponds to the average density coefficient in the premodern Near East. This estimate relies on an analogy between ancient and present-day settlements in traditional societies (the ethnoarchaeological method) as well as on an analysis of the layout of excavated sites; see Broshi, "Population of Western Palestine," 1–10; Finkelstein, "A Few Notes on Demographic Data," 47–52. It is commonly thought that biblical and postbiblical sources tend to supply inflated population numbers; see Byatt, "Josephus and Population Numbers," 56–58 (for Jerusalem); Broshi, "La population de l'ancienne Jérusalem," 5–14; idem, "Expansion of Jerusalem," 10–15. For additional discussion of population estimates and citations to the literature, see Tarler and Cahill, "David, City of," 65; Lipiński, *Itineraria Phoenicia,* 493–545; Asali, *Jerusalem in History,* 204; Peters, *Jerusalem,* 408, 564–65; Schölch, *Palästina im Umbruch,* 115; idem, "Jerusalem in the 19th Century," 228–48.

5. The first archaeological maps were drawn in the 1860s by the *Survey of Western Palestine.* The first accurate map with all known findspots appears in Kuemmel, *Karte der Materialien zur Topographie des alten Jerusalem* (1904), with a report in *Materialien zur Topographie* (1906); see more recently: Amiran, Shachar, and Kimhi, *Atlas of Jerusalem* (1973); Bahat, *Illustrated Atlas of Jerusalem* (1990). In 1992, Bieberstein drew Jerusalem maps I–III of the *Tübinger Atlas des Vorderen Orients,* B IV 7 (TAVO) and Map IV of that series in collaboration with Burgoyne; it was reprinted in Mittmann and Schmitt, *Tübinger Bibelatlas* (2001). For a simplified version, see Ben-Dov, *Historical Atlas of Jerusalem* (2002).

6. Avni, "Urban Limits," 373–96.


## Chapter 3. The Chalcolithic Period and the Bronze Age

1. Ahituv, *Canaanite Toponyms,* 122.

2. Knudtzon, *Die El-Amarna-Tafeln* I, 856–79 nos. 285–90.

3. See Mazar et al., "Cuneiform Tablet."

4. Liwak, "Israel und Juda," 55.
5. Relative chronologies after the Chalcolithic period are derived primarily from typological studies of pottery based on stratified assemblages in the region. The chronology of the Holy Land in the Bronze and Iron Ages is determined mainly by that of Egypt (A. Mazar, *Archaeology*, 28–29). Although various dates have been suggested for the beginning of the Bronze Age and the different sub-periods (such as Stager, "Periodization," I, 22–41; II, 17–60; King and Stager, *Life in Biblical Israel*, xxiii), we have adopted here the chronology of Stern, *New Encyclopedia* IV, 1529.
6. Franken, "Jerusalem in the Bronze Age," 17–41.
7. Kenyon, *Jerusalem: Excavating 3000 Years*, 19–25, 63–77.
8. Shiloh, *City of David* I, 11–15, 25–29.
9. Weill, *La cité de David*, 118–25.
10. Reich and Shukron, "On the History of the Gihon," 211–23.
11. Crowfoot and Fitzgerald, *Excavations in the Tyropoeon Valley*, 12–20; Alt, "Taltor von Jerusalem," 74–98 was the first to identify this gate with the Valley Gate mentioned in Neh 2:13.
12. Broshi and Gophna, "The Settlements and Populations of Palestine," 41–53; Zwickel, *Biblische Landes- und Altertumskunde*, 118.
13. Knauf, "Jerusalem in the Late Bronze and Early Iron Ages," 75–90.
14. Vincent and Steve, *Jérusalem* I, 260–64.
15. Cf. Reich, "On the History of the Gihon Spring," 330–33 (Hebrew; English summary, 83*).
16. Humbert de Dijon was the first Christian pilgrim to mention the well, in his travel report; see Kaeppeli and Benoit, "Un pèlerinage dominicain inédit du XIV$^i$ siècle," 532.
17. Channel II is covered by large fieldstones.
18. Rosen, "Flint Implements," 257–67.
19. Vincent, *Jérusalem sous terre*, 27–32.
20. Callaway, *Pottery*; Kenyon and Holland, *Excavations at Jericho* IV, 124–243, and, more generally, Amiran, *Ancient Pottery of the Holy Land*, 41–57; Weippert, *Palästina*, 148–54.

## Chapter 4. The Iron Age

1. For a recent survey of the history of the city from King David through the Six Day War, see Montefiore, *Jerusalem*.
2. The term "Jebusite" appears in the Bible and is meant to distinguish the original Canaanite inhabitants of the city from the conquering Israelites; see Hübner, "Jerusalem und die Jebusiter," 31–42.

3. Finkelstein, "Campaign of Shoshenq I," 109–35.

4. Traditionally, the expansion of the city towards the north occurred when Solomon erected the First Temple on top of Mount Moriah. According to recent reevaluations, however, the settlement may have spread north as early as the Late Bronze Age. See Knauf, "Jerusalem in the Late Bronze and Early Iron Ages," 75–90.

5. The paucity of archaeological remains has caused many in the field to argue that the importance attributed to Jerusalem of the time of King Solomon and the glory of the monarchy in general were based in a myth created hundreds of years later. The main proponent of this view (Finkelstein, "State Formation in Israel and Judah," 35–52; idem, "Rise of Jerusalem and Judah," 105–15; idem, "Campaign of Shoshenq I," 109–35; and Finkelstein and Silberman, *Bible Unearthed,* 21–24) is challenged by a majority of archaeologists, as his theory seems untenable from a literary point of view (e.g., Rainey, "Stones for Bread," 140–49; Cahill, "David's Jerusalem," 34–41, 63; idem, "Jerusalem at the Time of the United Monarchy," 13–80; idem, "Jerusalem in David and Solomon's Time," 20–31, 62–63; Dever, "Excavating the Hebrew Bible," 67–77; Vieweger, "Review," 1182–86; Na'aman, "Cow Town or Royal Capital?" 43–47, 67; Steiner, "It's Not There," 24–44, 63). Regarding the controversy over the chronology of the tenth–ninth centuries B.C.E. ("high" versus "low" chronology), Jerusalem does not provide any clear material evidence that would allow us to favor one theory over the other. E. Mazar's interpretations of her widely publicized recent excavations south of the Temple Mount ("Ophel") describing a Solomonic wall and on the Southeast Hill ("City of David") claiming the discovery of King David's palace, have not gained scholarly support. See E. Mazar, "Did I Find David's Palace?" 16–27, 70. In response see Finkelstein et al., "Has King David's Palace Been Found?," 142–64. See also E. Mazar, Solomonic Wall.

6. The gate that was expected to be found within the area of the southern protrusion could not be located.

7. Avigad identified his wall with the "Broad Wall," mentioned in the context of the reconstruction of the city's fortifications under Nehemiah (Neh 3:8). As mentioned above, however, the Broad Wall was already dismantled in the seventh century.

8. Avigad area A: Geva, *Jewish Quarter Excavations* I, 37–82.

9. Avigad area W: ibid., I, 131–59; Avigad area X-2: ibid., I, 199–215.

10. Kenyon area A: Kenyon, *Digging Up Jerusalem,* 144–49.

11. Shiloh areas E and D: Shiloh, *City of David* I, 7–15.

12. Reich and Shukron areas A, J, C, R: Reich and Shukron, "Excavations at the Gihon Spring," 327–39; idem, "System of Rock-cut Tunnels," 5–17; idem, "History of the Gihon," 211–23.

13. See Paul and Dever, *Biblical Archaeology*, 65–73.

14. Since the Temple has recently aroused renewed interest among scholars, in particular in discussions regarding the size of Jerusalem in the Late Bronze and Early Iron Ages, we feel obliged to at least marginally address the issue. For analogous material from other contemporary sites: Fritz, "Temple Architecture," 38–49 compares the Solomonic Temple as described in the biblical text to archaeological remains of temples uncovered in Syria and elsewhere in the Near East.

15. According to Laperrousaz, "Quelques résultats récents," 150–59, the wall section should be dated to the preexilic period; Dunand, "Byblos, Sidon, Jérusalem," 64–70 dates it to the Persian period; Tsafrir, "Location of the Seleucid Akra," 501–21 identifies it with the remains of the Akra.

16. Based on his detailed analysis of the biblical texts, Zwickel (*Salomonischer Tempel*, 55–71, pl. 4b) visually reconstructs the Solomonic temple — both its architectural components and furnishings.

17. See Fritz, "Temple Architecture," 38–49.

18. Abu 'Assaf, *Der Tempel von 'Ain Dara*; see also King and Stager, *Life in Biblical Israel*, 334–36.

19. Paul and Dever, *Biblical Archaeology*, 61, 73–77.

20. Shiloh, *City of David* I, 15–21.

21. On houses, see Shiloh, *City of David* I, "Four-Room House," 180–90; idem, "Casemate Wall," 3–15; Netzer, "Domestic Architecture," 193–201.

22. For the ceramics from Stratum II at Lachish, Stratum V at En Gedi, Stratum VI at Arad, and Stratum V at Ramat Rachel; see Shiloh, *City of David* I, 29.

23. The inscription was discovered in 1880 by a boy walking through the tunnel. It is now located in the Istanbul Archaeological Museum (inv. no. 2195).

24. When the Jews returned from the Babylonian exile, they brought with them the square Aramaic letters with which Hebrew is written to this day.

25. It is likely that the upper portion would have mentioned the king or some other sponsor of the project.

26. Hebrew *zdh* is perhaps 'cavity,' 'crack,' 'split,' or 'overlap'; the etymology and meaning are still disputed; see Lancaster and Long, "Where They Met," 15–26.

27. Younger, Jr., "Siloam Tunnel Inscription," 543–56; idem, "Shiloam Inscription," 145–46, no. 2.28; Amiran, "Water Supply," 78.

28. Herodotus, *History* III, 60.

29. Knauf, "Hezekiah or Manasseh?" 281–87.

30. In the first decade of the twentieth century, G. Dalman, director of the German Protestant Institute of Archaeology in Jerusalem, began the first tomb-survey in Silwan, but never published a report. Between 1968 and 1971, D. Ussishkin surveyed the entire area again: Ussishkin, *Village of Sil-*

*wan.* For a summary on Iron Age tombs see Barkay, *Necropolis of Jerusalem*, 195–232; regarding burial practices see Bloch-Smith, *Judahite Burial Practices.*

31. Barkay, *Ketef Hinnom*, 19–31.

32. Barkay and Kloner, "Jerusalem Tombs," 22–39.

33. Ibid., 29, 36; Barkay, "Burial Headrests," 48–50.

34. Keel, "Peculiar Headrests," 50–53; Keel et al., *Studien zu den Stempelsiegeln* II, 66–75.

35. Barkay and Kloner, "Jerusalem Tombs," 22–39.

36. An ornamental bone object in the form of a pomegranate with an inscription reading "Belonging to the Temp[le of YWHW]H, holy to the priests" was purchased by the Israel Museum in Jerusalem in 1989. It was believed to represent the only material evidence associated with Solomon's Temple. We did not include the artifact in our survey, as it has been proven to be a fake. See Goren et al., "Re-examination."

37. Shoham, "'Lmlk' Seal Impressions," 75–80; Avigad and Barkay, "'Lmlk' and Related Seal Impressions," 243–66. For recent lists of the distribution of these impressions, see Garfinkel, "2 Chr 11:5–10," 69–73; Vaughn, *Theology, History and Archaeology*, 185–97.

38. Gilbert-Peretz, "Ceramic Figurines," 29–41; Yezerski and Geva, "Iron Age II Clay Figurines," 63–84. For the changing interpretations of these figurines, see Holland, "Study of Palestinian Iron Age Baked Clay Figurines," 121–55.

39. On the differences between family and state religion and the evolving interrelationship throughout the history of Israelite religion, see Albertz, *History of Israelite Religion*, which includes references to earlier-held views and alternative theories; see also Keel and Küchler, *God and Goddeses.*

40. For the results of the Ketef Hinnom excavations, see Barkay, *Ketef Hinnom.*

41. The text and nature of the silver plaques are described in detail by Barkay, *Ketef Hinnom*, 29–31, and more recently, with revisions, Barkay et al., "Amulets from Ketef Hinnom," 41–71; see also Jaroš, *Die ältesten Fragmente.*

## Chapter 5. The Babylonian and Persian Periods

1. Regarding the status of the province, see also the discussions by Sacchi, "L'esilio," 131–48; idem, "Re vassalli," 147–52; and Na'aman, "Royal Vassals or Governors?" 35–44.

2. The discussion regarding the exact date (587 or 586 B.C.E.) depends on how the beginning of the kingship is calculated. We follow here Galil (*Chronology*, 108–18), who comments on this extensively.

3. Ackroyd, "The Jewish Community in Palestine," 160–1.

4. In 1996 the temple in Elephantine, Egypt was discovered by C. von Pilgrim; see his summary "Tempel des Jahu," 303–317, and Rosenberg, "The Jewish Temple," 4–13.

5. Sachau, *Drei aramäische Papyrusurkunden*, no. 1; Cowley, *Aramaic Papyri*, 108–26, nos. 30–33; Porten, "Jews in Egypt," 390; Modrzejewski, *Jews of Egypt*.

6. See discussion of fortifications in chapters 3 and 4.

7. Kenyon area A: Kenyon, *Digging Up Jerusalem*, 183–84. Shiloh area G: Shiloh, *City of David* I, 20–21.

8. Crowfoot and Fitzgerald, *Excavations in the Tyropoeon Valley*, 12–23.

9. Clermont-Ganneau, *Archaeological Researches* I, 239–46.

10. Dunand, "Byblos, Sidon, Jérusalem, 69–70.

11. For a complete study of Persian seals and seal impressions, see Stern, *Material Culture*, 196–214.

12. On the various coins, see Stern, *Material Culture*, 217–35; on the *yhd* coins, see Meshorer, *Ancient Jewish Coinage* I, 13–34.

## Chapter 6. The Hellenistic Period

1. In contrast to the chronological division used by the *New Encyclopedia* IV, 1529, we include the Herodian period within the Hellenistic sequence of rulers; Herod and other members of his dynasty adopted the cultural and artistic traditions of other Late Hellenistic rulers. Since it is the material remains that constitute the primary focus of this volume, the present chronology is not based on the political events of the city.

2. Hengel, *Judaism and Hellenism*; idem, "Interpenetration of Judaism and Hellenism," 167–228; Feldman, "How Much Hellenism?" 83–111; Hayes and Mandell, *Jewish People*; Sacchi, *History*, 214–49; regarding Jerusalem specifically, see: Hengel, "Jerusalem als jüdische und hellenistische Stadt," 269–306.

3. Will, "Succession to Alexander," 23–61; idem, "Formation of the Hellenistic Kingdoms," 101–17; Walbank, "Monarchies," 62–100.

4. Regarding the Ptolemaic and Seleucid dynasties and the wars between them, see Turner, "Ptolemaic Egypt," 118–74; Musti, "Syria," 175–220; Heinen, "Syrian-Egyptian Wars," 412–45; regarding Palestine, see Hengel, "Political and Social History," 35–78.

5. Bickerman, "La charte séleucide," 4–35 [*Studies* II, 44–85].

6. The Jews in the ancient Diaspora were literate (spoke, read, and wrote) in Greek. See Levine, *Jerusalem*, 270–76.

7. Schürer, *History* I, 125–63; on Antiochus IV, see Mørkholm, "Antiochus IV," 278–91.

8. Schürer, *History* I, 146–54; Levine, *Jerusalem*, 75–78.

9. Schürer, *History* I, 155.

10. Ibid., 155–73; Millar, "Background to the Maccabean Revolution," 1–21; Bickerman, *God of the Maccabees*; Bar Kochva, *Judas Maccabaeus*; Sievers, *Hasmoneans and Their Supporters*; Sacchi, *History*, 250–83; Levine, *Jerusalem*, 78–82.

11. The Jewish festival of Hanukkah commemorates these events.

12. Schürer, *History* I, 174–88.

13. Ibid., 219–28.

14. The Pharisees, generally hostile to the Hasmoneans, briefly attained an influential position under the devout Queen Salome Alexandra (76–67 B.C.E.).

15. Schürer, *History* I, 243–53.

16. Judaea: namely, at this time, the central hill country and desert, Jerusalem, and the coastal plain.

17. The city was destroyed on the eighth of Elul (September 26th). This date does not correspond exactly to the date of the destruction of the First Temple mentioned in the biblical account. The destruction of the First Temple is reported to have taken place on the seventh (2 Kgs 25:8–9) or tenth day of the fifth month (Jer 52:12–13, cf. Josephus, *Ant.* X, 135; *War* V, 250). The attack on the Temple Mount began on the eighth of Lous (Av) and ended on the tenth (*War* VI, 220–270). The combined data led rabbis to converge on the ninth of Av. See discussions in Babylonian Talmud, Ta'anit 29a; Mishnah, Ta'anit 4, 6; Tosefta, Ta'anit 4, 10.

18. Pfanner, *Titusbogen*. According to the inscription on the arch, it was erected after the death of Titus.

19. Crowfoot, "Excavations on Ophel" [1], 156–66.

20. Geva, "The First Wall," 724–29. Mazar and Eshel ("Who Built the First Wall of Jerusalem?," 263–68) date the wall to the first half of the second century, as they assume it preceded the gymnasium, which they locate in west Jerusalem in the newly built Israeli section of the city. This assumption, however, contradicts Josephus (*Ant.* XII, 241), who locates it underneath the Akra, that is, on the Southeast Hill, within the city wall. For a good overview on Hellenistic fortifications, see McNicoll and Milner, *Hellenistic Fortifications*.

21. Avigad area W: Geva, *Jewish Quarter Excavations* I, 131–97, 241–42.

22. Avigad area X-2: Geva, *Jewish Quarter Excavations* I, 199–242.

23. C. N. Johns, "Citadel, Jerusalem," 122–52; Re'em, "Excavations in the Citadel 2000–2001," 7–15.

24. Bliss and Dickie, *Excavations at Jerusalem*, 14–47, 83–100, 128–31, 312–29. The later excavations, conducted by B. Pixner, were limited to the area of the

Essene Gate; he identified the Byzantine gate as the Herodian gate, which completely defied the archaeological evidence; see Pixner, Chen, and Margalit, "Mount Zion," 85–95; Pixner, "History of the 'Essene Gate' Area," 96–104.

25. Zelinger's "Yehiel." Zelinger, "Jerusalem, the Slopes of Mount Zion."

26. The Second Wall was certainly pre-Herodian, since Josephus (*Ant.* XIV, 476) describes how Herod had to overcome the obstacle of both walls to conquer the city in 37 B.C.E.

27. The wall would have run east of the Golgotha hill, since Herodian period tombs can be attested in this area. In other words, this section was extramural at the time of Jesus's crucifixion.

28. Robinson, *Biblical Researches* I, 465–67; Robinson, *Later Biblical Researches*, 179–80.

29. Sukenik and Mayer, *Third Wall of Jerusalem*.

30. Hamrick, "Northern Barrier Wall," 213–32.

31. Ben-Arieh and Netzer, "Excavations along the 'Third Wall,'" 97–107.

32. Tzaferis et al., "Jerusalem, the Third Wall," 130–33.

33. See discussion in this chapter, under Necropolis.

34. Jewish barrier wall: Hamrick, "Northern Barrier Wall," 213–32; Roman barrier wall: Kenyon, "Letters to the Editor," 265–66; McNulty, "North Wall," 141–44.

35. Vincent, "Encore la troisième enceinte," 90–126; Vincent and Steve, *Jérusalem* I, 146–74; Hubbard, "Topography," 133–35, 149–51.

36. Fischer, "Die Mauern und Tore," 233–43.

37. Schmitt, "Die dritte Mauer Jerusalems," 153–70; and more recently stated by Augustin, "Die dritte Mauer Jerusalems," 23–43. Levine, *Jerusalem*, 315–18 summarizes the different views regarding the location of the Third Wall.

38. Geva, "The Acra," 723–24. It is rather surprising that Josephus, *Ant.* XII, 252 does not mention the earlier construction; see also Sievers, "Jerusalem, the Akra, and Josephus," 195–209.

39. Wightman, "Temple Fortresses in Jerusalem, Part I, 29–40 and "Temple Fortresses in Jerusalem, Part II," 7–35; Murphy-O'Connor, "Where was the Antonia Fortress?" 78–89; Levine, *Jerusalem*, 194–96; Netzer, *Architecture of Herod*, 120–26.

40. Since Mark Antony was defeated by Augustus in the Battle of Actium in 31 B.C.E., and soon after committed suicide, the naming would have occurred before this date.

41. Theoderich, Guide 4; see Wilkinson, *Jerusalem Pilgrimage*, 278.

42. The discussion regarding the Herodian extension of the Antonia by L.-H. Vincent and Marie Aline de Sion was convincingly refuted by Benoit, "L'Antonie," 135–67.

43. Compare with the western wall of the Temple Mount, located slightly further south, and the Herodian construction in Hebron at the Tomb of Abraham and at Mambre; see Roller, *Building Program*, 162–64, 186–88; Lichtenberger, *Baupolitik*, 143–49; Japp, *Baupolitik*, 112–14, 138–39.

44. See discussion in chapter 7, under Arched Gateways.

45. On the Hasmonean palace, see Pixner, "Trial of Jesus," 66–80; on the Herodian palace, see Roller, *Building Program*, 176, 180; Lichtenberger, *Baupolitik*, 93–98. The remains of one of the three towers protecting Herod's palace in Jerusalem can be seen in the Citadel near Jaffa Gate. See fig. 12.3.

46. Bahat, "Herodian Temple," 38–58.

47. For Herod's building policy, see Roller, *Building Program*; Lichtenberger, *Baupolitik*, 131–42; Japp, *Baupolitik*; Netzer, *Architecture of Herod*, 137–78.

48. For a historical overview, see Avni and Seligman, *Temple Mount*. For an architectural study, see Ritmeyer, *The Quest*, 232–400. For the underground areas, see Gibson and Jacobson, *Temple Mount*.

49. The easternmost Single Gate is a later addition. On Hulda: Mishnah, Middot 1, 3 (see note 52).

50. Shani and Chen, "On the Umayyad Dating of the Double Gate," 1–40.

51. The stairs were excavated by Benjamin Mazar beginning in 1968. See Mountain of the Lord, 130; 140–48.

52. References to rabbinic literature are kept here to a minimum. Regarding the use of rabbinic literature in the study of Second Temple Jerusalem, see Levine, *Jerusalem*, 349–50.

53. For excavations conducted by Mazar that exposed the pillar and overpass, refuting the original interpretation of the arch, see B. Mazar, *Mountain of the Lord*, 132. Y. Billig and R. Reich exposed a significant segment of the street below the overpass; see Reich and Billig, "Excavations along the Western Wall," 41–44, and Reich and Billig, "Robinson's Arch." They determined that the road was planned as part of Herod's general building program of the Temple Mount. It was paved, however, only in the last generation before the destruction of the city in 70 C.E. The city's primary north–south artery ran 100 meters west and parallel to the street below the overpass. It served as one of the major commercial hubs used by the local population and visiting pilgrims. See Weksler-Bdoalh et al., "Western Wall Plaza Excavations." For the southern continuation of the parallel street, see Reich, "The Dung Gate Area."

54. Wilson and Warren, *Recovery of Jerusalem*, 15–16, 111–14.

55. Ibid., 16–17, 76–94.

56. Vincent and Steve, *Jérusalem* II–III, 552–53, 568.

57. Mare, *Archaeology*, 158.

58. Ådna, *Jerusalemer Tempel*.

59. Kaufman, "Where the Ancient Temple of Jerusalem Stood," 40–59.

60. Josephus, *War* V, 194; VI, 125 tells us that the Greek inscriptions alternated with Latin inscriptions, however none in Latin has survived.

61. Fry, *Warning Inscriptions;* Segal, "Penalty of the Warning Inscription," 79–84.

62. The Jewish Quarter excavations were conducted by N. Avigad between 1969 and 1978; see Avigad, *Discovering Jerusalem;* idem, *Herodian Quarter;* Geva, *Jewish Quarter Excavations* I–III.

63. Avigad area E: Avigad, *Discovering Jerusalem,* 83–88 and Geva, *Jewish Quarter Excavations* III.

64. Avigad area M: Avigad, *Discovering Jerusalem,* 193–94.

65. Avigad area P: ibid., 95–120.

66. Avigad area B: ibid., 120–39.

67. Galor, "Roman-Byzantine Dwelling," 17–34; Galor, "Domestic Architecture," 44–57.

68. Hachlili, *Ancient Jewish Art and Archaeology,* 65–71; Avigad, *Discovering Jerusalem,* 144–50.

69. Since Reich's seminal study on *miqva'ot* of the Second Temple Period, the corpus of 800 pools identified as ritual baths has doubled in size; see Amit, "'Jerusalem' *Miqva'ot,*" 35–48; Reich, *Miqwa'ot* (unfortunately unpublished).

70. The stepped pool, popularly referred to as the "Siloam Pool," was uncovered on the Southeast Hill, and may have functioned as a ritual pool. Major remodeling occurred during the Byzantine period. Reich, "The Pool of Siloam."

71. A. Mazar, "Survey of the Aqueducts to Jerusalem," 210–44.

72. Jerusalem Talmud, Yoma 41a; Babylonian Talmud, Yoma 31a; Babylonian Talmud, Zevahim 54b; Lamentations Rabbah 4, 4.

73. The most comprehensive study on burials was published by Kloner and Zissu (*Necropolis,* 2007). Relevant in this context are also Rahmani, *Catalogue of Jewish Ossuaries;* and Hachlili, *Jewish Funerary Customs.* For an excellent study of Jerusalem's necropolis during late antiquity, see Avni, "Urban Limits," 373–96.

74. Schick, "New Discoveries," 198–200; Netzer, *Architecture of Herod,* 132–4; Kloner and Zissu, *Necropolis,* 469–70. We accept Netzer's identification as Herod's Family Tomb.

75. Avigad, *Ancient Monuments,* 37–78; Barag, "The 2000–2001 Exploration of the Tombs," 78–95, 104–10; Kloner and Zissu, *Necropolis,* 243–45 no. 6-3.

76. Jotham-Rothschild, "Tombs of Sanhedria" [1], 23–38; idem, "Tombs of Sanhedria" [2], 16–22; Rahmani, "Jewish Rock-Cut Tombs," 93–104; Kloner and Zissu, *Necropolis,* 407–24.

77. Avigad, "Jewish Rock-Cut Tombs," 119–25, no. 1 (Hebrew; English summary, 72*); Kloner and Zissu, *Necropolis,* 179–81 no. 2-[5–9].

78. Avigad, *Ancient Monuments*, 79–90; Kloner and Zissu, *Necropolis*, 246 no. 6-4.

79. Avigad, *Ancient Monuments*, 91–133; Kloner and Zissu, *Necropolis*, 242–43 no. 6-2.

80. de Saulcy, *Voyage en Terre Sainte* II, 206–10; Vincent and Steve, *Jérusalem* I, 146–74; Hachlili, *Funerary Customs*, 36–37, 120–26; Kloner and Zissu, *Necropolis*, 231–34 no. 5-1.

81. The tomb was so famous that it was mentioned in the second century C.E. by Pausanias, *Description of Greece* VIII, 16:5, and again in the fourth century C.E. by Eusebius, *Ecclesiastical History* II, 12:3.

82. Rahmani, "Jason's Tomb," 61–100; Kloner and Zissu, *Necropolis*, 389–91 no. 23-3.

83. Vincent and Steve, *Jérusalem* I, 342–6; Kloner and Zissu, *Necropolis*, 356–57 no. 14-1. The identification with Herod's Family Tomb is not convincing for us; see above note 74.

84. See Rahmani, *Catalogue of Jewish Ossuaries;* corpus-like catalogues of oother collections are still lacking.

85. Reich, "Ossuary Inscriptions from the Caiaphas Tomb"; Horbury, "Caiaphas"; and VanderKam, *From Joshua to Caiaphas*, 426–37 no. 37.

86. Wilkinson, "Stone Tables," 7–21.

87. Magen, *Stone Vessel Industry*; Avigad, *Discovering Jerusalem*, 125–27.

88. See Hershkovitz, "Jerusalemite Painted Pottery," 31–34.

89. Avigad, *Discovering Jerusalem*, 117, 185–86.

90. Ibid., 107–17. Only a few isolated vessels of this type are known; one is in the Eretz Israel Museum, Tel Aviv, the other one is in the Metropolitan Museum of Art, New York.

91. See Levine, *Jerusalem*, 395.

92. According to Levine, *Jerusalem*, 272–73, the inscription indicates an established Diaspora community of pilgrims within the city of Jerusalem. See also Levine, *Ancient Synagogue*, 52–58; Kloppenborg Verbin, "Dating Theodotos," 243–80.

## Chapter 7. The Roman Period

1. Schäfer, "Hadrian's Policy in Judaea," 281–303.

2. Isaac, "Roman Colonies in Judaea," 31–54.

3. Isaac, "Cassius Dio," 68–76.

4. Smallwood, *Jews under Roman Rule*, 439–40.

5. Ibid., 428–66; Schäfer, *Der Bar Kokhba-Aufstand;* idem, *Bar Kokhba War Reconsidered*.

6. Mildenberg, "Bar Kochba in Jerusalem?" 1–6; idem, *Coinage of the Bar Kokhba War*.

7. Bowersock, "Roman Perspective on the Bar Kochba War," 131–41.

8. Lifshitz, "Jérusalem," 444–89. Geva, "Aelia Capitolina," 759–66.

9. Archaeological remains of the wall between New Gate and Damascus Gate: Vincent, "Troisième enceinte," 532–35; remains were uncovered west and east of Herod's Gate: idem, "Troisième enceinte," 101–106, as well as in a recent excavation carried out ca. 120 meters east of the gate. See Avni, Baruch, and Weksler-Bdolah, "Jerusalem," 76*–79*, and Baruch and Zissu, "Jerusalem," [20 March 2006]. The walls are mentioned by the Bordeaux Pilgrim, 593–94.

10. Wilson, "Camp of the Tenth Legion," 138–44 [*Golgotha*, 142–48]; Lifshitz, "Jérusalem sous la domination romaine," 469–70; Tsafrir, "Jerusalem," 547; Geva, "Camp of the Tenth Legion," 239–54; Isaac, "Roman Army in Jerusalem," 635–40; Zangenberg, "Aelia Capitolina," 33–52; Burger, "Madaba Map," 33–45; Belayche, "Du Mont du Temple au Golgotha," 387–413.

11. Tushingham, *Excavations in Jerusalem* I, 60–61, figs. 66–67, pl. 119.

12. Bar, "Aelia Capitolina," 8–19.

13. E. Mazar, *Complete Guide*, 66–68.

14. Mazar, "Hadrian's Legion."

15. Shaikh Badr (Givat Ram): Arubas and Goldfus, "Kilnworks," 95–107; Khirbat Salih (Ramat Rahel): Aharoni, *Ramat Rahel* I–II. On the stamp tiles, see Barag, "Brick Stamp-Impressions," 244–67; Adler, "Brick and Tile Stamp Impressions," 117–32.

16. Many Roman cities in the East had only one major thoroughfare running from north to south. See, for example, the street networks in Hippos and Gadara; see Hoffmann and Kerner, *Gadara, Gerasa*, 9–12 (Gerasa), 119–24 (Gadara), and Segal, "Horbat Susita," 13*–17* (Hippos).

17. For excavation of decumanus, see Abu Riya, "Jerusalem," 134–35; Gershuny, "Jerusalem," 135–36. For excavation of cardo, see Weksler-Bdolah et al., "Jerusalem."

18. Excavated in 1937–38 by Hamilton, "North Wall," 1–26, and in 1964–66 by Hennessy, "Damascus Gate," 22–27; the final report by Wightman, *Damascus Gate;* excavated again in 1979–84 by Magen, "Roman Jerusalem," 48–56, and "Damascus Gate," 281–86; see also Geva and Bahat, "Damascus Gate Area," 223–35; on the arches of Jerusalem, see Arnould, *Arcs romains.*

19. Other than Magness, "North Wall," 328–39, who suggests that the Hadrianic city extended north of the present-day Damascus Gate, scholars agree that the triple-arched gateway marked the northernmost limit of Aelia Capitolina.

20. See the very convincing arguments in favor of this theory in Eliav, "Urban

Layout," 241–77; for a more recent version of this publication, see idem, *God's Mountain*, 94–124.

21. Avni, "Urban Limits," 377. On the differences between Roman and Byzantine period tombs, see Avni and Greenhut, *Akeldama Tombs*.

22. Nock, "Cremation and Burial," 321–59; Morris, *Death-ritual*, 56–60.

23. Citadel: Johns, "Citadel, Jerusalem," 153, 156. Armenian Quarter: see description in this chapter under Camp of the Tenth Legion. Jewish Quarter: Avigad, *Discovering Jerusalem*, 205–7.

24. Arubas and Goldfus, "Kilnworks," 95–107.

25. B. Mazar, *Mountain of the Lord*, 215; Peleg: "Roman Marble Sculpture," 129–49.

26. Ibid., 133–36, no. A2.

27. On Roman board games see Bell, *Board and Table Games*, 30–32; and more recently Hübner, *Spiele und Spielzeug*, 77–78.

## Chapter 8. The Byzantine Period

1. The most important sources come from the anonymous Bordeaux Pilgrim (333 C.E.), Egeria (ca. 400 C.E.), Jerome (404 C.E.), the archdeacon Theodosius (518–530 C.E.), the Breviarius of Jerusalem (ca. 550 C.E.), the anonymous Piacenza Pilgrim (ca. 570 C.E.), and the Bishop Arculf (ca. 680 C.E.); see Wilkinson, *Jerusalem Pilgrims*.

2. See Kaplony, *Haram*, 23–31.

3. Antiochus of Mar Saba, *Prise de Jérusalem* 23; Eutychius, *Annales* 268. Cf. Schick, *Christian Communities*, 20–48.

4. See Donner, *Mosaic Map*; Piccirillo and Alliata, *Madaba Map*.

5. This underlying orientation is embedded in the very words used in biblical Hebrew for *east*, literally, "in front of" (Gen 12:8); *west*, "behind" (ibid.); *north*, "on the left hand" (Gen 14:15); and *south*, "on the right hand" (1 Sam 23:24). See Harley and Woodward, *History of Cartography*, 113–14.

6. Mentioned only by the excavators Kenyon and E. Mazar.

7. Bliss and Dickie, *Excavations at Jerusalem*, 85–96, 314–15, 325–29.

8. Ibid., 14–47, 83–100, 128–31, 312–29. Regarding the new excavations by Y. Zelinger, see Zelinger, "Jerusalem, the Slopes of Mount Zion" (2010).

9. Hamilton, "Excavations against the North Wall of Jerusalem," 1–26.

10. Krautheimer, *Early Christian and Byzantine Architecture*, 23–37.

11. For an overview, see Tsafrir, "Jerusalem," 525–615; ibid., "Ecclesiastical Architecture."

12. Ibid.

13. Vincent and Abel, *Bethléem*; Richmond, "Church of the Nativity," 63–66;

Freeman-Grenville, *Basilica of the Nativity*. The conventional reconstruction of the Constantinian basilica features an octagonal structure at the church's eastern end. The archaeological data, however, support a polygonal apse; see Weber-Dellacroce and Weber, "'Dort, wo sich Gottes Volk versammelt,'" 251 and fig. 7, based on Richmond, "Church of the Nativity," 63–72. It should be emphasized that the present church — despite frequent references in scholarly and popular literature — does not date to the reign of Justinian (527–565 C.E.), but rather to the second half of the fifth century C.E. The church is neither mentioned by Procopius, nor is the architectural decoration (capitals and friezes) typical of the time of Justinian. See Restle, "Bethlehem," 601–12, more recently supported by Weiland, "Die Kapitelle," 813–27 (regarding the "wrong" date, see esp. 816–17).

14. Most likely only completed during the reign of Constantine's sons.

15. In contrast to Eusebius's description, some of the decorative elements were reused from the destroyed temple.

16. Given the topographical conditions, the church is oriented to the west.

17. Although in most churches the apse is oriented to the east, here, building constraints and the location of the basilica in relation to the tomb guided the orientation of the apse.

18. The literature regarding the church is endless; see Bieberstein and Bloedhorn, *Jerusalem* II, 186–216; Corbo, *Santo Sepolcro* I–III (excavation reports, 1950s–1970s; and Corbo's later report, "Santo Sepolcro," 391–422. See also Patrich, "Early Church of the Holy Sepulchre," 101–17; Broshi, "Excavations in the Holy Sepulchre," 118–22; as well as the recent monograph by Krüger, *Grabeskirche*.

19. The empress Helena arrived only after construction had already begun in Jerusalem. Eusebius, a contemporary witness, mentions the dedications of the Church of the Nativity in Bethlehem and the Eleona Church. The connection between the construction of the church on top of the holy tomb and Helena is not made before Ambrosius's eulogy for Theodosius I (395 C.E.), which mentions the legendary discovery of the Cross.

20. Vincent, "Les récentes fouilles d'Ophel" [1], 219–65.

21. The Jerusalem bishops and patriarchs were buried beside the crypt, in a previously Herodian tomb.

22. The report of the pilgrim Arculf was written by Abbot Adomnan, *The Holy Places* (ed. Wilkinson, *Jerusalem Pilgrims*, 93–116; regarding the Imbomon, see ibid., 100–101; 194, pl. 2). Only a very small part of the foundations of the outer wall was discovered; see Corbo, *Ricerche*, 135–49.

23. Pixner, "Church of the Apostles," 30–34. The map shows the Crusader church; the Byzantine church was 14 meters shorter on the west side.

24. Corbo, *Ricerche*, 3–49.

25. Vincent and Abel, *Jérusalem nouvelle* II/4, 1007–13.

26. Ibid., II/4, 860–64.

27. Ibid., II/4, 673–84.

28. Clermont-Ganneau, *Archaeological Researches* I, 332–34; Vincent and Abel, *Jérusalem nouvelle* II/4, 929.

29. Vincent and Abel, *Jérusalem nouvelle* II/4, 745–65.

30. Ibid., II/4, 845–52, 968; Stutchbury, "Excavations in the Kidron Valley," 101–13.

31. Vincent and Abel, *Jérusalem nouvelle* II/4, 855–60, 872–74.

32. Pixner, "Pit of Jeremiah," 118–21, 148.

33. Vincent and Abel, *Jérusalem nouvelle* II/4, 866–68, 966.

34. Avner, Lavas, and Rosidis, "Jerusalem, Mar Elias," 89*–92*.

35. Schick, "Discovery of a Beautiful Mosaic Pavement," 257–60 (St. Polyeuctus); Baramki, "Byzantine Remains," 56–58 (unidentified chapel); Tzaferis, Feig, Onn, and Shukron, "Excavations at the Third Wall," 287–92; Amit and Wolff, "An Armenian Monastery," 293–98. Because of the limited excavation areas, the relationship between the complexes that have been exposed is not always clear; see Reich, "Ancient Burial Ground," 111–18, esp. 117–18; Reich and Shukron, "Western Extramural Quarter of Byzantine Jerusalem," 193–201.

36. Vincent and Abel, *Jérusalem nouvelle* II/4, 911, 928, 966. On the new excavation by G. Barkay, see his *Ketef Hinnom*, 13.

37. Avigad, *Discovering Jerusalem*, 229–46.

38. Avigad, "Building Inscription," 145–51.

39. Crowfoot and Fitzgerald, *Excavations in the Tyropoeon Valley*, 27–55; Crowfoot, "Ophel Again," 74.

40. B. Mazar, *Mountain of the Lord*, 244–60; Ben-Dov, *In the Shadow of the Temple*, 243–59; E. Mazar, *Temple Mount Excavations* II. E. Mazar's supposed "Monastery of the Virgins" in Area XV is not confirmed by archaeological or literary sources.

41. Regarding the earthquakes, see Amiran, Arieh, and Turcotte, "Earthquakes," 260–305, esp. 266–67.

42. Reich and Shukron, "The Western Extramural Quarter of Byzantine Jerusalem," 193–201.

43. Avni, "Urban Limits," 373–96.

44. Vincent, "Tombeau des prophètes," 72–88.

45. Avni, "Urban Limits," 379.

46. Tzaferis et al., "Excavations at the Third Wall," 287–92; Amit and Wolff, "Armenian Monastery," 293–98.

47. Iliffe, "Cemeteries and a 'Monastery,'" 70–80.

48. Avni and Greenhut, *Akeldama Tombs*.

49. Avni, "Urban Limits," 379–80.

50. Ibid., 381.

51. For a complete catalogue on Jerusalem mosaics, see Avi-Yonah, "Mosaic Pavements," 162–78 [= *Art in Ancient Palestine*, 309–25]; A. and R. Ovadiah, *Hellenistic, Roman and Early Byzantine Mosaic Pavements*, 77–87.

52. Brandenburg, "Christussymbole," 74–138.

53. In addition to the Jerusalem workshop, A. and R. Ovadiah (*Hellenistic, Roman and Early Byzantine Mosaic Pavements*, 179–82) identify three more in ancient Palestine: in Gaza, Sycomina (Shiqmona), and Scythopolis (Bet Shean).

54. On the discovery of the chapel with the mosaic, see Vincent, "Une mosaïque byzantine," 436–44; idem, "Une mosaïque d'Orphée," 100–103. See also Ovadiah and Mucznik, "Orpheus from Jerusalem," 152–66.

55. Piccirillo and Israeli, "Architecture and Liturgy," 48–113.

56. Israeli, "Christian Images," 114–65.

## Chapter 9. The Early Islamic Period

1. The Christian and Muslim chronologies do not offer the same date for the conquest of Jerusalem.

2. For recent publications on the Early Islamic period, especially its history, see Elad, *Medieval Jerusalem*; Prawer and Ben-Shammai, *History of Jerusalem*.

3. For a succinct and in-depth summary of the first decades of Muslim rule in Jerusalem, see Grabar, *Shape of the Holy*, 44–51. In order to avoid confusion we are using here *Haram* or *Haram al-Sharif* for the whole area and *al-Aqsa* or *al-Jami al-Aqsa* only for the congregational mosque at the southern end.

4. The provincial capital during the Umayyad period was the newly founded city of Ramla; the seat of the caliphate at this time was in Damascus.

5. Goitein, "Historical Background," 104–8; Busse, "Tempel, Grabeskirche und Haram al-Sharif," 1–27; Rosen-Ayalon, *Early Islamic Monuments*; Raby and Johns, *Bayt al-Maqdis* I and Johns, *Bayt al-Maqdis* II. More generally, on the artistic climate of the period, see Ettinghausen and Grabar, *Art and Architecture of Islam*, 17–25; and R. Hillenbrand, *Islamic Architecture*.

6. A very useful description of Fatimid Jerusalem appears in Grabar, *Shape of the Holy*, 135–69.

7. van Ess, *Chiliastische Erwartungen*; Halm, "Der Treuhänder Gottes," 11–72.

8. The destruction began on Safar 5, A.H. 400/September 28, 1009 C.E. In the same year St. Mary in Damascus and, shortly after, St. Mary and St. Cosmas in Cairo were destroyed; in the following year, the monastery al-Qusair near Cairo, St. Mary in Damiette, St. George in Lydda, in Fustat the Mu'allaqa and Mar Shanuda, and one of the churches in the Raya Monastery in Suez.

9. In addition, the rotunda was enclosed from the eastern side. The renovation began in 1033 C.E.; the inauguration took place in 1048 C.E.

10. The others occurred in A.H. 407/1016 C.E. and A.H. 460/1068 C.E. See also Amiran, Arieh, and Turcotte, "Earthquakes," 268–69.

11. See chapter 7.

12. For a complete and detailed historical and architectural documentation of the Haram area between 324 and 1099 C.E., see Kaplony, *Haram.*

13. Regarding the conscious decision of the Marwanid caliphs to erect the Dome of the Rock on the site of the former Temple, see Grabar, "Space and Holiness," 275–86; Kaplony, *Haram,* 38–48.

14. As "large beams" would be far too heavy to be supported by "planks" we suggest that Adomnan's *tabulae* refer to the decorated panels applied to the pillars.

15. On the two concurrent conceptions, one considering only the southern building as a mosque, the other the entire platform, see Kaplony, *Haram,* 32–37.

16. Regarding the historical, political, and religious reasons for the construction of the Dome of the Rock, see Grabar, "Umayyad Dome of the Rock," 33–62; Kaplony, *Haram,* 294–97, 473–96, 677–713.

17. On the different gates, see Kaplony, *Haram,* 330–33.

18. Columns, including bases and capitals, were spolia from Roman and Byzantine structures. See Wilkinson, *Column Capitals.*

19. On the physical and symbolic significance of the rock, see Kaplony, *Haram,* 346–63

20. This diameter is identical to the one in the Anastasis rotunda. See also Kaplony, *Haram,* 363–69.

21. For a detailed description of the various building phases, see Kaplony, *Haram,* 313–70, 497–536, 714–58.

22. See chapter 8. On the Dome of the Rock's inspiration from Christian martyria, see Grabar, "Umayyad Dome of the Rock," 240–41. Another inspiration for the octagonal plan of the Dome of the Rock may have been the recently excavated Kathisma church, half-way between Jerusalem and Bethlehem, where, according to tradition, Mary rested; see Avner, Lavas, and Rosidis, "Jerusalem, Mar Elias," 89*–92*.

23. On the importance of the mosaic decoration and inscriptions inside the Umayyad structure, see Grabar, "Umayyad Dome of the Rock," 241–50.

24. Busse, "Arabische Inschriften," 8–24; Rosen-Ayalon, *Early Islamic Monuments,* 16.

25. For a complete description and a theological analysis of the decoration, see especially Rosen-Ayalon, *Early Islamic Monuments,* 46–69. Grabar's interpretation of the decoration in the Dome of the Rock was recently criticized by Busse, "Oleg Grabar," 93–103.

26. Grabar, *Shape of the Holy*, 130–32; Kaplony, *Haram*, 298–307, 482–85.

27. The presence of the mihrab was mentioned in the tenth century; see Le Strange, *Palestine under the Moslems*, 151–53.

28. Rosen-Ayalon, "Early Source," 184–85.

29. See in this chapter Adomnan's description, under Religious Architecture.

30. Küchler, "Moschee und Kalifenpaläste," 120–43.

31. On the role of the mosque in its larger historical, religious, architectural, and art-historical framework, see Grabar, *Formation of Islamic Art*, 99–131.

32. The renovation was necessary after the earthquake of July 1927; Hamilton ("Once Again the Aqsa," 141–44) revised his original chronology, which appeared in Hamilton's *Structural History*.

33. Regarding the construction of the mosque, see Grabar, *Shape of the Holy*, 117-22 and Kaplony, *Haram*, 371-82.

34. On the Fatimid structure, see Kaplony, *Haram*, 770–89.

35. The excavations were conducted by B. Mazar and are described by Ben-Dov, "Omayyad Structures," 37–44; Ben-Dov, "Building Techniques," 75–91, 24*–25*; cf. now Bahat's overview, "Physical Infrastructure," 70–73. The "missing" Building I is the Aqsa Mosque; cf. the first map in Ben-Dov, "Omayyad Structures," 38.

36. Creswell, *Early Muslim Architecture*, 48.

37. Unfortunately, Ben-Dov never revised his plan of Building III — according to Johns ("Discoveries in Palestine," 93–94), because the latter found its western wall more to the west, beside the eastern Byzantine *cardo*. Cf. Bieberstein and Bloedhorn, *Jerusalem* II, 382–83 and Bieberstein, *Jerusalem, Architectural Development: Map III*. Our plan (fig. 9.15) is provisory until the publication of a final report; see recently Baruch and Reich, "Umayyad Buildings," 118–19, not including any map. The subtitle of E. Mazar's *Temple Mount Excavations in Jerusalem* — "*The Byzantine and Early Islamic Periods*" — is inexact since none of these Umayyad buildings are treated there.

38. Similar buildings were found at Khirbet al-Mafjar; see Hamilton, *Khirbet al-Mafjar*, 28, fig. 8; for Jabal Sais, Qasr al-Hair al-Gharbi, and Qasr Ruba, see Creswell, *Early Muslim Architecture*, figs. 533, 563, 661.

39. Building III may have had four gates.

40. Reich and Billig, "Jerusalem, Robinson's Arch," 88–90; E. Mazar, "Roman-Byzantine Bathhouse," 87–102; Baruch and Reich, "Umayyad Buildings," 117–32.

41. B. Mazar, *Excavations in the Old City of Jerusalem (2nd and 3rd Seasons)*, 24; Sharon, "Arabic Inscriptions," 214–20.

42. Rosen-Ayalon, *Early Islamic Monuments*, 22-24; Rosen-Ayalon, "Art and Architecture in Jerusalem," 412.

43. Creswell, "Islam's Newly Revealed Artistic Inheritance," 94–95. For a more recent analysis, see R. Hillenbrand, "Umayyad Woodwork," 271–310.

44. Currently in the collection of the Museum of the Haram al-Sharif; see Busse, "Arabische Inschriften," 11–12, 17–20.

## Chapter 10. The Crusader and Ayyubid Periods

1. For a history of the Crusades, see Riley-Smith, *Atlas;* idem, *Oxford Illustrated History;* idem, *First Crusaders;* idem, *What Were the Crusades?;* for the conquest of Jerusalem, see Lobrichon, *1099, Jérusalem conquise.*

2. Boas, *Jerusalem*, 44.

3. Ibid.

4. Ibid., 45. Al-Mu'azzam believed that it would be more difficult for the Franks to hold the city if it lacked defenses; see Wightman, *Walls of Jerusalem*, 277.

5. First noticed by Robinson, *Later Biblical Researches*, 188; partially exposed and recorded by Schick, "Recent Discoveries," 62–63; further sections by Tarler, De Groot, and Solar, "Jerusalem," 56–57.

6. This section of the forewall was excavated by Bahat and Ben-Arie, "Excavations at Tancred's Tower," 109–10.

7. Boas, *Jerusalem*, 46–47.

8. Abbot Daniel 14; Fulcher of Chartres I, 26,3.

9. Boas, *Jerusalem*, 73–78.

10. See Johns, "The Citadel," 121–90; Amiran and Eitan, "Excavations in the Courtyard of the Citadel," 9–17; Geva, "Excavations in the Citadel," 55–71.

11. Hawari, *Ayyubid Architecture*, 24.

12. Boas, *Jerusalem*, 49–68.

13. Theoderich 3 (11).

14. Ibid., 134–41.

15. Ibid.

16. Ibid., 83–93.

17. William of Tyre XI, 27.

18. See Bahat, "Two Recent Studies," 57; Boas, *Jerusalem*, 83.

19. Boas, *Jerusalem*, 142–55.

20. Boas, *Jerusalem*, 143 and n. 8 (on p. 238) compares Crusader structures in Jerusalem to similar buildings in Caesarea, which Pringle, *Churches* I, 182–83 suggested might be a merchant's cantina, with living quarters above it.

21. Boas, *Jerusalem*, 27–28.

22. Ibid., 26–27.

23. Schick, "Muristan," 42–56; Vincent and Abel, *Jérusalem nouvelle* II/4, 953–65.

24. Ben-Dov, "Restoration of St. Mary's Church," 140–42; A. Ovadiah, "Crusader Church," 136–39.

25. Boas, *Jerusalem*, 28–29.

26. B. Kühnel, *Crusader Art*; Folda, *Art of the Crusaders*. The recently published third volume of Denys Pringle's fundamental *Corpus of the Churches of the Crusader Kingdom of Jerusalem* describes all the Crusader churches of Jerusalem. For the architectural decoration, see especially Buschhausen, *Süditalienische Bauplastik*.

27. Categorized for the first time by Bieberstein and Bloedhorn, *Jerusalem* I, 204–209.

28. Yahya ibn Sa'id al-Antaki, 230–1.

29. Ibid., 230.

30. William of Tyre I, 6.

31. Parts of these brick walls can still be seen opposite the *aedicula*.

32. Boas, *Jerusalem*, 102–9; see Pringle, *Churches* III, 6–72 no. 283.

33. Clapham, "Latin Monastic Buildings," 3–18.

34. Given the limited availability of space, construction efforts focused on the rotunda and the adjacent choir with ambulatory and three radiate chapels in the area of the Holy Garden.

35. The nave was never built.

36. Ibn al-Athir XI, 363–66.

37. Boas, *Jerusalem*, 109–10; Pringle, *Churches* III, 397–417 no. 367.

38. Boas, *Jerusalem*, 111–13; Pringle, *Churches* III, 261–87 no. 336.

39. Ibid., 273–82.

40. Boas, *Jerusalem*, 113; Pringle, *Churches* III, 72–88 no. 284.

41. The present-day dome was erected after the Crusader period.

42. B. Kühnel, "Crusader Sculpture," 41–50. Kühnel (*Crusader Art*, 30–33) claims that the preserved aedicula was built at the beginning of the twelfth century C.E. and that the marble decoration was added at a later stage. There is no evidence, however, for different execution stages. On this, see also Pringle, *Churches* III, 86–87.

43. Boas, *Jerusalem*, 114–19; Pringle, *Churches* III, 142–56 no. 305.

44. Boas, *Jerusalem*, 122–25; Pringle, *Churches* III, 236–53 no. 334.

45. Boas, *Jerusalem*, 125; Pringle, *Churches* III 253–61 no. 335.

46. Boas, *Jerusalem*, 130; Pringle, *Churches* III 327–35 no. 344.

47. Bahat, "The Church of Mary Magdalene," 5–7 (p. 65*).

48. Boas, *Jerusalem*, 119–21; Pringle, *Churches* III, 287–306 no. 337.

49. Orfali, *Gethsémani*, 1–7; Pringle, *Churches* III, 358–65 no. 357.

50. Pringle, *Churches* III, 417–35 nos. 368–69.

51. Boas, *Jerusalem*, 121; Pringle, *Churches* III, 192–207 nos. 322–23.

52. Its façade can still be seen on David Street.

53. Bahat and Solar ("Une église croisée," 72–80) identify the church as that of St. Julian; Boas, *Jerusalem*, 129–30; also now Pringle, *Churches* III, 212–15 no. 327; for a more convincing identification, see Bieberstein, "St. Julian oder St. Johannes Evangelista?" 178–84.

54. Boas, *Jerusalem*, 125–126; Pringle, *Churches* III, 228–36 no. 333.

55. Vincent and Abel, *Jérusalem nouvelle* II/4, 949–50; Boas, *Jerusalem*, 128 ("St. Thomas"). On p. 126 Boas mentions "St. Thomas Alemannorum," which he locates on the Harat al-Maidan (Hayyei Olam Street); cf. Bahat and Reich, "Une église médiévale," 111–14; Pringle, *Churches* III, 386–89 no. 365.

56. Boas, *Jerusalem*, 126–28; Pringle, *Churches* III, 168–82 no. 318.

57. Boas, *Jerusalem*, 128; Pringle, *Churches*, III 189–92 no. 321.

58. Carswell, *Kütahya Tiles*, I, 4; Pringle, *Churches* III, 385–86 no. 364, dates the church to the second half of the thirteenth century c.e.

59. Boas, *Jerusalem*, 79–82.

60. Röhricht, "Karten und Pläne" [2], 35–36 (Florence?); Levy, "Medieval Maps of Jerusalem," 462 no. 7; Levy-Rubin, "Rediscovery of the Uppsala Map," 162–67.

61. Röhricht, "Karten und Pläne" [1], 138–40; Levy, "Medieval Maps of Jerusalem," 467 no. 8.

62. For Ayyubid Jerusalem see the epigraphic study by van Berchem, *Matériaux* II, as well as Rosen-Ayalon's "Art and Architecture in Ayyubid Jerusalem," 305–14 for all architectural matters; and Korn, *Ayyubidische Architektur* for this period. A complete catalogue of Ayyubid architecture in Jerusalem with detailed discussions was compiled recently by Hawari. Hawari, *Ayyubid Architecture*; see also Hillenbrand and Auld, *Ayyubid Jerusalem*.

63. Ibid., 22–26.

64. Ibid., 19–20.

65. Ibid., 20–21, 161–65 no. 19 (porch).

66. Ibid., 57–70 nos. 5–6; Pringle, *Churches* III, 422–24.

67. Hawari, *Ayyubid Architecture*, 84–96 no. 9 (Ayyubid); Pringle, *Churches* III, 413–14 (Crusader).

68. Hawari, *Ayyubid Architecture*, 103–11 no. 11 (Ayyubid); Pringle, *Churches* III, 129–32 (Ayyubid or Crusader).

69. Hawari, *Ayyubid Architecture*, 112–26 no. 12.

70. Ibid., 134–36 no. 15.

71. Ibid., 137–40 no. 17.

72. Ibid., 166–70 no. 20.

73. Ibid., 74–83 no. 8.

74. Ibid., 187–88 no. 2; and Pringle, *Churches* III, 143–45.

75. Hawari, *Ayyubid Architecture*, 35–44 no. 1; Pringle, *Churches* III, 125–29.

76. Hawari, *Ayyubid Architecture*, 49–51 no. 3.

77. Ibid., 146–60 no. 18.

78. Ibid., 141–45 no. 17.

79. Ollendorf, "Two Mamluk Tomb-Chambers," 245–50.

80. Though generally an important medium in Crusader Palestine, hardly anything has survived of the wall paintings in the Church of the Holy Sepulchre in Jerusalem; see G. Kühnel, *Wall Painting*; B. Kühnel, *Crusader Art*, 47–60; Boas, *Jerusalem*, 194.

81. The most important of extant works from the scriptorium is known as Queen Melissende's Psalter, a remarkable work that has been preserved with its silk and ivory binding; see Folda, *Art of the Crusaders*, 137–63; Boas, *Jerusalem*, 194–97.

82. The most complete work on Ayyubid Jerusalem is the epigraphic study of van Berchem, *Matériaux* II; and recently Korn, *Ayyubidische Architektur*. See also, Rosen-Ayalon, "Art and Architecture in Ayyubid Jerusalem," 305-14.

83. Keenan, "Local Trend in Crusader Art," 114–15; B. Kühnel, *Crusader Art*, 164–68.

84. See Levy, "Medieval Maps of Jerusalem," 418–507; Levy-Rubin, "Crusader Maps of Jerusalem," 230–38.

85. See C. Hillenbrand, *Crusades*, 150–61.

## Chapter 11. The Mamluk Period

1. For an excellent summary of the Mamluk history of Jerusalem, see Little, "Jerusalem under the Ayyubids and Mamluks," 177–99. For a more thorough treatment of Mamluk society, see Burgoyne, *Mamluk Jerusalem*, 53–76.

2. Little, "Jerusalem under the Ayyubids and Mamluks," 177–99; Burgoyne, *Mamluk Jerusalem*, 53–76.

3. Burgoyne, *Mamluk Jerusalem*, 75–76.

4. Ibid., 45, 48, 225.

5. Ibid., 570–71 no. 60.

6. Ibid., 606–12 no. 64.

7. For further information on hospices, see Bahat, "Hospices and Hospitals," 73–88.

8. Burgoyne, *Mamluk Jerusalem*, 117–26 no. 3.

9. Ibid., 129–40 no. 5.

10. Ibid., 144–53 no. 7.

11. Mujir al-Din, the chief *qadi* of Jerusalem as of A.H. 891/1486 C.E., published his history of Jerusalem and Hebron in A.H. 900/1495 C.E.

12. Burgoyne, *Mamluk Jerusalem*, 412–14 no. 37.

13. Ibid., 154–66 no. 8.

14. See Burgoyne, *Mamluk Jerusalem* 201–10 (al-Jawiliya); 223–39 no. 18 (al-Tankiziya); 299–307 no. 25 (al-Sallamiya); 384–98 no. 35 (al-Manjakiya); 443–55 no. 43 (al-Baladiya); 514–16 no. 51 (al-Subaybiya); 526–33 no. 54 (al-Ghadiriya); 534–41 no. 55 (al-Hasaniya).

15. Ibid., 589–605 no. 63.

16. Burgoyne, *Mamluk Jerusalem*, 258–69 no. 22.

17. Ibid., 88. We know of one significant synagogue that existed during Mamluk rule. The Ramban Synagogue was built by Nahmanides around 1270. See Ben-Eliezer, *Synagogues*, 11–13; Naor, *Jewish Quarter*, 116.

18. Ibid., 85.

19. Ibid., 178–83 no. 10.

20. Ibid., 244–48 no. 20.

21. Mujir al-Din, *Histoire de Jérusalem*, 379.

22. Burgoyne, *Mamluk Jerusalem*, 415–18 no. 38.

23. Ibid., 273–98 no. 24.

24. Ibid., 59; Meinecke, *Mamlukische Architektur* II 15 no. 4/40.

25. Burgoyne, *Mamluk Jerusalem*, 485–504 no. 48.

26. Ibid., 505–12 no. 49.

27. Ibid., 109–16 no. 2.

28. Ibid., 167–77 no. 9; 460–75 no. 45.

29. Abu Khalaf, *Islamic Art Through the Ages*, 57–73. On the typology of Mamluk ceramics, see Fehérvári, *Ceramics of the Islamic World*, 245–59.

30. According to Burgoyne (*Mamluk Jerusalem*, 237), this mosaic was the work of artists from Damascus. Rosen-Ayalon (*Islamic Art and Archaeology*, 112) suggests that it was created between A.H. 786 and 800.

31. For a detailed study of the manuscripts see Salameh, *Qur'an Manuscripts*.

32. E. Kühnel, *Islamic Arts*, 26.

33. al-Alfi, *al-Fann al-Islami*, 252.

34. Salameh, *Qur'an Manuscripts*, 89.

## Chapter 12. The Ottoman Period

1. R. Hillenbrand, "Structure, Style and Context," 1–23.

2. See Asali, *Jerusalem*, 200, and Cuneo, "Urban Structure," 211–20.

3. On the city wall, see Cuneo, "Urban Structure," 212–13; Myres, "Overview," 327–28; and R. Hillenbrand, "Structure, Style and Context," 3.

4. van Berchem, *Matériaux* II/1, 431–49 nos. 119–29.

5. Cohen, *Economic Life*, 4.

6. Schur, "Why Suleiman the Magnificent Built the Walls," 15–19; Cohen,

"Walls of Jerusalem" [1], 467–77; Cohen, "Walls of Jerusalem" [2], 52–64; Asali, *Jerusalem*, 200; Grabar, "al-Kuds," 344.

7. For a preliminary report on the Citadel during the Ottoman period, see Hawari, "Citadel," 493–518. M. K. Hawari is currently preparing a complete architectural and archaeological study of the Citadel from its earliest to latest phases.

8. Stephan, "Two Turkish Inscriptions from the Citadel," 132–35.

9. van Berchem, *Matériaux* II/1, 165–67 no. 53.

10. Ibid., 505.

11. Cuneo, "Urban Structure," 213; Natsheh, "Architecture," 599–601.

12. Prag, *Blue Guide, Jerusalem*, 41.

13. Myres, "Overview," 328.

14. Asali, *Jerusalem*, 201.

15. van Berchem, *Matériaux* II/1, 413, 421–22.

16. Peters, *Distant Shrine*, 204.

17. See Aslanapa, *Turkish Art*, 257–59; Behrens-Abouseif, "Sabil," 679–83. O. Aslanapa maintains that this type began in Anatolia at the beginning of the Seljuk period.

18. Aslanapa, *Turkish Art*, 259.

19. Dow, "Hammams," 519–24.

20. Burgoyne, *Mamluk Jerusalem*, 282, 287.

21. See Asali, *Jerusalem*, 202. Three of the endowments were initially in favor of the Dome of the Rock and the Aqsa Mosque, partly in the case of Hammam al-'Ain and Hammam al-Shifa', or wholly in the case of Hammam al-Jamal. Hammam al-Sayyida Maryam and Hammam al-Batrak were endowed in favor of the Khanqah al-Salahiya, and Hammam al-Sultan was endowed in favor of the Khassaki Sultan Takiya.

22. Ashbee, *Jerusalem*, 17.

23. Golvin, "Quelques notes," 114.

24. In the Qur'an: Surat al-Ma'idah 5:6.

25. Richmond, *Dome of the Rock*, 23–76; Atil, *Age of Sultan Süleyman*, 239; Blair and Bloom, *Art and Architecture*, 220.

26. See van Berchem, *Matériaux* II/2, 180–83 no. 196. Despite the flourishing tile industry at Iznik at this time, the tiles are thought to have been made locally. On this, see Atil, *Age of Sultan Süleyman*, 241.

27. van Berchem, *Matériaux* II/2, 340–42 nos. 243–44.

28. Natsheh, "Catalogue of Buildings," 742–46 no. 14; 792–801 nos. 16–17; 821–50 nos. 20–24; 913–16 no. 34; 968–71 no. 46; 987–95 nos. 51–53.

29. Catherwood according to Wilson, *Land of the Bible*, 477.

30. Heyd, *Ottoman Documents*, 139; Natsheh, "Catalogue of Buildings," 747–90 no. 15.

31. Peri, "Waqf," 47; see also Asali, *Some Islamic Monuments*, 9–25.
32. Heyd, *Ottoman Documents*, 146–47 no. 94; Myres, "al-'Imara al-'Amira," 539–81.
33. See description under Commercial and Domestic Construction in chapter 11.
34. Burgoyne, *Mamluk Jerusalem*, 415.
35. Ibid., 270–72.
36. Ben-Eliezer, *Synagogues*; Naor, *Jewish Quarter*, 116–44.
37. Kroyanker, *Jerusalem Architecture*, 24, 41, 68, 73–81, 119, 125–26, 132–38; Ben-Arieh, *New City*, 324–27.
38. Asali, "Cemeteries of Ottoman Jerusalem," 279–84.
39. For additional information on dress in Jerusalem in the Ottoman period, see Micklewright, "Costumes," 291–300.

# Bibliography

Note: Page numbers of English summaries of Hebrew texts are indicated with an asterisk.

## 1. Sources

ADOMNAN

*The Holy Places.* Translated and edited by J. Wilkinson. In *Jerusalem Pilgrims Before the Crusades.* Warminster, UK: Aris and Phillips, 1977, 93–116.

AMARNA LETTERS

Knudtzon, J. A. *Die El-Amarna-Tafeln* I. Leipzig: J. C. Hinrichs, 1908.

ANTIOCHUS OF MAR SABA

*La prise de Jérusalem par les Perses en 614.* Translated by G. Garitte. Corpus scriptorum christianorum orientalium 203; scriptores Iberici 12. Louvain: Secrétariat du CorpusSCO, 1960.

BORDEAUX PILGRIM

*Egeria's Travels to the Holy Land.* Translated with supporting documents and notes by J. Wilkinson. 3rd ed. London: Aris and Phillips, 1999, 22–34.

BREVIARIUS OF JERUSALEM

*Breviarius of Jerusalem.* In J. Wilkinson, ed. *Jerusalem Pilgrims*, 59–61.

CASSIUS DIO

*Historia Romana.* In M. Stern, ed. *Greek and Latin Authors on Jews and Judaism II. Edited with Introductions, Translations and Commentary.* II. *From Tacitus to Simplicius.* Jerusalem: Israel Academy of Sciences and Humanities, 1980. 391–92.

DANIEL

*The Pilgrimage of the Russian Abbot Daniel in the Holy Land 1106–1107* A.D. Annotated by Colonel Sir Ch. W. Wilson. Palestine Pilgrims' Text Society no. 6 (Library of the Palestine Pilgrims' Text Society 4,3). London: 1888.

EGERIA

*Egeria's Travels to the Holy Land.* Translated with supporting documents and notes by J. Wilkinson. 3rd ed. London: Aris and Phillips, 1999.

EUSEBIUS

*The Ecclesiastical History* I–II. Translated by K. Lake. 6th ed. Loeb Classical Library 153 and 265. Cambridge, MA and London: The Loeb Classical Library, 1975.

EUTYCHIUS

*Annales.* In *Extracts from Aristeas, Hecataeus, Origen and Other Early Writers.* Translated by A. Stewart. Palestine Pilgrims' Text Society no. 28 (Library of the Palestine Pilgrims' Text Society 11,1). London: 1895, 35–68.

EVLIYA ÇELEBI

"Evliya Tshelebi's Travels in Palestine, VI. Description of the Grand Mosque al-Aqsa (al-Masjidu-l-Aqsa)." Translated and annotated by S. H. Stephan. *Quarterly of the Department of Antiquities of Palestine* 9. 1942, 81–104.

FELIX FABRI

*Evagatorium in Terra Sanctae (circa 1480–1483* A.D.) I–II. Translated by A. Stewart. Palestine Pilgrims' Text Society no. 20 (Library of the Palestine Pilgrims' Text Society 7–10). London: 1892.

FULCHER OF CHARTRES

*A History of the Expedition to Jerusalem, 1095–1127.* Translated by F. R. Ryan
(Sisters of St. John); edited with an introduction by H. S. Fink. Knoxville:
University of Tennessee Press, 1969.

HERODOT

*[History] in Four Volumes* II. Books III–IV. Translated by A. D. Godley. Cambridge, MA and London: Cambridge Classical Library, 1921.

IBN AL-ATHIR

*The Chronicle of the Crusading Period from al-Kāmil fi'l-ta'rīkh II. The Years 541–
589/1146–1193: the Age of Nur al-Din and Saladin.* Translated by D. S.
Richards. Aldershot, UK: 2007.

JOSEPHUS, *ANTIQUITIES*

*Josephus in Nine Volumes* VII: *Jewish Antiquities, Books XII–XIV.* Translated by R.
Marcus. Cambridge, MA and London: The Loeb Classical Library, 1933,
365
*Josephus in Ten Volumes* VIII: *Jewish Antiquities, Books XV–XVII.* Translated by R.
Marcus. Cambridge, MA and London: The Loeb Classical Library, 1963,
410.
*Josephus in Ten Volumes* IX: *Jewish Antiquities, Books XVIII–XIX.* Translated by L.
H. Feldman. Cambridge, MA and London: The Loeb Classical Library,
1965, 433.
*Josephus in Ten Volumes* X: *Jewish Antiquities, Book XX. General Index to Volumes I–
X.* Translated by L. H. Feldman. Cambridge, MA and London: The Loeb
Classical Library, 1965, 456.

JOSEPHUS, *WAR*

*Josephus in Eight Volumes* II: *The Jewish War, Books I–III.* Translated by H. S. J.
Thackeray. London and New York: The Loeb Classical Library, 1927, 203.
*Josephus in Eight Volumes* III: *The Jewish War, Books IV–VII.* Translated by H. S. J.
Thackeray. London and New York: The Loeb Classical Library, 1928, 210.

MUJIR AL-DIN

*Histoire de Jérusalem et d'Hébron depuis Abraham jusqu'a la fin du XVᵉ siècle de J.-C.*
Fragments de la Chronique de Moudjir-ed-dyn traduits sur le texte arabe
par H. Sauvaire. Paris: 1876.

AL-MUQADDASI

*Description of Syria, including Palestine, by Mukaddasi (circ. 985* A.D.*).* Translated from the Arabic and annotated by Guy Le Strange. Palestine Pilgrims' Text Society no. 4 (Library of the Palestine Pilgrims' Text Society 3,3). London: 1892.

NĀSIR-I-KHUSRAU

*Diary of a Journey through Syria and Palestine by Nāsir-i-Khusrau, in 1047* A.D. Translated from the Persian and annotated by Guy Le Strange. Palestine Pilgrims' Text Society no. 9 (Library of the Palestine Pilgrims' Text Society 4,1). London: 1888.

OTTOBONIAN GUIDE

*Ottobonian Guide.* In J. Wilkinson, ed. *Jerusalem Pilgrims,* 92–93.

PAUSANIAS

*Description of Greece in Four Volumes* III. *Books VI–VIII (1–21).* Translated by W. H. S. Jones. London and Cambridge, MA: The Loeb Classical Library, 1933.

PIACENZA PILGRIM

*Travels from Piacenza.* In J. Wilkinson, ed. *Jerusalem Pilgrims,* 79–89.

PLINY THE ELDER

*Natural History.* In M. Stern, ed. *Greek and Latin Authors* I, 471.

THEODERICH

*Guide to the Holy Land.* Translated by A. Stewart. 2nd ed., with new introduction, notes and bibliography by R. G. Musto. New York: Italica Press, 1986.

THEODOSIUS

*The Topography of the Holy Land.* In J. Wilkinson, ed. *Jerusalem Pilgrims,* 63–71.

AL-ʿUMARI

al-ʿUmari, Masalik al-absar. "A Medieval Arabic Description of the Haram of Jerusalem." Translated by L. A. Mayer. In *Quarterly of the Department of Antiquities of Palestine* 1 (1932), 44–51, 74–85.

WILLIAM OF TYRE

*Chronicon.* Édition critique par R. B. C. Huygens. Identification des sources historiques et détermination des dates par H. E. Mayer and G. Rösch. Turnhout: Corpus Christianorum, continuatio mediaevalis 63, 1986.

YAHYA IBN SA'ĪD D'ANTIOCHE

*Histoire.* Édition critique du texte arabe préparée par I. Kratchkovsky et traduction française annotée par F. Micheau and G. Troupeau. Turnhout: Patrologia Orientalia 47,4, 1997, 369–559.

## 2. General Bibliography

Abu 'Assaf, A. *Der Tempel von 'Ain Dara.* Damaszener Forschungen 3. Mainz: Philipp von Zabern, 1990.

Abu Khalaf, M. F. *Islamic Art Through the Ages. Masterpieces of the Islamic Musuem of al-Haram al-Sharif (al-Aqsa Mosque) in Jerusalem.* Jerusalem: Marwan F. Abu Khalaf, 1998.

Abu Riya, R. "Jerusalem, Street of Chain (A)." *Excavations and Surveys in Israel* 10 (1991), 134–35.

Ackroyd, P. "The Jewish Community in Palestine in the Persian Period." In *The Cambridge History of Judaism* I: *Introduction. The Persian Period.* Edited by W. D. Davies and L. Finkelstein. Cambridge, UK: Cambridge University Press, 1984, 130–161.

Adler, N. "Brick and Tile Stamp Impressions of the Tenth Legions from the Temple Mount Excavations." *New Studies on Jerusalem* 6 (2000), 117–32 (Hebrew; English summary, 10*).

Ådna, J. *Jerusalemer Tempel und Tempelmarkt im 1. Jahrhundert n. Chr.* Abhandlungen des Deutschen Palästina-Vereins 25. Wiesbaden: Harrassowitz, 1999.

Aharoni, Y. *Excavations at Ramat Rahel* I: *Seasons 1959 and 1960.* Rome: Centro di Studi Semitici, 1962.

——. *Excavations at Ramat Rahel* II: *Seasons 1961 and 1962.* Rome: Centro di Studi Semitici, 1964.

Ahituv, S. *Canaanite Toponyms in Ancient Egyptian Documents.* Jerusalem: Magnes, 1984.

Albertz, R. *A History of Israelite Religion in the Old Testament Period.* London: SCM Press, 1994.

al-Alfi, A. *al-Fann al-Islami.* Cairo: Dar al-Ma'arif, 1984.

Alt, A. "Das Taltor von Jerusalem." *Palästinajahrbuch* 24 (1928), 74–98.

Amiran, D. H. K., E. Arieh, and T. Turcotte."Earthquakes in Israel and Adjacent Areas: Macroseismic Observations since 100 B.C.E." *Israel Exploration Journal* 44 (1994), 260–305.

Amiran, D. H. K., A. Shachar, and I. Kimhi. *Atlas of Jerusalem.* Jerusalem: Massada, 1973.

Amiran, R. *Ancient Pottery of the Holy Land: From Its Beginnings in the Neolithic Period to the End of the Iron Age.* Jerusalem: Massada, 1969.

———. "The Water Supply of Israelite Jerusalem." In Yadin, *Jerusalem Revealed* (1975), 75–78.

Amiran, R., and A. Eitan. "Excavations in the Courtyard of the Citadel, Jerusalem, 1968–1969 (Preliminary Report)." *Israel Exploration Journal* 20 (1970), 9–17.

Amit, D. "'Jerusalem' *Miqva'ot* from the Hebron Hills in the Second Temple Period." In *Hikrei Eretz: Studies in the History of the Land of Israel Dedicated to Prof. Jehuda Feliks.* Edited by Y. Friedman, Z. Safrai, and J. Schwartz. Ramat-Gan: Bar Ilan University, 1997, 35–48 (Hebrew).

Amit, D., and S. R. Wolff. "An Armenian Monastery in the Morasha Neighborhood, Jerusalem." In H. Geva, *Ancient Jerusalem Revealed* (2000), 293–98.

Ariel, D. T. "Imported Stamped Amphora Handles, Coins, Worked Bone and Ivory, and Glass." *Excavations at the City of David 1978–1985* II. Directed by Yigal Shiloh. Qedem 30. Jerusalem: Institute of Archaeology, Hebrew University, 1990.

———. "Inscriptions." *Excavations at the City of David 1978–1985* VI. Directed by Yigal Shiloh. Qedem 41. Jerusalem: Institute of Archaeology, Hebrew University, 2000.

Arnould, C. *Les arcs romains de Jérusalem: Architecture, décor et urbanisme.* Fribourg: Éditions universitaires, 1997.

Arubas, B., and H. Goldfus. "The Kilnworks of the Tenth Legion Fretensis." In *The Roman and Byzantine Near East: Some Recent Archaeological Research* I. Edited by J. R. Humphrey. Ann Arbor, MI: Cushing-Malloy, 1995.

Asali, K. J. "The Cemeteries of Ottoman Jerusalem." In Auld and Hillenbrand, *Ottoman Jerusalem* I (2000), 279–84.

———. *Jerusalem in History.* Buckhurst Hill: Scorpion, 1989.

———. *Some Islamic Monuments in Jerusalem.* Amman, 1982 (Arabic).

Ashbee, C., ed. *Jerusalem 1918–1920. Being the Records of the Pro-Jerusalem Council during the Period of the British Military Administration.* London, 1921.

Aslanapa, O. *Turkish Art and Architecture.* London: Faber ad Faber, 1971.

Atil, E. *The Age of Sultan Süleyman the Magnificent.* Washington, DC: National Gallery of Art. New York: H. Abrams, 1987.

Augustin, C. "Die dritte Mauer Jerusalems. Überlegungen zu ihrer Baugeschichte und ihrem Verlauf." *Jahrbuch des Deutschen Evangelischen Instituts für Altertumswissenschaft des Heiligen Landes* 8 (2002), 23–43.

Auld, S., and R. Hillenbrand, eds. *Ottoman Jerusalem: The Living City, 1517–1917* I–II. London: on behalf of the British School of Archaeology in Jerusalem in cooperation with the Administration of Auqaf and Islamic Affairs, Jerusalem, by Altajir World of Islam Trust, 2000.

Avi-Yonah, M. *Art in Ancient Palestine: Selected Studies.* Jerusalem: Magnes, 1981.

———. "Mosaic Pavements in Palestine." *Quarterly of the Department of Antiquities of Palestine* 2 (1933), 162–78.

Avigad, N. *Ancient Monuments in the Kidron Valley.* Jerusalem: Bialik Institute, 1954 (Hebrew).

———. "A Building Inscription of the Emperor Justinian and the Nea in Jerusalem (Preliminary Report)." *Israel Exploration Journal* 27 (1977), 145–51.

———. *Discovering Jerusalem.* Jerusalem: Shikmona and Israel Exploration Society, 1983.

———. *The Herodian Quarter in Jerusalem: Wohl Archaeological Museum.* Jerusalem: Keter, 1989.

———. "The Inscribed Pomegranate from the 'House of the Lord," *Biblical Archaeology Review* 53/3 (1990), 157–166.

———. "Jewish Rock-Cut Tombs in Jerusalem and in the Judaean Hill-Country." *Eretz Israel* 8 (1967), 119–25 (Hebrew; English summary, 72*).

Avigad, N., and G. Barkay. "The 'lmlk' and Related Seal Impressions." In H. Geva, *Jewish Quarter Excavations* I (2000), 243–66.

Avner, R., G. Lavas, and I. Rosidis. "Jerusalem, Mar Elias–The Kathisma Church." *Excavations and Surveys in Israel* 113 (2001) (Hebrew; English summary, 89*–92*).

Avni, G. "The Urban Limits of Roman and Byzantine Jerusalem: A View from the Necropolis." *Journal of Roman Archaeology* 18 (2005), 373–96.

Avni, G., Y. Baruch, and S. Weksler-Bdolah. "Jerusalem, the Old City, Herod's Gate." *Hadashot Arkheologiyot* 13 (2001) (Hebrew; English summary, 76*–79*).

Avni, G., and Z. Greenhut. *The Akeldama Tombs: Three Burial Caves in the Kidron Valley, Jerusalem. Israel Antiquities Authority Reports* 1. Jerusalem: Israel Antiquities Authority, 1996.

Avni, G., and J. Seligman. *Temple Mount 1917–2001. Documentation, Research and Inspection of Antiquities.* Jerusalem: Israel Antiquities Authority, 2001.

Bahat, D. "The Church of Mary Magdalene and Its Quarter." *Eretz Israel* 18 (1985) 5–7 (Hebrew; English summary, 65*).

———. "The Herodian Temple." In *The Cambridge History of Judaism* III: *The Early Roman Period.* Edited by W. Horbury et al. Cambridge, UK: Cambridge University Press, 1999, 38–58, 1091–82.

——. "Hospices and Hospitals in Mamluk Jerusalem." In *Towns and Material Culture in the Medieval Middle East, 400–1453*. Edited by Y. Lev. Leiden: Brill, 2002, 73–88.

——. *The Illustrated Atlas of Jerusalem*. New York: Simon and Schuster, 1990.

——. "The Physical Infrastructure." In *The History of Jerusalem: The Early Muslim Period, 638–1099*. Edited by J. Prawer and H. Ben-Shammai. Jerusalem: Yad Izhak Ben-Zvi; New York: New York University Press, 1996, 38–101.

——. "Two Recent Studies of the Archaeology of Jerusalem." *Palestine Exploration Quarterly* 130 (1998), 51–62.

Bahat, D., and D. Ben-Arie. "Excavations at Tancred's Tower." In Yadin, *Jerusalem Revealed* (1975), 109–10.

Bahat, D., and M. Broshi. "Jerusalem, Old City, the Armenian Garden." *Israel Exploration Journal* 22 (1972), 171–72.

Bahat, D., and R. Reich. "Une église médiévale dans le quartier juif de Jérusalem." *Revue Biblique* 93 (1986), 111–14.

Bahat, D., and G. Solar. "Une église croisée récemment découverte à Jérusalem," *Revue Biblique* 85 (1978), 72–80.

Bar, D. "Aelia Capitolina and the Location of the Camp of the Tenth Legion." *Palestine Exploration Quarterly* 130 (1998), 8–19.

Bar-Kochva, B. *Judas Maccabaeus: The Jewish Struggle against the Seleucids*. Cambridge, UK: Cambridge University Press, 1989.

Barag, D. "Brick Stamp-Impressions of the Legio X Fretensis." *Bonner Jahrbücher* 167 (1967), 244–67.

——. "The 2000–2001 Exploration of the Tombs of Benei Hezir and Zechariah." *Israel Exploration Journal* 53 (2003), 78–110.

Baramki, D. C. "Byzantine Remains in Palestine II: A Small Monastery and Chapel outside the 'Third Wall.'" *Quarterly of the Department of Antiquities of Palestine* 5 (1936), 56–58.

Barkay, G. "Burial Headrests as a Return to the Womb: A Reevaluation." *Biblical Archaeology Review* 14.2 (1988), 48–50.

——. *Ketef Hinnom. A Treasure Facing Jerusalem's Walls*. Jerusalem: Israel Museum, 1986.

——. "The Necropolis of Jerusalem in the First Temple Period." In *The History of Jerusalem: The Biblical Period*. Edited by S. Ahituv and A. Mazar. Jerusalem: Yad Izhak Ben-Zvi, 2000, 195–232 (Hebrew).

Barkay, G., and A. Kloner. "Jerusalem Tombs from the Days of the First Temple." *Biblical Archaeology Review* 12.2 (1986), 22–57.

Barkay, G., et al. "The Amulets from Ketef Hinnom: A New Edition and Evaluation." *Bulletin of the American Schools of Oriental Research* 334 (2004), 41–71.

Baruch, Y., and R. Reich. "The Umayyad Buildings near the Foot of the Temple

Mount: A Re-examination." *New Studies on Jerusalem* 8 (2002), 117–32 (Hebrew; English summary, 15*–16*).

Baruch, Y., and B. Zissu. "Jerusalem, the Old City, Herod's Gate." *Hadashot Arkheologiyot,* 118 (2006) [20/3 2006].

Batz, S. "The Church of St. Theodore at Khirbet Beit Sila." *Israel Museum Studies in Archaeology* 1 (2002), 39–54.

Behrens-Abouseif, D. "Sabil, as an Architectural Term." *Encyclopaedia of Islam* VIII (1995) 679–681.

Belayche, N. "Du Mont du Temple au Golgotha: La Capitole de la colonie d'Aelia Capitolina." *Revue de l'Histoire des Religions* 214 (1997), 387–413.

Bell, R. C. *Board and Table Games from Many Civilizations* I. Oxford: Oxford University Press, 1960.

Ben-Arieh, S., and E. Netzer. "Excavations along the 'Third Wall' of Jerusalem, 1972–1974." *Israel Exploration Journal* 24 (1974), 97–107.

Ben-Arieh, Y. *Jerusalem in the 19th Century. Emergence of the New City.* Jerusalem, 1986.

———. *Jerusalem in the 19th Century. The Old City.* Jerusalem, 1984.

Ben-Dov, M. "Building Techniques in the Umayyad Palace near the Temple Mount, Jerusalem." *Eretz Israel* 11 (1973), 75–91 (Hebrew; English summary, 24*–25*).

———. *Historical Atlas of Jerusalem.* New York: Continuum, 2002.

———. *In the Shadow of the Temple.* Jerusalem: Keter, 1985.

———. "The Omayyad Structures near the Temple Mount." In *The Excavations in the Old City of Jerusalem: Preliminary Report of the 2nd and 3rd Seasons, 1969–1970.* Edited by B. Mazar. Jerusalem: Israel Exploration Society, 1971, 37–44.

———. "The Restoration of St. Mary's Church of the German Knights in Jerusalem." In *Ancient Churches Revealed.* Edited by Y. Tsafrir. Jerusalem: Israel Exploration Society, 1993, 140–42.

Ben-Eliezer, S. *The Synagogues of the Jewish Quarter. Destruction and Renewal.* Jerusalem: Rubin Mass, 1975.

Benoit, P. "L'Antonie d'Hérode le Grand et le forum oriental d'Aelia Capitolina." *Harvard Theological Review* 64 (1971), 135–67.

van Berchem, M. *Matériaux pour un Corpus Inscriptionum Arabicarum* II: *Syrie du Sud* 1: *Jérusalem "la ville."* Cairo: l'Institut français d'archéologie orientale, 1922.

———. *Matériaux pour un Corpus Inscriptionum Arabicarum* II: *Syrie du Sud,* 2: *Jérusalem "Haram."* Cairo: l'Institut français d'archéologie orientale, 1927.

Bickerman, E. J. "La charte séleucide de Jérusalem." *Revue des Études Juives* 100 (1935), 4–35 [= *Studies in Jewish and Christian History* II. Leiden: Brill, 1980, 44–85].

———. *The God of the Maccabees: Studies on the Meaning and Origin of the Maccabean Revolt.* Leiden: Brill, 1979.

Bieberstein, K. *Jerusalem, Architectural Development: Map I. From the Early Bronze Age to the Destruction by Nebukadnezar II (3100–587/586 B.C.).* Tübinger Atlas des Vorderen Orients B IV 7. Wiesbaden: L. Reichert, 1992.

———. *Jerusalem, Architectural Development: Map II. From the Re-erection in the Persian Period to the Destruction by Titus (539 B.C.–70 A.D.).* Tübinger Atlas des Vorderen Orients B IV 7. Wiesbaden: L. Reichert, 1992.

———. *Jerusalem, Architectural Development: Map III. From the Re-erection in the Hadrianic Period to the Eve of the Crusades (117–1099 A.D.).* Tübinger Atlas des Vorderen Orients B IV 7. Wiesbaden: L. Reichert, 1992.

———. "St. Julian oder St. Johannes Evangelista? Zur historischen Identifizierung einer neuentdeckten Kreuzfahrerkirche in der Altstadt Jerusalems." *Zeitschrift des Deutschen Palästina-Vereins* 103 (1987), 178–84.

Bieberstein, K., and H. Bloedhorn. *Jerusalem: Grundzüge der Baugeschichte vom Chalkolithikum bis zur Frühzeit der osmanischen Herrschaft* I–III. Tübinger Atlas des Vorderen Orients, Beiheft 100. Wiesbaden: L. Reichert, 1994.

Bieberstein, K., and M. H. Burgoyne. *Jerusalem, Architectural Development: Map IV. From the Arrival of the Crusaders to the Early Ottoman Period (1099–ca. 1750 A.D.).* Tübinger Atlas des Vorderen Orients B IV 7. Wiesbaden: L. Reichert, 1992.

Billig, Y., and R. Reich. "Excavations along the Western Wall of the Temple Mount, near Robinson Arch." *Judaea and Samaria Research Studies* 7 (1997), 41–44 (Hebrew; English summary, p. X*).

Blair, S. S., and J. M. Bloom. *The Art and Architecture of Islam 1250–1800.* New Haven: Yale University Press, 1994.

Bliss, F. J., and A. C. Dickie. *Excavations at Jerusalem, 1894–1897.* London: Palestine Exploration Fund, 1898.

Bloch-Smith, E. "Judahite Burial Practices and Beliefs about the Dead." *Journal for the Study of the Old Testament*, Supplement 123. Sheffield: JSOT Press, 1992.

Boas, A. *Jerusalem in the Time of the Crusaders: Society, Landscape and Art in the Holy City.* London: Routledge, 2001.

Bouchnik, R., et al. "Animal Bone Remains from the City Dump of Jerusalem from the Late Second Temple Period." *New Studies on Jerusalem* 10 (2004), 71–80 (Hebrew; English summary, 50*).

———. "Faunal Remains from the Late Second Temple Period. A View from the Village of Burnat and Jerusalem City Dump Assemblages." *New Studies on Jerusalem* 12 (2006), 109–122 (Hebrew; English summary, 16*).

———. "More Bones from the City Dump of Jerusalem from the Late Second

Temple Period." *New Studies on Jerusalem* 11 (2006), 175–185 (Hebrew; English summary, 40*–41*).

Bowersock, G. W. "A Roman Perspective on the Bar Kochba War." In *Approaches to Ancient Judaism* II. Edited by W. S. Brown. Judaic Studies 9. Chico, CA: Scholars, 1980, 131–141.

Brandenburg, H. "Christussymbole im frühchristlichen Bodenmosaiken." *Römische Quartalschrift* 64 (1969), 74–138.

Broshi, M. "Along Jerusalem's Walls." *Biblical Archaeologist* 40 (1977), 11–17.

——. "Excavations in the Holy Sepulchre in the Chapel of St. Vartan and the Armenian Martyrs." In *Ancient Churches Revealed*. Edited by Y. Tsafrir. Jerusalem: Israel Exploration Society, 1993, 118–22.

——. "The Expansion of Jerusalem in the Reigns of Hezekiah and Manasseh." *Biblical Archaeology Review* 4.2 (1978), 10–15.

——. "La population de l'ancienne Jérusalem." *Revue Biblique* 82 (1975), 5–14.

——. "The Population of Western Palestine in the Roman-Byzantine Period." *Bulletin of the American Schools of Oriental Research* 236 (1979), 1–10.

Broshi, M., and R. Gophna. "The Settlements and Population of Palestine during the Early Bronze Age II–III." *Bulletin of the American Schools of Oriental Research* 253 (1984), 41–53.

Burger, J. A. "The Madaba Map and the Courses of Jerusalem's Main North-South Streets: A Historical Geographical View." *Old Testament Essays* 6 (1993), 33–45.

Burgoyne, M. H. *Mamluk Jerusalem: An Architectural Study*. London: on behalf of the British School of Archaeology in Jerusalem, by the World of Islam Festival Trust, 1987.

Buschhausen, H. *Die süditalienische Bauplastik im Königreich Jerusalem von König Wilhelm II. bis Kaiser Friedrich II*. Denkschriften der Öesterreichischen Akademie der Wissenschaft (der philosophisch-historischen Klass) 108. Vienna: Österreichische Akademie der Wissenschaften, 1989.

Busse, H. "Die arabischen Inschriften im und am Felsendom in Jerusalem." *Das Heilige Land* 109.1–2 (1977), 8–24.

——. "Oleg Grabar, The Shape of the Holy, und andere neue Bücher über das frühislamische Jerusalem." *Islam* 75 (1998), 93–103.

——. "Tempel, Grabeskirche und Haram ash-Sharif. Drei Heiligtümer und ihre gegenseitigen Beziehungen in Legende und Wirklichkeit." In *Jerusalemer Heiligtumstraditionen in altkirchlicher und frühislamischer Zeit*. Edited by H. Busse and G. Kretschmar. Abhandlungen des Deutschen Palästina-Vereins (8). Wiesbaden: Harrassowitz, 1987, 1–27.

Byatt, A. "Josephus and Population Numbers in 1st Century Palestine." *Palestine Exploration Quarterly* 105 (1973), 56–58.

Cahill, J. "David's Jerusalem: Fiction or Reality? It Is There: The Archaeological Evidence Proves It." *Biblical Archaeology Review* 24.4 (1998), 34–41, 63.

———. "Jerusalem at the Time of the United Monarchy: The Archaeological Evidence." In *Jerusalem in Bible and Archaeology: The First Temple Period*. Edited by A. G. Vaughn and A. E. Killebrew. Atlanta: Society of Biblical Literature, 2003), 13–80.

———. "Jerusalem in David and Solomon's Time: It Really Was a Major City in the Tenth Century B.C.E." *Biblical Archaeology Review* 30.6 (2004), 20–31, 62–63.

Cahill, J. M., and Tarler, D. "Excavations Directed by Yigal Shiloh at the City of David, 1978–1985." In *Ancient Jerusalem Revealed*. Edited by H. Geva, Ancient Jerusalem Revealed. Jerusalem: Israel Exploration Society, exp. ed. 2000, 30–45.

Callaway, J. A. *Pottery from the Tombs at 'Ai (et-Tell)*. London: B. Quaritch, 1964.

Canaan, T. *Mohammedan Saints and Sanctuaries in Palestine*. London: Luzac, 1927.

Carswell, J. *Kütahya Tiles and Pottery from the Armenian Cathedral of St. James, Jerusalem* I–II. Oxford: Clarendon, 1972.

Clapham, A. W. "The Latin Monastic Buildings of the Church of the Holy Sepulchre, Jerusalem." *Antiquaries Journal* 1 (1921), 3–18.

Clermont-Ganneau, C. *Archaeological Researches in Palestine during the Years 1873–1874* I–II. London: Palestine Exploration Fund, 1899–96 [sic].

———. *Études d'archéologie orientale* I–II. Paris: Bouillon, 1895–97.

———. *Recueil d'archéologie orientale* I–VIII. Paris: Leroux, 1888–1924.

———. "La stèle de Dheban." *Revue Archéologique* 21 (1870), 184–207, 357–86.

———. "Une stèle du Temple de Jérusalem." *Revue Archéologique* 23 (1872), 214–34, 290–296.

Cohen, A. *Economic Life in Ottoman Jerusalem*. Cambridge 1989.

———. "The Walls of Jerusalem" [1]. In *The Islamic World. From Classical to Modern Times. Essays in Honor of Bernhard Lewis*. Edited by C. E. Bosworth et al. Princeton: Darwin Press, 1989, 467–477.

Conder, C. R. *The City of Jerusalem*. London: Palestine Pilgrims' Text Society, 1888.

Corbo, V. C. *Ricerche archeologiche al Monte degli Ulivi*. Pubblicazioni dello Studium Biblicum Franciscanum, collectio maior 16. Jerusalem: Tip. dei Padri Francescani, 1965.

———. *Il Santo Sepolcro di Gerusalemme: Aspetti archeologici dalle origini al periodo crociato I–III*. Studium Biblicum Franciscanum, collectio maior 29. Jerusalem: Franciscan Printing Press, 1982.

———. "Il Santo Sepolcro di Gerusalemme: Nova et Vetera." *Liber Annuus* 38 (1988), 391–422.

Cotton, H., et al., eds. *Corpus Inscriptionum Iudaeae/Palestinae. A Multi-lingual Corpus of the Inscriptions from Alexander to Muhammad* I. 1, 2. Jerusalem. Berlin–New York: Walter de Gruyter, 2010.

Cowley, A. E. *Aramaic Papyri of the Fifth Century* B.C. Oxford: Clarendon, 1923.

Creswell, K. A. C. *Early Muslim Architecture* I. *Umayyads,* A.D. 622–750. 2nd ed. Oxford: Clarendon, 1969.

———. "Islam's Newly Revealed Artistic Inheritance from Byzantium: Hellenistic Panels in the al-Aksa Mosque." *Illustrated London News* (Jan. 16, 1937), 94–95.

Crowfoot, J. W. "Excavations on Ophel, 1928." *Palestine Exploration Quarterly* 61 (1929), 9–16, 75–77, 156–66.

———. "Ophel Again." *Palestine Exploration Quarterly* 77 (1945), 66–104.

Crowfoot, J. W., and G. M. Fitzgerald. "Excavations in the Tyropoeon Valley, Jerusalem, 1927." *Annual of the Palestine Exploration Fund* 5. London: Palestine Exploration Fund, 1929.

Cuneo, P. "The Urban Structure and Physical Organization of Ottoman Jerusalem in the Context of Ottoman Urbanism." In Auld and Hillenbrand, *Ottoman Jerusalem* I (2000), 210–220.

Dalman, G. *Jerusalem und sein Gelände.* Gütersloh: C. Bertelsmann, 1930.

De Groot, A., and D. T. Ariel. "Extramural Areas." *Excavations at the City of David 1978–1985* V. Directed by Yigal Shiloh. Qedem 40. Jerusalem: Institute of Archaeology, Hebrew University, 2000.

———. "Stratigraphical, Environmental, and Other Reports." *Excavations at the City of David 1978–1985* III. Directed by Yigal Shiloh. Qedem 33. Jerusalem: Institute of Archaeology, Hebrew University, 1992.

———. Various reports. *Excavations at the City of David 1978–1985* IV. Directed by Yigal Shiloh. Qedem 35. Jerusalem: Institute of Archaeology, Hebrew University, 1996.

De Groot, A., and H. Bernick-Greenberg. *Excavations at the City of David 1978– 1985 Directed by Yigal Shiloh VIIa. Area E. Stratigraphy and Architecture.* Qedem 53. Jerusalem: Institute of Archaeology, Hebrew University, 2012.

De Groot, A., and H. Bernick-Greenberg. *Excavations at the City of David 1978– 1985 Directed by Yigal Shiloh VIIb. Area E. The Finds.* Qedem 54. Jerusalem: Institute of Archaeology, Hebrew University, 2012.

De Sandoli, S. *Corpus Inscriptionum Crucesignatorum Terrae Sanctae (1099–1291).* Pubblicazioni dello Studium Biblicum Franciscanum, collection maior 21. Jerusalem: Franciscan Printing Press, 1974.

Dearman, J. A. *Studies in the Mesha Inscription and Moab.* Atlanta: Scholars, 1989.

Dever, W. "Excavating the Hebrew Bible, or Burying It Again? On Israel Finkelstein, Neil Asher Silberman's 'The Bible Unearthed: Archaeology's New

Vision of Ancient Israel and the Origin of Its Sacred Texts.'" *Bulletin of the American Schools of Oriental Research* 322 (2001), 67–77.

Donner, H. *The Mosaic Map of Madaba. An Introductory Guide.* Palaestina antiqua 7. Kampen: Kok Pharos, 1992.

Dow, M. "The Hammams of Ottoman Jerusalem." In Auld and Hillenbrand, *Ottoman Jerusalem* I (2000), 519–24.

Drinkard, J. F., et al., eds. *Benchmarks in Time and Culture: An Introduction to Palestinian Archaeology Dedicated to Joseph A. Callaway.* Atlanta: Scholars, 1988.

Dunand, M. "Byblos, Sidon, Jérusalem. Monuments apparentés des temps achéménides." Volume of the *Sixth Congress of the International Organization for the Study of the Old Testament*, Rome, 1968. Vetus Testamentum Supplement 17. Leiden: Brill, 1969, 64–70.

Elad, A. *Medieval Jerusalem and Islamic Worship: Holy Places, Ceremonies, Pilgrimage.* Islamic History and Civilization, Studies and Texts 8. Leiden and Boston: Brill, 1999.

Elath, E. "Claude Reignier Conder." *Palestine Exploration Quarterly* 97 (1965), 21–41.

Eliav, Y. *God's Mountain: The Temple Mount in Time, Place, and Memory.* Baltimore: Johns Hopkins University Press, 2005.

———. "The Urban Layout of Aelia Capitolina: A New View from the Perspective of the Temple Mount." In *The Bar Kokhba War Reconsidered: New Perspectives on the Second Jewish Revolt.* Edited by P. Schäfer. Tübingen: Mohr Siebeck, 2003, 241–77.

Eshel, I., and K. Prag, eds. *Excavations by K. M. Kenyon in Jerusalem, 1961–1967* IV: *The Iron Age Cave Deposits on the South-East Hill and Isolated Burials and Cemeteries Elsewhere.* Oxford: for the British School of Archaeology in Jerusalem, Oxford University Press, 1995.

van Ess, J. *Chiliastische Erwartungen und die Versuchung der Gottlichkeit: Der Kalif al-Hakim (386–411 H.)* Heidelberg: C. Winter Universitätsverlag, 1977.

Ettinghausen, R., and O. Grabar. *The Art and Architecture of Islam, 650–1250.* Harmondsworth and New York: Penguin, 1987.

Fehérvári, G. *Ceramics of the Islamic World in the Tareq Rajab Museum.* London and New York: I. B. Tauris, 2000.

Feldman, L. H. "How Much Hellenism in Jewish Palestine?" *Hebrew Union College Annual* 57 (1986), 83–111.

———. "Josephus (C.E. 37–c. 100)." In *The Cambridge History of Judaism* III: *The Early Roman Period.* Edited by W. Horbury et al. Cambridge, UK: Cambridge University Press, 1999, 901–21, 1189–97.

Finkelstein, I. "The Campaign of Shoshenq I to Palestine: A Guide to the 10th

Century B.C.E. Polity." *Zeitschrift des Deutschen Palästina-Vereins* 118 (2002), 109–35.

———. "A Few Notes on Demographic Data from Recent Generations and Ethnoarchaeology." *Palestine Exploration Quarterly* 122 (1990), 47–52.

———. "The Rise of Jerusalem and Judah: The Missing Link." *Levant* 33 (2001), 105–15.

———. "State Formation in Israel and Judah: A Contrast in Context, a Contrast in Trajectory." *Near Eastern Archaeology* 62 (1999), 35–52.

Finkelstein, I., and N. A. Silberman. *The Bible Unearthed: Archaelogy's New Vision of Ancient Israel and the Origin of Its Sacred Texts.* New York and London: Free Press, 2001.

Finkelstein, I., Z. Herzog, L. Singer-Avitz, and D. Ussishkin. "Has King David's Palace in Jerusalem been Found?" *Tel Aviv* 34 (2007), 142–64.

Fischer, J. "Die Mauern und Tore des biblischen Jerusalem." *Theologische Quartalschrift* 111 (1932), 233–43.

Folda, J. *The Art of the Crusaders in the Holy Land.* New York: Cambridge University Press, 1995.

Franken, H. J. "Jerusalem in the Bronze Age, 3000–1000 B.C." In Asali, *Jerusalem in History* (1989), 11–41.

Franken, H. J., and M. L. Steiner. *Excavations in Jerusalem, 1961–1967 II: The Iron Age Extramural Quarter on the South-East Hill.* Oxford: Oxford University Press, 1990.

Freeman-Grenville, G. S. P. *The Basilica of the Nativity in Bethlehem.* Jerusalem: Carta, 1993.

Fritz, V. "Temple Architecture: What Can Archaeology Tell Us about Solomon's Temple?" *Biblical Archaeology Review* 13.4 (1987), 38–49.

Fry, V. R. L. *The Warning Inscriptions from the Herodian Temple.* Ann Arbor, MI: University Microfilms International, 1985.

Galil, G. *The Chronology of the Kings of Israel and Judah.* Leiden: Brill, 1996.

Galor, K. "Domestic Architecture in Roman and Byzantine Galilee and Golan." *Near Eastern Archaeology* 66 (2003), 44–57.

———. "The Roman-Byzantine Dwelling in the Galilee and the Golan–'House' or 'Apartment'?" *Archaeologia transatlantica* 18 (2000), 17–34.

Galor, K., and G. Avni. *Unearthing Jerusalem: 150 Years of Archaeological Research in the Holy City.* Winona Lake, IN: Eisenbrauns, 2011.

Garfinkel, Y. "2 Chr 11:5–10: Fortified Cities List and the 'lmlk' Stamps. Reply to Nadav Na'aman." *Bulletin of the American Schools of Oriental Research* 271 (1988), 69–73.

Gershuny, L. "Jerusalem, Street of Chain (B)." *Excavations and Surveys in Israel* 10 (1991), 135–36.

Geva, H. "The Acra." In *The New Encyclopedia of Archaeological Excavations in the*

*Holy Land* II. Edited by E. Stern. Jerusalem: Israel Exploration Society and Carta; New York: Simon and Schuster, 1993, 723–24.

———. "Aelia Capitolina." In E. Stern, ed. *New Encyclopedia* II (1993), 759–66.

———, ed. *Ancient Jerusalem Revealed.* Jerusalem: Israel Exploration Society, exp. ed. 2000.

———. "The Camp of the Tenth Legion in Jerusalem: An Archaeological Reconsideration." *Israel Exploration Journal* 34 (1984), 239–54.

———. "Excavations in the Citadel of Jerusalem, 1979–1980. Preliminary Report." *Israel Exploration Journal* 33 (1983), 55–71.

———. "The First Wall." In E. Stern, ed. *New Encyclopedia* II (1993), 724–29.

———. *Jewish Quarter Excavations in the Old City of Jerusalem: Conducted by Nahman Avigad, 1969–1982* I: *Architecture and Stratigraphy: Areas A, W and X-2. Final Report.* Jerusalem: Israel Exploration Society, 2000.

———. *Jewish Quarter Excavations in the Old City of Jerusalem: Conducted by Nahman Avigad, 1969–1982* II: *The Finds from Areas A, W, and X-2, Final Report.* Jerusalem: Israel Exploration Society, 2003.

———. *Jewish Quarter Excavations in the Old City of Jerusalem: Conducted by Nahman Avigad, 1969–1982* III: *Area E and Other Studies, Final Report.* Jerusalem: Israel Exploration Society, 2006.

———. *Jewish Quarter Excavations in the Old City of Jerusalem; Conducted by Nahman Avigad, 1969–1982* IV. *The Burnt House of Area B and Other Studies. Final Report.* Jerusalem: Israel Exploration Society, 2010.

———. "Twenty-five Years of Excavations in Jerusalem, 1967–1992: Achievements and Evaluation." In H. Geva, *Ancient Jerusalem Revealed* (2000), 1–28.

Geva, H., and D. Bahat. "Architectural and Chronological Aspects of the Ancient Damascus Gate Area." *Israel Exploration Journal* 48 (1998), 223–35.

Gibson, S. "British Archaeological Work in Jerusalem between 1865 and 1967: An Assessment." In Galor and Avni, *Unearthing Jerusalem* (2011), 23–57.

Gibson, S., and D. M. Jacobson. *Below the Temple Mount in Jerusalem. A Sourcebook on the Cisterns, Subterranean Chambers and Conduits of the Haram al-Sharif.* British Archaeological Reports, International Series 637. Oxford, 1996.

Gilbert-Peretz, D. "Ceramic Figurines." In De Groot and Ariel, *Excavations at the City of David, 1978–1985* IV (1996), 29–86.

Goitein, S. D. "The Historical Background of the Erection of the Dome of the Rock." *Journal of the American Oriental Society* 70 (1950), 104–108.

Golvin, L. "Quelques notes sur le Suq al-Qattanin et ses annexes à Jérusalem." *Bulletin d'Études Orientales* 20 (1967), 101–117.

Goren, H. *For Jerusalem's Sake.* Jerusalem: Ariel, 1998 (Hebrew).

———. "Scientific Organizations as Agents of Change: The Palestine Exploration

Fund, the 'Deutsche Verein zur Erforschung Palästinas' and Nineteenth-century Palestine." *Journal of Historical Geography* 27 (2001), 153–65.

———. "Titus Tobler's Legacy: Two Sources." *Bulletin of the Anglo-Israel Archaeology Society* 14 (1994–95), 57–62.

———. "'Undoubtedly, the best connoisseur of Jerusalem in our times.' Conrad Schick as 'Palästina-Wissenschaftler.'" In Hübner, *Palaestina exploranda* (2006), 105–28.

Goren, Y., et al. "A Re-examination of the Inscribed Pomegranate from the Israel Museum." *Israel Exploration Journal* 55/1 (2005), 3–20.

Grabar, O. *The Formation of Islamic Art.* Revised ed. New Haven: Yale University Press, 1987.

———. "al-Kuds. B. Monuments." *Encyclopaedia of Islam* V (1986) 339–44.

———. *The Shape of the Holy: Early Islamic Jerusalem.* Princeton, NJ: Princeton University Press, 1996.

———. "Space and Holiness in Medieval Jerusalem." In L. I. Levine, ed. *Jerusalem. Its Sanctity and Centrality to Judaism, Christianity, and Islam.* New York: Continuum, 1999, 275–86.

———. "The Umayyad Dome of the Rock in Jerusalem." *Ars Orientalis* 3 (1959), 33–62 [= Bloom, J. M., ed. *Early Islamic Art and Architecture.* Aldershot, UK and Burlington, VT: Ashgate, 2002, 223–56].

Gröber, K. *Palästina, Arabien und Syrien. Baukunst, Landschaft, Volksleben.* Berlin, 1925.

Gutfeld, O. *Jewish Quarter Excavations in the Old City of Jerusalem; Conducted by Nahman Avigad, 1969–1982 V. The Cardo (Area X) and the Nea Church (Areas D and T). Final Report.* Jerusalem: Israel Exploration Society, 2012.

Guthe, H. *Ausgrabungen bei Jerusalem.* Leipzig: K. Baedeker, 1883.

Hachlili, R. *Ancient Jewish Art and Archaeology in the Land of Israel.* Leiden: Brill, 1988.

———. *Jewish Funerary Customs, Practices and Rites in the Second Temple Period.* Journal for the Study of Judaism, Supplement 94. Leiden and Boston 2005.

Halm, H. "Der Treuhänder Gottes. Die Edikte des Kalifen al-Hakim." *Islam* 63 (1986), 11–72.

Hamilton, R. W. "Excavations against the North Wall of Jerusalem." *Quarterly of the Department of Antiquities of Palestine* 10 (1944), 1–26.

———. *Khirbat al Mafjar: An Arabian Mansion in the Jordan Valley.* Oxford: Clarendon, 1959.

———. "Once Again the Aqsa." In Raby and Johns, *Bayt al-Maqdis* I (1992), 141–44.

———. "Street Levels in the Tyropoeon Valley" [1]. *Quarterly of the Department of Antiquities of Palestine* 1 (1932), 105–110.

——. "Street Levels in the Tyropoeon Valley" [2]. *Quarterly of the Department of Antiquities of Palestine* 2 (1933), 34–40.

——. *The Structural History of the Aqsa Mosque: A Record of Archaeological Gleanings from the Repairs of 1938–1942.* Jerusalem: Department of Antiquities of Palestine, 1949.

Hamrick, E. W. "The Northern Barrier Wall in Site T." In A. D. Tushingham, *Excavations in Jerusalem, 1961–1967* I. Toronto: Royal Ontario Museum, 1985, 213–32.

Harley, J. B., and D. Woodward, eds. *The History of Cartography* I: *Cartography in Prehistoric, Ancient, and Medieval Europe and the Mediterranean.* Chicago: University of Chicago Press, 1987.

Hawari, M. K. *Ayyubid Jerusalem (1187–1250): An Architectural and Archaeological Study.* Oxford: Archaeopress, 2007.

——. "The Citadel (Qal'a) in the Ottoman Period. An Overview." In Auld and Hillenbrand, *Ottoman Jerusalem* I (2000), 493–518.

Hayes, J. H., and S. R. Mandell. *The Jewish People in Classical Antiquity: From Alexander to Bar Kokhba.* Louisville: Westminster John Knox Press, 1998.

Heinen, H. "The Syrian-Egyptian Wars and the New Kingdoms of Asia Minor." In *The Cambridge Ancient History* I: *The Hellenistic World.* Edited by F. W. Walbank et al. Cambridge, UK: Cambridge University Press, 1984, 412–45.

Hengel, M. "The Interpenetration of Judaism and Hellenism in the pre-Maccabean Period." In *The Cambridge History of Judaism* II: *The Hellenistic Age.* Edited by W. D. Davies and L. Finkelstein. Cambridge, UK: Cambridge University Press, 1989, 167–228.

——. "Jerusalem als jüdische und hellenistische Stadt." In *Hellenismus. Beiträge zur Erforschung von Akkulturation und politischer Ordnung in den Staaten des hellenistischen Zeitalters. Akten des Internationalen Hellenismus-Kolloquiums 8.–14. März 1994 in Berlin.* Edited by B. Funck. Tübingen: Verlag J. C. B. Mohr (Paul Siebeck), 1996, 269–306.

——. *Judaism and Hellenism: Studies in Their Encounter in Palestine during the Early Hellenistic Period.* 2nd revised ed. London: SCM Press, 1974; Philadelphia: Fortress, 1981.

——. "The Political and Social History of Palestine from Alexander to Antiochus III (333–187 B.C.E.)." In *The Cambridge History of Judaism* II: *The Hellenistic Age.* Edited by W. D. Davies and L. Finkelstein. Cambridge, UK: Cambridge University Press, 1989, 35–78.

Hennessy, J. B. "Preliminary Report on Excavations at the Damascus Gate Jerusalem, 1964–1966." *Levant* 2 (1970), 22–27.

Hershkovitz, M. "Jerusalemite Painted Pottery from the Last Second Temple Period." In *The Nabateans in the Negev.* Edited by R. Rosenthal-Heginbottom. Reuben and Edith Hecht Museum, University of Haifa, Catalogue 22. Haifa, 2003, 45–50 (Hebrew, English summary 31*–34*).

Heyd, U. *Ottoman Documents on Palestine, 1552–1615: A Study of the Firman according to Muehimme Defteri*. Oxford: Clarendon, 1960.

Hillel, D. *The Natural History of the Bible: An Environmental Exploration of the Hebrew Scriptures*. New York: Columbia University Press, 2006.

Hillenbrand, C. *The Crusades: Islamic Perspectives*. Edinburgh: University of Edinburgh Press, 1999.

Hillenbrand, R. *Islamic Architecture: Form, Function and Meaning*. Edinburgh: University of Edinburgh Press, 1994.

———. "Structure, Style and Context in the Monuments of Ottoman Jerusalem." In Auld and Hillenbrand, *Ottoman Jerusalem* I (2000), 1–23.

———. "Umayyad Woodwork in the Aqsa Mosque." In Johns, *Bayt al-Maqdis* II (1999), 271–310.

Hillenbrand, R., and S. Auld, eds. *Ayyubid Jerusalem. The Holy City in Context, 1187–1250*. London: on behalf of the British School of Archaeology in Jerusalem in cooperation with the Administration of Auqaf and Islamic Affairs, Jerusalem, by Altajir World of Islam Trust, 2009.

Hoffmann, A., and S. Kerner, eds. *Gadara, Gerasa und die Dekapolis*. Mainz: Philipp von Zabern, 2002.

Holland, T. A. "A Study of Palestinian Iron Age Baked Clay Figurines with Special Reference to Jerusalem." *Levant* 9 (1977), 121–55.

Horbury, W. "The 'Caiaphas'-Ossuaries and Joseph Caiaphas." *Palestine Exploration Quarterly* 126 (1994), 32–48.

Hubbard, R. P. S. "The Topography of Ancient Jerusalem." *Palestine Exploration Quarterly* 98 (1966), 130–54.

Hübner, U. "The German Protestant Institute of Archaeology (Deutsches Evangelisches Institut für Altertumswissenschaft des Heiligen Landes)." In Galor and Avni, *Unearthing Jerusalem* (2011), 23–57.

———. "Jerusalem und die Jebusiter." *Kein Land für sich allein: Studien zum Kulturkontakt in Kanaan, Israel/Palästina*. Edited by U. Hübner and E. A. Knauf. Freiburg: Universitätsverlag, 2002, 31–42.

———. *Spiele und Spielzeug im antiken Palästina*. Freiburg: Universitätsverlag, Göttingen: Vandenhoeck & Ruprecht, 1992.

Iliffe, J. H. "Cemeteries and a 'Monastery' at the Y.M.C.A., Jerusalem." *Quarterly of the Department of Antiquities of Palestine* 4 (1935), 70–80.

Isaac, B. "Cassius Dio on the Revolt of Bar Kokhba." *Scripta Classica Israelica* 7 (1983–84), 68–76.

———. "The Roman Army in Jerusalem and Its Vicinity." *Studien zu den Militärgrenzen Roms III. Vorträge des 13. Internationalen Limeskongresses Aalen 1983*. Stuttgart: Theiss, 1986, 635–40.

——. "Roman Colonies in Judaea: The Foundation of Aelia Capitolina." *Talanta* 12–13 (1980–81), 31–54.

Israeli, Y. "Christian Images and Symbols." In *The Cradle of Christianity.* Edited by Y. Israeli and D. Mevorah. Jerusalem: Israel Museum, 2000, 114–65.

Issar, A., and M. Zohar. *Climate Change: Environment and Civilization in the Middle East.* Berlin and New York: Springer, 2004.

Japp, S. *Die Baupolitik Herodes' des Grossen: Die Bedeutung der Architektur für die Herrschaftslegitimation eines römischen Klientelkönigs.* Internationale Archäologie 64; Rahden/Westf.: M. Leidorf, 2000.

Jaroš, K. *Die ältesten Fragmente eines biblischen Textes. Zu den Silberamuletten von Jerusalem.* Mainz: Philipp von Zabern, 1997.

Johns, C. N. "The Citadel, Jerusalem: A Summary of Work since 1934." *Quarterly of the Department of Antiquities of Palestine* 14 (1950), 121–90.

——. "Discoveries in Palestine since 1939." *Palestine Exploration Quarterly* 80 (1948), 81–101.

——. "Excavations at the Citadel, Jerusalem, Interim Report, 1935." *Quarterly of the Department of Antiquities of Palestine* 5 (1936), 127–31.

——. "Jerusalem: Ancient Street Levels in the Tyropoeon Valley within the Walls." *Quarterly of the Department of Antiquities of Palestine* 1 (1932), 97–100.

Johns, J., ed. *Bayt al-Maqdis* II: *Jerusalem and Early Islam.* Oxford: Oxford University Press, 1999.

Jotham-Rothschild, J. "The Tombs of Sanhedria" [1]. *Palestine Exploration Quarterly* 84 (1952), 23–38.

——. "The Tombs of Sanhedria" [2]. *Palestine Exploration Quarterly* 86 (1954), 16–22.

Kaeppeli, T., and P. Benoit. "Un pèlerinage dominicain inédit du XIVe siècle, Le liber de locis et conditionibus Terrae sanctae et Sepulcro d'Humbert de Dijon O.P. (1332)." *Revue Biblique* 62 (1955), 513–40.

Kaplony, A. *The Haram of Jerusalem, 324–1099: Temple, Friday Mosque, Area of Spiritual Power.* Stuttgart: Franz Steiner, 2002.

Kaufman, A. S. "Where the Ancient Temple of Jerusalem Stood." *Biblical Archaeology Review* 9.2 (1983), 40–59.

Keel, O. "The Peculiar Headrests for the Dead in First Temple Times." *Biblical Archaeology Review* 13.3 (1987), 50–53.

Keel, O., et al. *Studien zu den Stempelsiegeln aus Palästina-Israel* II. Freiburg: Universitätsverlag, 1989.

Keel, O., and M. Küchler. *Gods and Goddesses and Images of God in Ancient Israel.* Minneapolis: Augsburg Fortress, 1998.

——. *Orte und Landschaften der Bibel. Ein Handbuch und Studien-Reiseführer zum*

*Heiligen Land II. Der Süden.* Zürich and Göttingen: Vandenhoeck and Ruprecht, 1982.

Keenan, N. "A Local Trend in Crusader Art in Jerusalem." In Yadin, *Jerusalem Revealed* (1975), 114–15.

Kenyon, K. M. *Digging Up Jerusalem.* London: Praeger, 1974.

——. *Jerusalem: Excavating 3000 Years of History.* London: Thames and Hudson, 1967.

——. "Letters to the Editor." *Israel Exploration Journal* 25 (1975), 265–66.

Kenyon, K. M., and T. A. Holland. *Excavations at Jericho* IV: *The Pottery Type Series and Other Finds.* London: British School of Archaeology in Jerusalem, 1982.

King, P. J., and L. E. Stager. *Life in Biblical Israel.* Louisville and London: Westminster John Knox, 2001.

Kloner, A., and B. Zissu. *The Necropolis of Jerusalem in the Second Temple Period.* Leuven: Peeters, 2007.

Kloppenborg Verbin, J. S. "Dating Theodotos ('CIJ' II 1404)." *Journal of Jewish Studies* 51 (2000), 243–80.

Knauf, E. A. "Hezekiah or Manasseh? A Reconsideration of the Siloam Tunnel and Inscription." *Tel Aviv* 28 (2001), 281–87.

——. "Jerusalem in the Late Bronze and Early Iron Ages." *Tel Aviv* 27 (2000), 75–90.

Knudtzon, J. A. *Die El-Amarna-Tafeln* I. Leipzig: J. C. Hinrichs, 1908.

Korn, L. *Ayyubidische Architektur in Ägypten und Syrien: Bautätigkeit im Kontext von Politik und Gesellschaft 564–658/1169–1260* I–II. Heidelberg: Heidelberger Orientverlag, 2004.

Krautheimer, R. *Early Christian and Byzantine Architecture.* 4th rev. ed. Harmondworth, Middlesex and New York: Penguin Books, 1986.

Kroyanker, D. *Jerusalem Architecture.* London: Tauris Parke; New York: Vendome Press, in association with the Jerusalem Institute for Israel Studies, 1994.

Krüger, J. *Die Grabeskirche zu Jerusalem: Geschichte–Gestalt–Bedeutung.* Regensburg: Schnell und Steiner, 2000.

Küchler, M. "Moschee und Kalifenpaläste Jerusalems nach den Aphrodito-Papyri." *Zeitschrift des Deutschen Palästina-Vereins* 107 (1991), 120–43.

Kühnel, B. *Crusader Art of the Twelfth Century: A Geographical, an Historical, or an Art Historical Notion?* Berlin: Gebr. Mann, 1994.

——. "Crusader Sculpture at the Ascension Church on the Mount of Olives in Jerusalem." *Gesta* 16 (1977), 41–50.

Kühnel, E. *Islamic Arts.* London: G. Bell, 1970.

Kühnel, G. *Wall Painting in the Latin Kingdom of Jerusalem.* Berlin: Gebr. Mann, 1988.

Kuemmel, A. *Karte der Materialien zur Topographie des alten Jerusalem.* Leipzig: Deutscher Verein zur Erforschung Palästinas, 1904.

——. *Materialien zur Topographie des alten Jerusalem, Begleittext zu der "Karte der Materialien zur Topographie des alten Jerusalem."* Halle: Deutscher Verein zur Erforschung Palästinas, 1906.

Lancaster, S. P., and G. A. Long. "Where They Met: Separations in the Rock Mass near Siloam Tunnel's Meeting Point." *Bulletin of the American Schools of Oriental Research* 315 (1999), 15–26.

Laperrousaz, E.-M. "Quelques résultats récents des fouilles archéologiques conduites à Jerusalem et aux alentours de la Ville Sainte." *Revue des Études Juives* 129 (1970), 145–59.

Le Strange, G. *Palestine under the Moslems: A Description of Syria and the Holy Land from* A.D. 650 *to* 1500. London: A. P. Watt, 1890.

Levine, L. I. *The Ancient Synagogue: The First Thousand Years.* New Haven: Yale University Press, 2000.

——. *Jerusalem: A Portrait of the City in the Second Temple Period (538* B.C.E.–70 C.E.*).* Philadelphia: Jewish Publication Society, 2002.

Levy, M. "Medieval Maps of Jerusalem." In *The History of Jerusalem. Crusaders and Ayyubids (1099–1250).* Edited by J. Prawer and H. Ben-Shammai. Jerusalem: Yad Izhak Ben Zvi, 1991, 418–507.

Levy, T. E., ed. *The Archaeology of Society in the Holy Land.* New York: Leicester University Press, 1995.

Levy-Rubin, M. "Crusader Maps of Jerusalem." In *Knights of the Holy Land.* Edited by S. Rozenberg. Jerusalem: Israel Museum, 1999, 230–38.

——. "The Rediscovery of the Uppsala Map of Jerusalem." *Zeitschrift des Deutschen Palästina-Vereins* 111 (1995), 162–67.

Lichtenberger, A. *Die Baupolitik Herodes des Grossen.* Abhandlungen des Deutschen Palästina-Vereins 26. Wiesbaden: Harrassowitz, 1999.

Lifshitz, B. "Jérusalem sous la domination romaine. Histoire de la ville depuis la conquête de Pompée jusqu'à Constantin (63 a.C.–325 p.C.)." *Aufstieg und Niedergang der Römischen Welt* II.8. Edited by W. Haase and H. Temporini. Berlin and New York: W. de Gruyter, 1977, 444–89.

Lipiński, E. *Itineraria Phoenicia.* Orientalia Lovaniensia Analecta 127. Leuven and Dudley, MA: Peeters, 2004.

Little, D. P. "Jerusalem under the Ayyubids and Mamluks, 1187–1516 A.D." In Asali, *Jerusalem in History* (1989), 177–99.

Liwak, R. "Israel und Juda." In *Herrscherchronologien der antiken Welt. Namen, Daten, Dynastien.* Edited by W. Eder and J. Renger. Der Neue Pauly, Supplement 1. Stuttgart, 2004, 55–58

Lobrichon, G. *1099, Jérusalem conquise.* Paris: Seuil, 1998.

Macalister, R. A. S., and J. G. Duncan. "*Excavations of the Hill of Ophel Jerusalem,*

*1923–1925: being the Joint Expedition of the Palestine Exploration Fund and the 'Daily Telegraph.'" Annual of the Palestine Exploration Fund* 4. London: Palestine Exploration Fund, 1926.

Magen, M. "Excavations at the Damascus Gate, 1979–1984." In H. Geva, *Ancient Jerusalem Revealed* (2000), 281–86.

———. "Recovering the Roman Jerusalem. The Entryway beneath Damascus Gate." *Biblical Archaeology Review* 14.3 (1988), 48–56.

Magen, Y. *The Stone Vessel Industry in the Second Temple Period: Excavations at Hizma and the Jerusalem Temple Mount.* Jerusalem: Israel Exploration Society, 2002.

Magness, J. "The North Wall of Aelia Capitolina." In *The Archaeology of Jordan and Beyond: Essays in Honor of James A. Sauer.* Edited by L. E. Stager, J. A. Greene, and M. D. Coogan. Cambridge, MA: Harvard University Press, 2000, 328–39.

Mare, W. H. *The Archaeology of the Jerusalem Area.* Grand Rapids, MI: Baker Book House, 1987.

Mazar, A. *Archaeology of the Land of the Bible, 10,000–586* B.C.E. New York: Doubleday, 1990.

———. "A Survey of the Aqueducts to Jerusalem." In *Aqueducts of Israel.* Edited by D. Amit, Y. Hirschfeld, and J. Patrich. Journal of Roman Archaeology, Supplementary Series 46. Portsmouth, 2002, 210–244.

Mazar, B. *The Excavations in the Old City of Jerusalem: Preliminary Report of the 2nd and 3rd Seasons, 1969–1970.* Jerusalem: Israel Exploration Society, 1971.

———. *The Mountain of the Lord.* Garden City, NY: Doubleday, 1975.

Mazar, B., and H. Eshel. "Who Built the First Wall of Jerusalem?" *Israel Exploration Journal* 48 (1998), 263–68.

Mazar, E. *The Complete Guide to the Temple Mount Excavations.* Jerusalem: Shoham Academic Research and Publication, 2002.

———. "Did I Find King David's Palace?" *Biblical Archaeology Review* 32.1 (2006), 16–27, 70.

———. *Discovering the Solomonic Wall in Jerusalem: A Remarkable Archaeological Adventure.* Jerusalem: Shoham Academic Research and Publication, 2011.

———. "Hadrian's Legion." British Archaeological Reports 32/6 (2006), 52–58, 82–83.

———. "The Roman-Byzantine Bathhouse at the Foot of the Western Wall of the Temple Mount Precinct." *New Studies on Jerusalem* 6 (2000), 87–102 (Hebrew; English summary, 9*).

———. *The Temple Mount Excavations in Jerusalem, 1968–1978, Directed by Benjamin Mazar. Final Reports* II: *The Byzantine and Early Islamic Periods.* Qedem 43. Jerusalem: Institute of Archaeology, Hebrew University, 2003.

———. *The Temple Mount Excavations in Jerusalem, 1968–1978, Directed by Ben-*

*jamin Mazar. Final Reports Volume III. The Byzantine Period.* Qedem 46. Jerusalem: Institute of Archaeology, Hebrew University, 2007.

———. *The Temple Mount Excavations in Jerusalem, 1968–1978, Directed by Benjamin Mazar. Final Reports Volume IV. The Tenth Legion in Aelia Capitolina.* Qedem 52. Jerusalem: Institute of Archaeology, Hebrew University, 2011.

Mazar, E., et al. "A Cuneiform Tablet from the Ophel in Jerusalem." *Israel Exploration Journal* 60 (2010), 4–21.

Mazar, E. and B. Mazar. *Excavations in the South of the Temple Mount: The Ophel of Biblical Jerusalem.* Qedem 29. Jerusalem: Institute of Archaeology, Hebrew University, 1989.

McNicoll, A. W., and N. P. Milner. *Hellenistic Fortifications from the Aegean to the Euphrates.* Oxford: Clarendon Press; New York: Oxford University Press, 1997.

McNulty, I. B. "The North Wall outside Jerusalem" *Biblical Archaeologist* 42 (1979), 141–44.

Meinecke, M. *Die mamlukische Architektur in Ägypten und Syrien (648/1250 bis 923/1517)* I–II. Glückstadt: J. J. Augustin, 1992.

Meshorer, Y. *Ancient Jewish Coinage* I: *Persian Period through Hasmoneans.* New York: Amphora Books, 1982.

Micklewright, N. "Costume in Ottoman Jerusalem." In Auld and Hillenbrand, *Ottoman Jerusalem* I (2000), 291–300.

Mildenberg, L. "Bar Kochba in Jerusalem?" *Schweizer Münzblätter* 27 (1977), 1–6.

———. *The Coinage of the Bar Kokhba War.* Aarau: Verlag Sauerländer, 1984.

Millar, F. "The Background to the Maccabean Revolution: Reflections on Martin Hengel's 'Judaism and Hellenism.'" *Journal of Jewish Studies* 29 (1978), 1–21.

Mittmann, S., and G. Schmitt, eds. *Tübinger Bibelatlas.* Stuttgart: Deutsche Bibelgesellschaft, 2001.

Montefiore, S. S. *Jerusalem: The Biography.* New York: Alfred A. Knopf, 2012.

Modrzejewski, J. M. *The Jews of Egypt: From Rameses II to Emperor Hadrian.* Philadelphia: Jewish Publication Society, 1995.

Moorey, P. R. S. *A Century of Biblical Archaeology.* Cambridge, UK: Lutterworth, 1991.

Mørkholm, O. "Antiochus IV." In *The Cambridge History of Judaism* II: *The Hellenistic Age.* Edited by W. D. Davies and L. Finkelstein. Cambridge, UK: Cambridge University Press, 1989, 278–91.

Morris, I. *Death-ritual and Social Structure in Classical Antiquity.* Cambridge, MA: Cambridge University Press, 1992.

Murphy-O'Connor, J. "Where Was the Antonia Fortress?" *Revue Biblique* 111 (2004), 78–89.

Musée d'Art et d'Essay, Palais de Tokyo. *Félix de Saulcy et la Terre Sainte.* Paris: Ministère de la culture, Éditions de la réunion des musées nationaux, 1982.

Musti, D. "Syria and the East Domenico." In *The Cambridge Ancient History* I: *The Hellenistic World.* Edited by F. W. Walbank et al. Cambridge, UK: Cambridge University Press, 1984, 175–220.

Myres, D. "al-'Imara al-'Amira. The Charitable Foundation of Khassaki Sultan (959/1552)." In Auld and Hillenbrand, *Ottoman Jerusalem* I (2000), 539–81.

———. "An Overview of the Islamic Architecture of Ottoman Jerusalem." In Auld and Hillenbrand, *Ottoman Jerusalem* I (2000), 325–54.

Na'aman, N. "Cow Town or Royal Capital? Evidence for Iron Age Jerusalem." *Biblical Archaeology Review* 23.4 (1997), 43–47, 67.

———. "Royal Vassals or Governors? On the Status of Sheshbazzar and Zerubbabel in the Persian Empire." *Henoch* 22 (2000), 35–44.

Naor, M. *The Jewish Quarter in Jerusalem.* Jerusalem: The Company for the Reconstruction and Development of the Jewish Quarter in the Old City of Jerusalem, 1987.

Natsheh, Y. "The Architecture of Ottoman Jerusalem." In Auld and Hillenbrand, *Ottoman Jerusalem* I (2000), 583–655.

———. "Catalogue of Buildings." In Auld and Hillenbrand, *Ottoman Jerusalem* II (2000), 657–1085.

Netzer, E. *The Architecture of Herod, the Great Builder.* Texte und Studien zum Antiken Judentum 117. Tübingen 2006.

———. "Domestic Architecture in the Iron Age." In *The Architecture of Ancient Israel, from the Prehistoric to the Persian Periods, in Memory of Immanuel (Munya) Dunayevsky.* Edited by A. Kempinski and R. Reich. Jerusalem: Israel Exploration Society, 1992, 193–201.

Nock, A. D. "Cremation and Burial in the Roman Empire." *Harvard Theological Review* 25 (1932), 321–59.

Orfali, G. *Gethsémani, ou Notice sur l'Eglise de l'agonie ou de la prière, d'après les fouilles récentes accomplies par la Custodie franciscaine de Terre Sainte (1909–1920).* Paris: A. Picard, 1924.

Ollendorf, F. "Two Mamluk Tomb-Chambers in Western Jerusalem." *Israel Exploration Journal* 32 (1982), 245–50.

Ovadiah, A. "A Crusader Church in the Jewish Quarter of the Old City of Jerusalem." In *Ancient Churches Revealed.* Edited by Y. Tsafrir. Jerusalem: Israel Exploration Society, 1993, 136–39.

Ovadiah, A., and S. Mucznik. "Orpheus from Jerusalem: Pagan or Christian Image?" *Jerusalem Cathedra* 1 (1981), 152–66.

Ovadiah, A., and R. Ovadiah. *Hellenistic, Roman and Early Byzantine Mosaic Pavements in Israel.* Rome: L'Erma" di Bretschneider, 1987.

Pastor, J. *Land and Economy in Ancient Palestine.* London and New York: Routledge, 1979.

Patrich, J. "The Early Church of the Holy Sepulchre in the Light of Excavations and Restoration." In *Ancient Churches Revealed.* Edited by Y. Tsafrir. Jerusalem: Israel Exploration Society, 1993, 101–17.

Paul, S. M., and W. G. Dever, eds. *Biblical Archaeology.* Jerusalem: Keter, 1973.

Peleg, O. "Roman Marble Sculpture from the Temple Mount Excavations." *New Studies on Jerusalem* 7 (2001), 129–49 (Hebrew; English summary, 11*–12*).

Peri, O. "The Waqf as an Instrument to Increase and Consolidate Political Power. The Case of Khasseki Sultan Waqf in Late Eighteenth-Century Ottoman Jerusalem." *Studies in Islamic Society. Contributions in Memory of Gabriel Baer.* Edited by G. R. Warburg and G. G. Gilbar. Haifa 1984, 47–62.

Peters, F. E. *Children of Abraham: Judaism, Christianity, Islam.* Princeton, NJ: Princeton University Press, 1982.

——. *The Distant Shrine. The Islamic Centuries in Jerusalem.* AMS Studies in Modern Society 22; New York 1993.

——. *Jerusalem: The Holy City in the Eyes of Chroniclers, Visitors, Pilgrims, and Prophets from the Days of Abraham to the Beginnings of Modern Times.* Princeton, NJ: Princeton University Press, 1985.

——. *Jerusalem and Mecca: The Typology of the Holy City in the Near East.* New York University Studies in Near Eastern Civilization 11. New York and London: New York University Press, 1986.

——. *The Monotheists: Jews, Christians, and Muslims in Conflict and Competition* I–II. Princeton, NJ: Princeton University Press, 2003.

Pfanner, M. *Der Titusbogen.* Mainz: Philipp von Zabern, 1983.

Piccirillo, M., and E. Alliata. *The Madaba Map Centenary, 1897–1997: Travelling through the Byzantine Umayyad Period.* Studium Biblicum Franciscanum, collectio maior 40. Jerusalem: Studium Biblicum Franciscanum, 1999.

Piccirillo, M., and Y. Israeli. "The Architecture and Liturgy of the Early Church." *The Cradle of Christianity.* Edited by Y. Israeli and D. Mevorah. Jerusalem: Israel Museum, 2000, 48–113.

Pierotti, E. *Jerusalem Explored being a Description of the Ancient and Modern City with Numerous Illustrations consisting of Views, Ground Plans, and Sections.* London: Bell and Daldy; Cambridge: Deighton, Bell and Co., 1864.

von Pilgrim, C. "Tempel des Jahu und 'Strasse des Königs.' Ein Konflikt in der späten Perserzeit auf Elephantine." In *Egypt. Temple of the Whole World–Ägypten. Tempel der gesamten Welt. Studies in Honour of Jan Assmann.* Edited by S. Meyer. Numen Book Series, Studies in the History of Religions 97. Leiden and Boston: Brill, 2003, 303–317.

Pixner, B. "Church of the Apostles Found on Mt. Zion." *Biblical Archaeology Review* 16.3 (1990), 17–35, 60.

———. "The History of the 'Essene Gate' Area." *Zeitschrift des Deutschen Palästina-Vereins* 105 (1989), 96–104.

———. "The Pit of Jeremiah Rediscovered?" *Christian News from Israel* 27 (1979–82), 118–21, 148.

———. "Was the Trial of Jesus in the Hasmonean Palace? A New Solution to a Thorny Topographical Problem of Jerusalem." In *Jerusalem, City of the Ages*. Edited by A. L. Eckardt. Lanham, MD: University Press of America; New York: American Academic Association for Peace in the Middle East, 1987, 66–80.

Pixner, B., D. Chen, and S. Margalit. "Mount Zion: The 'Gate of the Essenes' Re-excavated." *Zeitschrift des Deutschen Palästina-Vereins* 105 (1989), 85–95.

Porten, B. "The Jews in Egypt." In *The Cambridge History of Judaism* I: *Introduction. The Persian Period*. Edited by W. D. Davies and L. Finkelstein. Cambridge, UK: Cambridge University Press, 1984, 372–400.

Prag, K. *Blue Guide, Jerusalem*. London: A. and C. Black; New York: W. W. Norton, 1989.

———. *Excavations by K. M. Kenyon in Jerusalem 1961–1967* V: *Discoveries in Hellenistic to Ottoman Jerusalem*. London: Council for British Research in the Levant, 2008.

Prawer, J., and H. Ben-Shammai, eds. *The History of Jerusalem: The Early Muslim Period, 638–1099*. Jerusalem: Yad Izhak Ben-Zvi; New York: New York University Press, 1996.

Pringle, D. *The Churches of the Crusader Kingdom of Jerusalem: A Corpus* I–II. Cambridge, UK: Cambridge University Press, 1993–98.

———. *The Churches of the Crusader Kingdom of Jerusalem: A Corpus* III: *The City of Jerusalem*. Cambridge UK: Cambridge University Press, 2007.

———. *The Churches of the Crusader Kingdom of Jerusalem: A Corpus* IV: *The Cities of Acre and Tyre*. Cambridge UK: Cambridge University Press, 2009.

Raby, J., and J. Johns, eds. *Bayt al-Maqdis* I: *'Abd al-Malik's Jerusalem*. Oxford: University of Oxford, 1992.

Rahmani, L. Y. *A Catalogue of Jewish Ossuaries from the Collections of the State of Israel*. Jerusalem: Israel Antiquities Authority, 1994.

———. "Jason's Tomb." *Israel Exploration Journal* 17 (1967), 61–100.

Rainey, A. F. "Stones for Bread: Archaeology versus History." *Near Eastern Archaeology* 64 (2001), 140–49.

Re'em, A. "Excavations in the Citadel 2000–2001." In *New Discoveries at the Citadel of Jerusalem. Palaces and Fortifications*. Edited by B. Zissu. Jerusalem: Israel Antiquities Authority, 2002, 7–15 (Hebrew).

Reich, R. "The Ancient Burial Ground in the Mamilla Neighborhood, Jerusalem." In Geva, *Ancient Jerusalem Revealed* (2000), 111–18.

——. "The Dung Gate Area." In E. Stern, ed. *New Encyclopedia* V (2008), 1808–9.

——. "The Israel Exploration Society (IES)." In Galor and Avni, *Unearthing Jerusalem* (2011), 117–124.

——. *Miqwa'ot in Eretz-Israel in the Second Temple and the Mishnah and Talmud Periods.* PhD diss., Jerusalem, Hebrew University, 1990.

——. "On the History of the Gihon Spring in the Second Temple Period." *Eretz Israel* 19 (1987), 330–333 (Hebrew; English summary, 83*).

——. "Ossuary Inscriptions from the Caiaphas Tomb." *Atiqot* 21 (1992), 72–77.

——. "The Pool of Siloam." In *The New Encyclopedia of Archaeological Excavations in the Holy Land* V (supplementary vol.). Edited by E. Stern. Jerusalem: Israel Exploration Society and Carta; New York: Simon and Schuster, 2008, 1807.

Reich, R., and G. Bar-Oz. "The Jerusalem City Dump in the Late Second Temple Period. A Quantitative Study." *New Studies on Jerusalem* 12 (2006), 83–98 (Hebrew; English summary, 14*–15*).

Reich, R., and Y. Billig. "Jerusalem, Robinson's Arch." *Excavations and Surveys in Israel* 20 (2000): 135.

Reich, R., and Y. Billig. "The Robinson's Arch Area." In The New Encyclopedia of Archaeological Excavations in the Holy Land V (supplementary vol.) Edited by E. Stern. Jerusalem: Israel Exploration Society and Carta; New York: Simon and Schuster, 2008, 1809–11.

Reich, R., and E. Shukron. "Channel II in the City of David, Jerusalem: Some of Its Technical Features and Their Chronology." In *Cura aquarum in Israel: Proceedings of the 11th International Conference on the History of Water Management and Hydraulic Engineering in the Mediterranean Region. Israel, 7–12 May 2001.* Edited by C. Ohlig, Y. Peleg, and T. Tsuk. Siegburg: Deutschen Wasserhistorischen Gesellschaft, 2002, 1–6.

——. "The Excavations at the Gihon Spring and Warren's Shaft System in the City of David." In Geva, *Ancient Jerusalem Revealed* (2000), 327–39.

——. "The History of the Gihon Spring in Jerusalem." *Levant* 36 (2004), 211–23.

——. "Jerusalem, City of David." *Hadashot Arkheologiyot* 115 (2003), 69–71 (Hebrew; English summary, 51*–53*).

——. "Jerusalem, The Gihon Spring." *Hadashot Arkheologiyot* 108 (1998), 136–137.

——. "The System of Rock-cut Tunnels near Gihon in Jerusalem Reconsidered." *Revue Biblique* 107 (2000), 5–17.

——. "The Western Extramural Quarter of Byzantine Jerusalem." In *The Armenians in Jerusalem and the Holy Land.* Edited by M. E. Stone, R. R. Ervine, and N. Stone. Hebrew University Armenian Studies 4; Leuven, 2002, 193–201.

Restle, M. "Bethlehem." *Reallexikon zur Byzantinischen Kunst* I. Stuttgart: Hiersemann, 1966, 599–612.

Richmond, E. T. "The Church of the Nativity: the Plan of the Constantinian Church." *Quarterly of the Department of Antiquities of Palestine* 6 (1939), 63–72.

——. *The Dome of the Rock in Jerusalem. A Description of Its Structure and Decoration.* Oxford: Clarendon, 1924.

Riley-Smith, J. S. C., ed. *Atlas of the Crusades.* London: Times Books, 1991.

——. *The First Crusaders, 1095–1131.* Cambridge, UK and New York: Cambridge University Press, 1995.

——, ed. *The Oxford Illustrated History of the Crusades.* Oxford and New York: Oxford University Press, 1995.

——. *What Were the Crusades?* Houndmills, Basingstoke, Hampshire, UK and New York: Palgrave Macmillan, 2002.

Ritmeyer, L. *The Quest. Revealing the Temple Mount in Jerusalem.* Jerusalem: Carta, 2006.

Robinson, E. *Biblical Researches in Palestine, Mount Sinai and Arabia Petraea* I–III. London: Murray, 1841.

——. *Later Biblical Researches in Palestine and in the Adjacent Regions.* Boston: Crocker and Brewster, 1856.

Röhricht, R. "Karten und Pläne zur Palästinakunde aus dem 7.–16. Jarhundert" [1]. *Zeitschrift des Deutschen Palästina-Vereins* 14 (1891), 8–12, 87–92, 137–41.

——. "Karten und Pläne zur Palästinakunde aus dem 7.–16. Jarhundert" [2]. *Zeitschrift des Deutschen Palästina-Vereins* 15 (1892), 34–39, 185–92.

Roller, D. W. *The Building Program of Herod the Great.* Berkeley: University of California Press, 1998.

Rosen, S. A. "Flint Implements." In De Groot and Ariel, *Excavations at the City of David: Final Report, 1978–1985* IV. Qedem 35. Jerusalem: Institute of Archaeology, Hebrew University, 1996, 257–67.

Rosen-Ayalon, M. "Art and Architecture in Ayyubid Jerusalem." *Israel Exploration Journal* 40 (1990), 305–14.

——. "Art and Architecture in Jerusalem in the Early Islamic Period." In Prawer and Ben-Shammai, *The History of Jerusalem: The Early Muslim Period, 638–1099.* Jerusalem: Yad Izhak Ben-Zvi; New York: New York University Press, 1996, 386–412.

———. *The Early Islamic Monuments of al-Haram al-Sharif: An Iconographic Study.* Qedem 28. Jerusalem: Institute of Archaeology, Hebrew University, 1989.

———. "An Early Source on the Construction of the Dome of the Chain on the Temple Mount." *Cathedra* 11 (1979), 184–85.

———. *Islamic Art and Archaeology of Palestine.* Walnut Creek, CA: Left Coast, 2006.

———. "Récentes découvertes d'archéologie islamique." *Archéologie, Art et Histoire de Palestine.* Edited by E.-M. Laperrousaz. Paris: Cerf, 1988, 210–15.

Rosenberg, S. "The Jewish Temple at Elephantine." *Near Eastern Archaeology* 67 (2004), 4–13.

Sacchi, P. "L'esilio e la fine della monarchia Davidica." *Henoch* 11 (1989), 131–48.

———. *The History of the Second Temple Period.* Sheffield: Sheffield Academic Press, 2000.

———. "Re Vassalli o governatori? Una discussione." *Henoch* 23 (2001), 147–52.

Sachau, E. *Drei aramäische Papyrusurkunden aus Elephantine.* Berlin: Königl. Akademie der Wissenschaften, in Kommission bei G. Reimer, 1907.

Salameh, K. *The Qur'an Manuscripts in the Al-Haram Al-Sharif Islamic Museum, Jerusalem.* Reading, UK: Garnet; Paris: UNESCO, 2001.

de Saulcy, F. *Jérusalem.* Paris: A. Morel et Cie, 1882.

———. *Narrative of a Journey round the Dead Sea and in the Bible Lands, in 1850 and 1851* I–II. Philadelphia: Parry and M'Millan, 1854.

———. *Voyage autour de la Mer Morte et dans les terres bibliques, exécuté de décembre 1850 à avril 1851* I–II. Paris: J. Baudry, 1853.

———. *Voyage en Terre Sainte* I–II. Paris, Didier et cie, 1865.

Schäfer, P. *Der Bar Kokhba-Aufstand: Studien zum zweiten jüdischen Krieg gegen Rom, Texte und Krieg gegen Rom.* Texte und Studien zum Antiken Judentum 1. Tübingen: J. C. B. Mohr, 1981.

———, ed. *The Bar Kokhba War Reconsidered. New Perspectives on the Second Jewish Revolt.* Texte und Studien zum Antiken Judentum 100. Tübingen: Mohr Siebeck, 2003.

———. "Hadrian's Policy in Judaea and the Bar Kokhba Revolt: a Reassessment." *A Tribute to Geza Vermes: Essays on Jewish and Christian Literature and History.* Edited by P. R. Davies and R. T. White. Sheffield: JSOT Press, 1990.

Schick, C. "The Aqueducts from Siloam." *Palestine Exploration Quarterly* 18 (1886), 88–91.

———. *Beit el Makdas oder der alte Tempelplatz zu Jerusalem, wie er jetzt ist.* Jerusalem: Selbstverlag des Verfassers, 1887.

———. "Discovery of a Beautiful Mosaic Pavement with Armenian Inscription, North of Jerusalem." *Palestine Exploration Quarterly* 26 (1894), 257–260.

———. "The Muristan, or the Site of the Hospital of St. John of Jerusalem." *Palestine Exploration Quarterly* 34 (1902), 42–56.

———. "New Discoveries in the North of Jerusalem." *Palestine Exploration Quarterly* 11 (1879), 198–200.

———. "Recent Discoveries in Jerusalem." *Palestine Exploration Quarterly* 21 (1889), 62–63.

———. *Die Stiftshütte, der Tempelplatz der Jetztzeit.* Berlin: Weidmann, 1896.

Schick, R. *The Christian Communities of Palestine from Byzantine to Islamic Rule: A Historical and Archaeological Study.* Princeton, NJ: Darwin, 1995.

Schmitt, G. "Die dritte Mauer Jerusalems." *Zeitschrift des Deutschen Palästina-Vereins* 97 (1981), 153–70.

Schölch, A. "Jerusalem in the 19th Century, 1831–1917 A.D." In Asali, *Jerusalem in History* (1989), 228–48.

———. *Palästina im Umbruch 1856–1882.* Berliner Islamstudien 4. Stuttgart, 1986.

Schürer, E. *The History of the Jewish People in the Age of Jesus Christ (175 B.C.–A.D. 135)* I. Revised by G. Vermes and F. Millar. Edinburgh: T. and T. Clark, 1973.

Schur, N. "Why Suleiman the Magnificent Built the Walls of Jerusalem." *Zev Vilnay's Jubilee Volume II.* Edited by E. Schiller. Jerusalem 1987, 15–19.

Segal, A. "Horbat Susita." *Excavations and Surveys in Israel* 115 (2003), (Hebrew; English summary, 13*–17*).

Segal, P. "The Penalty of the Warning Inscription from the Temple of Jerusalem." *Israel Exploration Journal* 39 (1989), 79–84.

Seligman, J. "The Departments of Antiquities and the Israel Antiquities Authority (1918–2006): The Jerusalem Experience." In Galor and Avni, *Unearthing Jerusalem* (2011), 125–146.

Shani, R., and D. Chen. "On the Umayyad Dating of the Double Gate in Jerusalem." *Muqarnas* 18 (2001), 1–40.

Shanks, H. "Everything You Ever Knew About Jerusalem Is Wrong (Well, Almost)." *Biblical Archaeology Review* 25.6 (1999), 20–29.

Sharon, M. "Arabic Inscriptions from the Excavations at the Western Wall." *Israel Exploration Journal* 23 (1973), 214–20.

Shiloh, Y. "The Casemate Wall, the Four Room House, and Early Planning in the Israelite City." *Bulletin of the American Schools of Oriental Research* 268 (1987), 3–15.

———. *Excavations at the City of David I: 1978–1982, Interim Report of the First Five Seasons.* Qedem 19. Jerusalem: Institute of Archaeology, Hebrew University, 1984.

———. "The Four-Room House, Its Situation and Function in the Israelite City." *Israel Exploration Journal* 20 (1970), 180–90.

Shoham, Y. "'Lmlk' Seal Impressions and Concentric Circles." In Ariel, *Excavations at the City of David, 1978–1985* VI (2000) 75–80.

Sievers, J. *The Hasmoneans and Their Supporters: From Mattathias to the Death of John Hyrcanus I.* Atlanta: Scholars, 1990.

———. "Jerusalem, the Akra, and Josephus." In *Josephus and the History of the Greco-Roman Period: Essays in Memory of Morton Smith.* Edited by F. Parente and J. Sievers. Leiden: Brill, 1994, 195–209.

Silberman, N. A. *Digging for God and Country: Exploration, Archeology and the Secret Struggle for the Holy Land, 1799–1917.* New York: Knopf, 1982.

———. "In Search of Solomon's Lost Treasures." *Biblical Archaeology Review* 6.4 (1980), 30–41.

Simons, J. *Jerusalem in the Old Testament: Researches and Theories.* Leiden: Brill, 1952.

Sivan, R., and G. Solar. "Excavations in the Jerusalem Citadel, 1980–1988." In Geva, *Ancient Jerusalem Revealed* (2000), 168–76.

Smallwood, E. M. *The Jews under Roman Rule: From Pompey to Diocletian.* Leiden: Brill, 1976.

Smith, H. B., and R. D. Hitchcock. *The Life, Writings and Character of Edward Robinson.* New York: A. D. F. Randolph, 1863.

Steiner, M. L. *Excavations by K. M. Kenyon in Jerusalem, 1961–1967* III: *The Settlement in the Bronze and Iron Ages.* Sheffield: Sheffield Academic Press, 2001.

———. "It's Not There: Archaeology Proves a Negative." *Biblical Archaeology Review* 24.4 (1998), 24–44, 63.

Stephan, S. H. "Two Turkish Inscriptions from the Citadel of Jerusalem." *Quarterly of the Department of Antiquities of Palestine* 2 (1933), 132–35.

Stern, E. *Material Culture of the Land of the Bible in the Persian Period, 538–332* B.C. Warminster: Aris and Phillips, 1982.

———, ed. *The New Encyclopedia of Archaeological Excavations in the Holy Land* I–IV; V. Jerusalem: Israel Exploration Society and Carta; New York: Simon and Schuster, 1993; 2008.

Stern, M. *Greek and Latin Authors on Jews and Judaism. Edited with Introductions, Translations and Commentary* I. *From Herodotus to Plutarch.* Jerusalem: Israel Academy of Sciences and Humanities, 1976.

———. *Greek and Latin Authors on Jews and Judaism. Edited with Introductions, Translations and Commentary* II. *From Tacitus to Simplicius.* Jerusalem: Israel Academy of Sciences and Humanities, 1980.

Strobel, A. *Conrad Schick. Ein Leben für Jerusalem. Zeugnisse über einen erkannten Auftrag.* Fürth in Bayern: Flacius-Verlag, 1988.

Stutchbury, H. E. "Excavations in the Kidron Valley." *Palestine Exploration Quarterly* 93 (1961), 101–13.

Sukenik, E. L., and L. A. Mayer. "A New Section of the Third Wall, Jerusalem." *Palestine Exploration Quarterly* 76 (1944), 145–51.

——. *The Third Wall of Jerusalem: An Account of Excavations.* Jerusalem: University Press, 1930.

Tarler, D., and J. M. Cahill. "David, City of." *Anchor Bible Dictionary* II. New York: Doubleday, 1992, 52–67.

Tarler, D., A. De Groot, and G. Solar. "Jerusalem: Excavations between Nablus Gate and the New Gate." *Hadashot Arkheologiyot* 69–71 (1979), 56–57 (Hebrew).

Thomas, P. A. "The Success and Failure of Robert Alexander Stewart Macalister." *Biblical Archaeologist* 47 (1984), 33–36.

Tobler, T. "Analekten aus Palästina." *Das Ausland* 39 (1866), 250–255, 273–279.

——. *Bibliographia geographica Palaestinae zunächst kritische Übersicht gedruckter und ungedruckter Beschreibungen der Reisen ins Heilige Land.* Leipzig: S. Hirzel, 1867.

——. *Denkblätter aus Jerusalem.* St. Gallen: Scheitlin, 1853.

——. *Dritte Wanderung nach Palästina im Jahre 1857: Ritt durch Philistäa, Fussreisen im Gebirge Judäas und Nachlese in Jerusalem.* Gotha: Justus Perthes, 1859.

——. *Golgatha, seine Kirchen und Klöster.* St. Gallen: Bern, Huber und Comp., 1851.

——. *Ein Grundriss von Jerusalem nach Catherwood und Robinson, mit einem neu eingezeichneten Gassennetze und etlichen Theils zum ersten Male erscheinenden, Theils berichtigten Gräberplänen nach den Beobachtungen von Doktor Titus Tobler.* Zürich: Topographische Anstalt von Johannes Wurster und Comp., 1849; 2nd ed., St. Gallen and Bern, 1853.

——. *Lustreise ins Morgenland* I–II. Zürich: Orell & Füssli, 1839.

——. *Die Siloahquelle und der Ölberg, mit einer artistischen Beilage.* St. Gallen: Scheitlin und Zollikofer, 1852.

——. *Topographie von Jerusalem und seiner Umgebungen* I–II. Berlin: G. Reimer, 1853.

Trimbur, D. "The École Biblique et Archéologique Française: A Catholic, French, and Archaeological Institution" In Galor and Avni, *Unearthing Jerusalem* (2011), 95–108.

Tsafrir, Y. "The Development of Ecclesiastical Architecture in Palestine." In *Ancient Churches Revealed.* Edited by Y. Tsafrir. Jerusalem: Israel Exploration Society, 1993.

——. "Jerusalem." In *Reallexikon zur Byzantinischen Kunst* III. Stuttgart: Hiersemann, 1978, 525–615.

——. "The Location of the Seleucid Akra in Jerusalem." *Revue Biblique* 82 (1975), 501–21.

Tubb, J. N., and R. L. Chapman. *Archaeology and the Bible.* London: British Museum Press, 1990.

Turner, E. G. "Ptolemaic Egypt." In *The Cambridge Ancient History* I: *The Hellenistic World*. Edited by F. W. Walbank et al. Cambridge, UK: Cambridge University Press, 1984, 118–74.

Tushingham, A. D. *Excavations in Jerusalem, 1961–1967* I. Toronto: Royal Ontario Museum, 1985.

Tzaferis, V., N. Feig, A. Onn, and E. Shukron. "Excavations at the Third Wall, North of the Jerusalem Old City." In Geva, *Jewish Quarter Excavations* I (2000), 287–92.

Ussishkin, D. *The Village of Silwan: The Necropolis from the Period of the Judean Kingdom*. Jerusalem: Israel Exploration Society, 1993.

VanderKam, J. *From Joshua to Caiaphas: High Priests after the Exile*. Minneapolis: Fortress Press; Assen: Van Gorcum, 2004.

Vaughn, A. *Theology, History and Archaeology in the Chronicler's Account of Hezekiah*. Atlanta: Scholars, 1999.

Vernoit, S. "The Rise of Islamic Archaeology." *Muqarnas* XIV. Leiden: Brill, 1997, 1-10.

Vieweger, D. [Review of] "Finkelstein, Israel u. Neil Asher Silberman, Keine Posaunen vor Jericho." *Theologische Literaturzeitung* 129 (2004), 1182–86.

Vincent, H. *Jérusalem sous terre: Les récentes fouilles d'Ophel*. London: H. Cox, 1911.

———. "Une mosaïque byzantine à Jérusalem." *Revue Biblique* 10 (1901), 436–44.

———. "Une mosaïque d'Orphée." *Revue Biblique* 11 (1902), 100–103.

———. "Les récentes fouilles d'Ophel" [1]. *Revue Biblique* 20 (1911), 219–65, 566–91.

———. "Les récentes fouilles d'Ophel" [2]. *Revue Biblique* 21 (1912), 86–111, 424–53, 544–74.

———. "Le tombeau des prophètes." *Revue Biblique* 10 (1901), 72–88.

———. *Underground Jerusalem: Discoveries on the Hill of Ophel (1909–1911)*. London: H. Cox, 1911.

Vincent, L.-H. "Encore la troisième enceinte de Jérusalem." *Revue Biblique* 54 (1947), 90-126.

———. "La troisième enceinte de Jerusalem." *Revue Biblique* 36 (1927), 516–48.

Vincent, L.-H., and F.-M. Abel. *Bethléem: Le sanctuaire de la Nativité*. Paris: V. Lecoffre, 1914.

———. *Jérusalem nouvelle: Recherches de topographie, d'archéologie et d'histoire* II, 1–4. Paris: J. Gabalda, 1914–26.

Vincent, L.-H., and M. A. Steve. *Jérusalem de l'Ancien Testament: Recherches d'archéologie et d'histoire* I–III. Paris: J. Gabalda, 1954–56.

de Vogüé, C. J. M. *Les églises de la Terre Sainte*. Paris: V. Didron, 1860.

———. *Le Temple de Jérusalem: Monographie du Haram-ech-Chérif*. Paris: Noblet et Baudrie, 1864.

Walbank, F. W. "Monarchies and Monarchic Ideas." In *The Cambridge Ancient History* I: *The Hellenistic World*. Edited by F. W. Walbank et al. Cambridge, UK: Cambridge University Press, 1984, 62–100.

Warren, C., and C. R. Conder. *The Survey of Western Palestine: Jerusalem*. London: Palestine Exploration Fund, 1884.

Watson, C. M. *The Life of Major-General Sir Charles William Wilson, Royal Engineers*. London: John Murray, 1909.

Watzinger, C. *Denkmäler Palästinas. Eine Einführung in die Archäologie des Heiligen Landes I. Von den Anfängen bis zum Ende der israelitischen Königszeit*. Leipzig: Hinrichs'sche Buchhandlung, 1933.

Weber-Dellacroce, B., and W. Weber. "'Dort, wo sich Gottes Volk versammelt' — Die Kirchenbauten konstantinisicher Zeit." In *Imperator Caesar Flavius Constantinus — Konstantin der Grosse, Ausstellungskatalog*. Edited by A. Demandt and J. Engemann. Mainz: Philipp von Zabern, 2007, 244–55.

Wehnert, J. "Die Auswanderung der Jerusalemer Christen nach Pella — historisches Faktum oder theologische Konstruktion?" *Zeitschrift für Kirchengeschichte* 102 (1991), 231–55.

Weiland, A. "Die Kapitelle der Geburtskirche in Bethlehem." *Acta XIII Congressus Internationalis Archaeologiae Christianae, Split-Poreč 1994* III. Città del Vaticano, 1998, 813–27.

Weill, R. *La cité de David: Compte rendu des fouilles exécutées à Jérusalem, sur la site de la ville primitive, campagne de 1913–1914*. Paris: P. Geuthner, 1920.

———. *La cité de David: Compte rendu des fouilles exécutées à Jérusalem, sur la site de la ville primitive II, campagne de 1923–1924*. Paris: P. Geuthner, 1947.

Weippert, H. *Palästina in vorhellenistischer Zeit*. Munich: C. H. Beck, 1988.

Weiss, E., et al. "A Dump near the Temple? Two Difficulties Regarding the City Dump Adjacent to the Second Temple." *New Studies on Jerusalem* 12 (2006), 99–107 (Hebrew; English summary, 15*).

Weksler-Bdolah, S., et al. "Jerusalem, the Western Wall Plaza Excavations, 2005–2009. Preliminary Report." *Hadashot Archeologiyot* 121, 2009 [23/9/2009].

Wightman, G. J. *The Damascus Gate, Jerusalem: Excavations by C.-M. Bennett and J. B. Hennessy at the Damascus Gate, Jerusalem, 1964–66*. British Archaeological Reports International Series 519. Oxford: British Archaeological Reports, 1989.

———, ed. *Jerusalem Pilgrimage 1099–1185*. London: Hakluyt Society, 1988.

———. "Stone Tables in Herodian Jerusalem." *Bulletin of the Anglo-Israel Archaeology Society* 13 (1993–94), 7–23.

———. "Temple Fortresses in Jerusalem, Part I: The Ptolemaic and Seleucid Akras." *Bulletin of the Anglo-Israel Archaeology Society* 9 (1989/90), 29–40.

———. "Temple Fortresses in Jerusalem, Part II: The Hasmonean Baris and

Herodian Antonia." *Bulletin of the Anglo-Israel Archaeology Society* 10 (1990/91), 7–35.

———. *The Walls of Jerusalem: From Canaanites to the Mamluks.* Sydney: Meditarch, 1993.

Wilkinson, J. *Column Capitals in al Haram al Sharif (from 138 A.D. to 1118 A.D.).* Jerusalem: Adm. of Wakfs and Islamic Affairs, Islamic Museum, al-Haram al-Sharif, 1987.

———. *Jerusalem as Jesus knew it. Archaeology as Evidence.* London: Thames and Hudson, 1978.

———, ed. *Jerusalem Pilgrims Before the Crusades.* Warminster, UK: Aris and Phillips, 1977.

Will, E. "The Formation of the Hellenistic Kingdoms." In *The Cambridge Ancient History* I: *The Hellenistic World.* Edited by F. W. Walbank et al. Cambridge, UK: Cambridge University Press, 1984, 101–17.

———. "The Succession to Alexander." In *The Cambridge Ancient History* I: *The Hellenistic World.* Edited by F. W. Walbank et al. Cambridge, UK: Cambridge University Press, 1984, 23–61.

Williams, W. W. *The Life of General Sir Charles Warren.* Oxford: B. Blackwell, 1941.

Wilson, C. W. "The Camp of the Tenth Legion at Jerusalem and the City of Aelia." *Palestine Exploration Quarterly* 37 (1905), 138–44.

———. *Golgotha and the Holy Sepulchre.* London: Palestine Exploration Fund, 1906.

———. *Ordnance Survey of Jerusalem.* London: George E. Eyre and William Spottiswoode for Her Majesty's Stationery Office, 1865.

———. *Picturesque Palestine, Sinai and Egypt* I. London: J. S. Virtue, 1880.

Wilson, C. W., and C. Warren. *The Recovery of Jerusalem: A Narrative of Exploration and Discovery in the Holy Land.* London: R. Bentley, 1871.

Wilson, J. *The Lands of the Bible Visited and Described.* Edinburgh, 1847.

Yadin, T. *Jerusalem Revealed: Archaeology in the Holy Land 1968-1974.* Jerusalem: Israeli Exploration Society, 1975

Yezerski, I., and H. Geva. "Iron Age II Clay Figurines." In Geva, *Jewish Quarter Excavations* II (2003), 63–84.

Younger, Jr., K. L. "The Shiloam Inscription." In *The Context of Scripture* II: *Monumental Inscriptions from the Biblical World.* Edited by W. W. Hallo and K. L. Younger, Jr. Leiden: Brill, 2000, 145–46.

———. "The Siloam Tunnel Inscription. An Integrated Reading." *Ugarit-Forschungen* 26 (1994), 543–56.

Zangenberg, J. "Aelia Capitolina. Aspekte zur Geschichte Jerusalems in römischer Zeit (70–ca. 320 n. Chr.)." *Natur und Mensch. Jahresmitteilungen der naturhistorischen Gesellschaft Nürnberg* (1992), 33–52.

Zelinger, Y. "Jerusalem, the Slopes of Mount Zion. Preliminary Report." *Hada-shot Archeologiyot* 122 (2010).

Zwickel, W. *Einführung in die biblische Landes- und Altertumskunde.* Darmstadt, Wissenschaftliche Buchgesellschaft, 2002.

———. *Der Salomonische Tempel.* Mainz: Philipp von Zabern, 1999.

# Index